1996

University of St. Francis

S0-BOL-438

3 0301 00086608 3

The essays in this book, written for this volume by an international team of distinguished Whitman scholars, examine a variety of contemporary issues in Whitman's life and art. These scholars bring to their analyses a multiplicity of approaches mirroring at once the diversity of contemporary scholarship and the range of subjects that Whitman affords for such examination.

Writing out of a common concern for redefining Whitman in current terms, the authors of these essays address a wide-ranging series of issues befitting a poet of his stature and ambiguity: Whitman and photography, Whitman and feminist scholarship, Whitman and modernism, Whitman and the poetics of address, Whitman and the poetics of present participles, Whitman and Borges, Whitman and Isadora Duncan, Whitman and the Civil War, Whitman and the politics of his era, and Whitman and the changing nature of his style in his later years.

This volume is addressed to an audience of students and general readers and is written accordingly in a nontechnical style designed to promote accessibility to the study of Whitman. It includes a chronology of Whitman's life and Suggestions for Further Reading designed to provide background and additional information for such readers.

THE CAMBRIDGE
COMPANION TO
WALT WHITMAN

Cambridge Companions to Literature

Continued on page following Index

THE CAMBRIDGE
COMPANION TO
WALT WHITMAN

EDITED BY
EZRA GREENSPAN
University of South Carolina

LIBRARY
College of St. Francis
JOLIET, ILLINOIS

 CAMBRIDGE
UNIVERSITY PRESS

Published by the Press Syndicate of the University of Cambridge
The Pitt Building, Trumpington Street, Cambridge CB2 1RP
40 West 20th Street, New York, NY 10011-4211, USA
10 Stamford Road, Oakleigh, Melbourne 3166, Australia

© Cambridge University Press 1995

First published 1995

Printed in the United States of America

Library of Congress Cataloging-in-Publication Data
The Cambridge companion to Walt Whitman / edited by Ezra Greenspan.
p.   cm. – (Cambridge companions to literature)
Includes bibliographical references and index.
ISBN 0-521-44343-1. – ISBN 0-521-44807-7 (pbk.)
1. Whitman, Walt, 1819–1892 – Criticism and interpretation.
I. Greenspan, Ezra.   II. Series
PS3238.C16   1995
811′.3—dc20   94-23452
                                                                      CIP

A catalog record for this book is available from the British Library.

ISBN   0-521-44343-1 hardback
ISBN   0-521-44807-7 paperback

8 11. 3
G 795 c

CONTENTS

156,498

CONTENTS

ILLUSTRATIONS

CONTRIBUTORS

FERNANDO ALEGRÍA – is the Sadie Dernham Patek Professor in the Humanities, Emeritus, at Stanford University. His scholarly books include *Walt Whitman en Hispanoamérica* and *Nueva historia de la novela hispano-americana*.

RUTH L. BOHAN – teaches in the art history department at the University of Missouri–St. Louis. She is the author of *The Société Anonyme's Brooklyn Exhibition: Katherine Dreier and Modernism in America*. Her current project is a book on Whitman and the visual arts.

SHERRY CENIZA – teaches in the English department at Texas Tech University. She is the author of articles on Whitman and other topics and of a recently completed book manuscript, *Walt Whitman and "Woman under the New Dispensation."*

ED FOLSOM – teaches in the English department at the University of Iowa. He is the longtime editor of the *Walt Whitman Quarterly Review*. His recent works include, as editor, *Walt Whitman: The Centennial Essays* and, as author, *Walt Whitman's Native Representations*.

EZRA GREENSPAN – teaches in the English department at the University of South Carolina. He is the author of *Walt Whitman and the American Reader*, among other works, and is currently writing a cultural biography of the publisher George Palmer Putnam.

STEPHEN RAILTON – teaches in the English department at the University of Virginia. His most recent book is *Authorship and Audience: Literary Performance in the American Renaissance*. He is currently at work on a study of Samuel Clemens's career as "Mark Twain."

DAVID REYNOLDS – teaches in the English department at Baruch College and the Graduate School of the City University of New York. His books include *Beneath the American Renaissance: The Subversive Imagination in the Age of Emerson and Melville.* He is currently at work on a cultural biography of Whitman.

M. WYNN THOMAS – teaches in the English department at the University of Wales, Swansea. Among his books are *The Lunar Light of Whitman's Poetry* and *Wrenching Times* (a limited edition of Whitman's war poetry). He recently edited *The Page's Drift: R. S. Thomas at Eighty,* and his translations of Whitman's poetry into Welsh are to be published shortly.

ALAN TRACHTENBERG – teaches in the American Studies program at Yale University. His books include *Brooklyn Bridge: Fact and Symbol, The Incorporation of America: Culture and Society in the Gilded Age,* and *Reading American Photographs: Images as History from Mathew Brady to Walker Evans.*

JAMES PERRIN WARREN – teaches in the English department at Washington and Lee University. He is the author of *Walt Whitman's Language Experiment* and is currently writing a book called *Culture of Eloquence.*

1819	Born Walter Whitman on May 31 at West Hills, Long Island, the second of the eight children of Louisa Van Velsor and Walter Whitman.
1823	Family moves from its Long Island farm to Brooklyn, then still a village, where Whitman's father seeks to improve his fortunes.
1825–30	Attends public schools in Brooklyn.
1830–1	Begins doing odd jobs; formal schooling ends.
1831	Sent to begin formal apprenticeship at the printing office of the *Long Island Patriot,* a Democratic paper read by his father.
1832	Transferred to the printing office of the *Long Island Star,* the leading paper in Brooklyn, where he remains until 1835.
1836–8	Unable to find employment as a printer in Manhattan, reunites with his family, now back on Long Island, and begins his first period of school teaching.
1838	Launches his first publishing project as editor/proprietor of the *Long Islander,* a weekly newspaper.
1839–41	Suspends the *Long Islander,* works briefly as a writer for James Brenton's *Long Island Democrat,* and then returns to teaching on Long Island.
1841	Returns to Manhattan in the spring as a printer, finding employment in the printing office of Park Benjamin's popular weekly, the *New World.* Begins placing stories and poems with New York's leading magazine, the *Democratic Review.*
1842	Becomes editor in February of a penny daily, the New York *Aurora.* Fired in late April. Accepts an invitation from Park Benjamin to write a temperance novel; *Franklin Evans* published in November in the *New World*'s "Books for the People" series.

1843–5	Edits a variety of Manhattan papers and publishes occasional poems and stories in the press.
1845	Moves back to Brooklyn in August and reunites with his family. Begins contributing to the Brooklyn *Evening Star*.
1846–8	Becomes editor in February of the Brooklyn *Daily Eagle*, a position he holds for two years.
1848	Fired in January by publishers of the *Daily Eagle* for political views. Accepts an offer to write for the New Orleans *Crescent*. Spends the spring in New Orleans, then returns home to Brooklyn. Founds and edits a Free Soil newspaper, the Brooklyn *Freeman*.
1849	Resigns editorship of the *Freeman* in September. Writes freelance articles for the New York *Sunday Dispatch*.
1850	Edits briefly the New York *Daily News*, his last regular editorial position until after the publication of *Leaves of Grass*.
1851–4	Works as a house builder in Brooklyn and contributes occasional articles to the press. Works on free verse style and poems.
1855	Self-publishes the first edition of *Leaves of Grass*, issued in Brooklyn in July. Emerson's congratulatory letter soon follows.
1856	Publishes the second edition of *Leaves of Grass* in September. Visited at home by Bronson Alcott and Henry David Thoreau.
1857–9	Unable to find a publisher for the third edition of *Leaves of Grass*, returns to journalism as editor of the Brooklyn *Daily Times*.
1859	Leaves the *Daily Times* in the summer and returns to composition of poems and preparation of an expanded and revised edition of *Leaves of Grass* for the press.
1860	Publishes the third edition of *Leaves of Grass* with Thayer and Eldridge in Boston. Intends to issue a follow-up volume, tentatively titled *Banner at Day-Break*, but the plan falls through when Thayer and Eldridge fails in December, leaving Whitman without a publisher or clear direction.
1862	Journeys in December to northern Virginia to locate his soldier brother, reported as wounded in the New York *Herald*. Moved by the spectacle of war and comradeship, he chooses to remain near the front and relocates in Washington, D.C., his primary place of residence until 1873.

1863–4	Finds employment in a government office as a copyist and begins voluntary service as a male nurse in army hospitals. Unsuccessfully seeks a publisher for a book of hospital sketches while continuing to compose war poems. Begins a long friendship with Ellen and William Douglas O'Connor and with the people in their Washington circle.
1865	Publishes *Drum-Taps* in May and *Sequel to Drum-Taps* (featuring the newly composed "When Lilacs Last in the Dooryard Bloom'd") in the fall. Fired in June from his new clerkship in the Department of the Interior for the alleged obscenity of *Leaves of Grass,* but soon afterward employed in the office of the attorney general. Meets and befriends an ex-Confederate soldier, Peter Doyle, who becomes his most intimate friend during the remainder of his Washington years.
1866–7	Publishes the fourth edition of *Leaves of Grass* in New York.
1868	First foreign edition of Whitman's poetry, *Poems,* selected and edited by William Michael Rossetti, brought out in England.
1870	Book publication of *Democratic Vistas,* two parts of which had been issued several years previously in the *Galaxy.*
1871	Publishes the fifth edition of *Leaves of Grass* in Washington, D.C. Separate publication of *Passage to India.* Reads his new poem, "After All, Not to Create Only," written specially for the occasion, at the opening of the American Institute in New York.
1872	Reads a poem ("As a Strong Bird on Pinions Free") by invitation of students at the Dartmouth College commencement. Publishes *As a Strong Bird on Pinions Free and Other Poems* as a pamphlet in New York. A pirated edition (technically, the sixth) of *Leaves of Grass* published by John Camden Hotten in London (but not actually issued until the following year).
1873	Suffers his first paralytic stroke January 23. Left partially disabled and further depressed by the death of his mother in July, he moves in with his brother in Camden, New Jersey, which becomes his home for the rest of his life.
1874	Loses his government position and, with it, his main source of income.
1875	Hopes to be named official poet at the Centennial Exposition, to be held in Philadelphia, but is disappointed when Bayard Taylor, his onetime admirer, is chosen instead.

1876	Marks the Centennial by publishing *Two Rivulets* and an "Author's Edition" of *Leaves of Grass*. Anne Gilchrist, a widowed Englishwoman and admirer of Whitman and his poetry, moves to Philadelphia to be close to him. Whitman begins his recuperative visits to the Pennsylvania farm of the Staffords, with whose son he is particularly close.
1877	Receives visits from the English intellectual Edward Carpenter and the Canadian alienist Richard Maurice Bucke. The latter quickly becomes his vocal supporter, biographer, and all-purpose adviser.
1878	His health improved, he visits in Manhattan and travels up the Hudson to stay with his old friend and first biographer, John Burroughs.
1879	Travels for the first time across the Mississippi, stopping first briefly at St. Louis to visit with his favorite brother, Jeff, and his family before continuing as far west as Colorado. This, the longest trip of his life, dissolves into a fiasco; Whitman is stranded in St. Louis until given a loan from the publisher James Fields, with which to return east.
1880	Visits with Bucke in London, Ontario, his first trip outside the United States.
1881	Publishes the seventh edition of *Leaves of Grass* with James Osgood of Boston.
1882	Threatened with prosecution for obscenity by the Boston district attorney, Osgood removes *Leaves of Grass* from circulation. Whitman purchases the plates and arranges first with Rees Welsh, then with David McKay, both of Philadelphia, for its publication. Whitman's prose autobiography, *Specimen Days and Collect,* is published by McKay. Visited by Oscar Wilde, one of many notable men of letters to visit him during his last decade, as his reputation spreads nationally and internationally.
1883	Spends time at the Jersey shore with John Burroughs.
1884	Buys his own home, easily accessible to the Philadelphia ferry, at 328 Mickle Street, the residence of his final years.
1885–7	Quiet years of declining health spent mostly at or near home with friends and visitors.
1888	Horace Traubel, a frequent visitor at Mickle Street, begins to take notes of their conversations. With Traubel's help, Whitman publishes *Complete Poems and Prose* in an edition of

600 copies and *November Boughs*. Whitman suffers a stroke in June.

1889   Enjoys the public festivities held in Camden to celebrate his seventieth birthday.

1891   With Traubel's aid, publishes *Good-Bye My Fancy* and prepares for the press a final issue of *Leaves of Grass,* complete with annexes.

1892   Dies March 26.

I

EZRA GREENSPAN

Introduction

"Let America therefore celebrate its poets" was Herman Melville's way in 1850 of articulating the problematic situation of the poet and poetry in America just a few years before the appearance of Walt Whitman as a self-proclaimed national poet. Melville's words probably sounded shrill even then, and today, given the general reception by the country of its poets ever since it has become possible to talk of American poets, they barely manage to resonate. Both Melville and Whitman knew well that the situation of the poet and of letters in American society *was* an issue – and a complicated one, at that – in their time. For Whitman, in fact, it was a crucial issue, one to which he devoted his fullest energies from his days as a young journalist in the 1840s and as a brash young poet in the first edition of *Leaves of Grass* (1855) until the end of his life in 1892.

In this context, the widespread commemoration and celebration of Whitman, both in the United States and abroad in the centennial year of 1992, were themselves a phenomenon invested with intriguing cultural significance. One of the most interesting aspects of the centennial was the degree to which it passed from an act of commemoration to one of genuine celebration. It is one thing that academic conferences honoring Whitman were held from coast to coast; it is quite another – and one befitting Whitman himself, lover of the spoken word – that they were all surpassed by the marathon public readings of Whitman, and of poems inspired by or written in imitation of him, that went on for days in New York.

Personally speaking, I cannot help but believe that there was something appropriate about the public readings of Whitman in New York City. For one thing, Whitman was the ultimate New York poet – singer of movement and mobility, poet of ferries and bridges, coquette-lover of crowds, celebrator of diversity, master of self-advertising, and manipulator of images. For another, Whitman was uncannily a poet of the spoken word – a remark, I hope, that will not sound tautological. What I mean by this is that Whitman not only absorbed much of the flavor of the spoken arts – oratory, theater, opera, bardic poetry – into his own poetry but that he also had a deep sense – no matter if it was more fantasy that actuality – of addressing standing audiences that included "poets to come," who would, in turn, speak his thoughts or thoughts akin to his to future generations of listeners. A self-educated man and a self-created poet, Whitman was never one to fit the established cultural models and modes of artistic creation, publication, reception, and delivery. What could be more fitting, then, than all-night readings on the grass or out in the open or attended by mixed groups of fellow poets, critics, and simple lovers of the Whitmanesque word. In this context, 1992 brought Whitman's "followers" their ultimate poetic "present": his own voice, captured on a flawed but still audible recording, reading his obscure little poem "America." That we cannot know for sure that the old man's voice we hear passing over the words slowly and cherishingly is actually Whitman's would no doubt have given him reason to laugh; he had played the game of imposing false and multiple identities of himself on his listeners all his mature life. Why stop after life?

No less curious than the spectacle of Whitman celebrations around the country is the term itself. "Celebrate" was, after all, the first verb used in the opening poem of Whitman's first edition of *Leaves of Grass*. It was also one of the most fundamental concept terms in Whitman's poetry generally: His poetry articulated and performed a celebration of life. But Whitman was too shrewd an observer of his society not to be aware that celebration, as a rite of public affirmation, had become by the time of his generation a problematic matter. Holidays were no longer necessarily holy days; what was a secularized person to make of Christmas or Easter? For Whitman himself, more significant than either of those days was the Fourth of July, whose pageantry and histrionics alternately attracted and repelled him. At times, for lack of acceptable forums for public celebration, his own tendency was to revert to privatized substitutions, such as his nostalgic sentimentalization of Washington's separation from his troops or of Lafayette's heroic passage through Brooklyn during his return visit to America in 1824 (and to the special kiss he planted on the boy Whitman's forehead). At other times, his tendency was to seek out the crowds of people – on Broadway, on ferry crossings, in theaters, in army hospitals – and to observe with fascination the places of public architecture – the Crystal Palace, the Capitol, the White House – as grounds of potential celebration. The real celebration, though, Whitman was to find only in the complex and conflicted one he created in the pages of *Leaves of Grass*, whose strangely divided and uneven reception by the American reading public raised from a different perspective the problem of celebration in his society.

Seen in a larger context, the Whitman Centennial was but a part of the reevaluation of American culture currently going on everywhere from the academy to the Capitol. Clearly, we are today living through one of the cultural revisions that have periodically marked the political and cultural history of the United States during this century as new groups of people have entered our institutions and projected their voices and views into the language of societal debates. The current one, however, seems particularly far-reaching and unsettling in its criticism, challenging all groups to go back to first terms and, with the prefix "re" in the air, pressing them to reconsider and revise their basic premises. It is no coincidence that precisely at this time Walt Whitman, who relished a good fight with establishments, has again become one of the most current figures in American literary criticism. Even in the absence of major new biographical information, he is the subject of various new biographical studies, as well as more generally of the largest and most broadly conceived variety of critical studies he has ever received. Their meeting point, to the extent that one can see unity behind diversity, lies in the shared perception of the necessity to reformulate the terms in which we "see" Whitman.

Although Whitman is a typical instance of the way writers today generally have been coming in for their share of new scrutiny, the extraordinary amount of attention he has been receiving is particularly appropriate. Whitman liked to identify himself and his poetry with the country on the grand scale but, regardless of whether one today accepts him in his claim to representative stature, studies of him have typically gone beyond or through him to become analyses of American culture and society. His centrality to American culture readily raises discussions of him, as Emerson's raises his, to a higher, more inclusive level than is the case with their contemporaries. In fact, discussions of Whitman have often gone beyond even those of Emerson in tracing his influence across formal lines into the arts and music, fields in which Whitman has had a profound impact on the way creative people have expressed their sense of life. Whitman had a sharp eye and ear for the arts – photography, opera, drama, painting – as well as an uncanny appreciation for the creative process, a matter that he enjoyed foregrounding in his own creative work. But there is also a further reason for Whitman's centrality to studies of American culture. In his pursuit of an ideological commitment to reshaping the idea of culture along more open terms and, in doing so, to including peoples and subjects in his poetry previously kept out of or thought alien to culture, Whitman has become a natural subject for the citizens of our own more open, inclusive culture. The poet who self-consciously brought blacks, Native Americans, mothers, prostitutes, lovers, workers, American slang, and the latest technological gadgets into his poetry has today become a natural subject for an array of students and scholars working in such diverse fields as African-American, feminist, Native American, gay, semiotic, popular culture, and print culture studies, all of whom can readily align their subjects (and often their personal points of view) with Whitman's imposing target. Although they may differ over whether they like or approve of Whitman, they have all found that they cannot easily disregard him.

In assembling the following group of new critical essays on Whitman, I have attempted to elicit a broad variety of scholarly responses and kinds of responses to Whitman, one that will reflect the wide-open, decentralized situation of current thinking. Recognizing that a genuine attempt to cover all bases would require a multivolume format, I have made a virtue of necessity by compiling what Whitman himself might have called a "suggestive" volume, one designed to expose readers to a variety of critical perspectives on and approaches to the phenomenon of Whitman, and to do so via a medley of voices, accents, and critical discourses.

A few words about individual essays may be in order. Three of the essays offer strong new interpretations of different parts of Whitman's long career. Stephen Railton addresses the *I – you* relationship in Whitman's early poetry, a central topic in recent criticism, but figures it in novel terms as an act of poetic performance and traces its origins back to Whitman's uneasy homosexuality. M. Wynn Thomas offers an equally bold reevaluation in discussing Whitman's Civil War career. His far-ranging interpretation of the period that Whitman came to think of as the emotional and creative touchstone of his life understands Whitman as engaged in an ongoing act of "interconnection" – between soldiers and civilians, wounded men and their families, and himself and the reading public. Right at the center of these acts of connection he locates Whitman's soldier-brother George, whom most critics generally dismiss as Whitman's temperamental opposite but whom Thomas sees as Whitman's fraternal objective correlative to the events of the Civil War. Similarly, James Perrin Warren challenges the near consensus that has developed among post-Vietnam-age critics regarding the character and quality of Whitman's late poetry, whether defined as post-1860 or post–Civil War. He contests the view that Whitman entered a period of decline by proposing a countermodel of Whitman as an evolutionary rather than a revolutionary poet and by explicating "Passage to India," a poem now for several decades out of critical favor, along the lines of his model.

As I have mentioned, Whitman has long been a touchstone for critics trying to understand the culture of nineteenth-century America. Three of the essays track approaches to Whitman broadly different in their orientation but allied in their identification of Whitman with his period. Sherry Ceniza takes up the long-standing issue of Whitman's poetic treatment of women and gives it an intriguingly nonconformist feminist reading by analyzing the enthusiastic response of three independent-minded contemporary women reading the 1860 *Leaves of Grass*. Ironically, she finds, they found him more liberating than do most of their descendants today. David Reynolds takes a different tack in attempting to fix Whitman on the map of his society by juxtaposing him closely to leading midcentury social and political movements in which he moved or had an interest. More indirectly concerned with politics and ideology, I present in my essay a discursive analysis of a central device of his poetry: the present participles he used either in measured sequences or in patterned formations. First mastered in 1855 and never abandoned thereafter as a building block of his poetry, they served him well as a verbal construction through which he could express his sense of the conditions of American life.

The essays by Ed Folsom, Ruth Bohan, and Alan Trachtenberg all trace outlines of thinking regarding Whitman and nonprint media. Folsom analyzes Whitman's lifelong fascination with the new art of photography, whose developments were contemporaneous with Whitman's own life and, as Folsom shows, whose applications were one of the most resourceful experiments Whitman made in his self-presentational mode of book making. Projecting Whitman into the twentieth century, Trachtenberg presents a general overview of Whitman's influence on the moderns. As he persuasively demonstrates, it was so pervasive that its purview reads like an unending Whitmanian catalog. One of the early-twentieth-century creative spirits most profoundly influenced by Whitman, as Bohan shows, was Isadora Duncan. Cross-referencing Whitman's contribution to modern poetry and Duncan's contribution to modern dance, Bohan reads the Whitman–Duncan affinity as one of the seminal pairings of modern culture.

A particularly fascinating series of questions and issues underlies the contribution of Fernando Alegría. They relate to Whitman's status as the American author who has had the most considerable twentieth-century cultural influence not only at home but also abroad. Alegría first investigated Whitman's influence on Latin American writing in the 1950s and, in coming back to that subject now, is doing so at a time when internationalism has become an important matter in academic (as well as nonacademic) debates. His discussion centers on Whitman and Borges, one of Whitman's most sympathetic Latin American readers and translators. Fascinating as it is in its specific, nuanced analysis, it also can be read generically as a case study of the problems and challenges inherent in cross-cultural intersections of minds, sensibilities, and languages.

2

STEPHEN RAILTON

"As If I Were With You"—
The Performance of Whitman's Poetry

Every reader has noticed how often Walt Whitman says *I*. There are few pages of *Leaves of Grass* without at least some form of the first-person pronoun – *I, me, mine, my, myself*. Nor is there any hint of an apology in his acknowledgment of this fact: "I know perfectly well my own egotism . . . and cannot say any less."[1] Yet *I* is not the pronoun that most markedly distinguishes Whitman's poetry (as C. Carroll Hollis has calculated, for example, "on a percentage basis Dickinson uses even more"[2]). *You* is. Whitman doesn't say *you* as often as he says *I*, but he does use the second-person pronoun more pervasively than any other major poet. Even the assertion of his own egotism that I've just quoted is embedded in a larger thought that reveals the interdependence of his authorial *I* and the *you* of his reader:

> I know perfectly well my own egotism,
> And know my omnivorous words, and cannot say any less,
> And would fetch you whoever you are flush with myself.

To describe this awareness of and address to the reader, Hollis borrows a term from modern linguistics and calls it Whitman's "illocutionary" stance.[3] Ezra Greenspan borrows a term from classical grammar and calls it Whitman's "vocative technique."[4] A more colloquial way to indicate the crucial place *you* occupies in many of Whitman's poems is to say that they are performances. Whitman put it still more colloquially when he wrote in a notebook: "All my poems do. All I write I write to arouse in you a great personality."[5] Of course, as performances they were enacted imaginatively rather than literally. Despite Whitman's fantasies about being a national orator, speaking from real stages to packed houses, he seldom performed in front of live audiences. Even from the imaginative stage of a printed book, he was not widely read until after his death. But throughout his career he defined the goals of his poetry as public ones, and especially in the poems he wrote before the Civil War he conceived his poetry dramatically, as an address to the reader he refers to as the "listener up there" (1855, 85), the

7

you reading the book. That the performance was imaginary did not matter to someone who had so impressive an imagination: What the many *you*'s establish is how real and present his reader was in Whitman's mind. *You* is what I want to explore here. What does *you* do? What is the role that Whitman's reader plays in his imagination and his poetry? Who is *you*? Can we be specific about the way he conceived his reader? And what does Whitman mean when he says that the aim of his performance is to fetch *you* flush with himself?

That shift in the stanza I quoted earlier, from the first person to the second, from an apparent self-absorption to a real concern with an other, is a very common pattern in Whitman's poetry. The first word of "Song of Myself," for instance, is *I*, but the last word is *you*, and the poem's opening stanza announces this larger pattern explicitly:

> I celebrate myself,
> And what I assume you shall assume,
> For every atom belonging to me as good belongs to you.
>
> (1855, 25)

Looked at closely, both these stanzas reveal how anxious is the relationship they assert between *I* and *you*. The eternal present tense of "I celebrate myself" or "I know my own egotism" has to yield to time (the future tense of "shall assume") and chance (the conditional tense of "would fetch"). What looks at first like amplitude betrays its incompleteness; neither the celebrated self nor his own egotism is enough. As these tense changes indicate, the reader stands outside the circle Whitman is trying to draw. In "Song of Myself" *I* is everything, the whole cosmos, except *you*. Hundreds of other persons are referred to in the poem – prostitutes and presidents, runaway slaves and Texas Rangers – but they can be treated as parts of the self. *You*, on the other hand, though not strictly speaking "in" the poem at all, exists as a separate consciousness. Therefore *you* is the poem's only other character. *You* may in fact be the more important character. As the first line gives way to the second, it suddenly becomes unclear what the poem is about. Is its focus the self and the universe, or the self and the other, the poet and the reader? Which is the occasion for the poem – all that the *I* is or the one thing *I* isn't, that is, *you*?

As the first poem in the first edition of *Leaves of Grass*, "Song of Myself" is the place where Whitman premiered his identity as "Walt Whitman." Thinking of the poem as a performance might help with a problem that all the commentary on it has been unable to resolve. "Song of Myself" is one of the world's great long poems, but none of the many attempts to define its structure have been convincing. Unlike other long poems, as Quentin Anderson has pointed out, "Song of Myself" cannot tell a story without fatally compromising the claims to imperial selfhood that Whitman puts in for his *I*.[6] But if we conceive it generically as an epic poem, we will continue to expect a narrative structure of some kind. We are less likely to bring such expectations to a performance. "Song of Myself" is not a poem about "what happened"; instead, the poem itself, like any performance, is what is happening as it is being read. That is the when of the poem: the "this day and night" the reader spends with the poet, reading the poem (1855, 26). The dramatically charged space between Whitman and the reader is the where of the poem. The poem doesn't have a plot; it is a plot – it is organized around the reader, whose assumptions Whitman seeks to make over in his own image. Looking at "Song of Myself" for its structural design, in the way we can look for the structure of the *Iliad* or *Paradise Lost* or even *The Prelude,* will continue to frustrate critics because its design is essentially outward-looking, rhetorical, strategic. But once this distinction is grasped, we can realize that, like many other epic-length poems, this one announces its argument in its opening lines, as the poet advances out of the self to engage the reader's attention and to commit himself to a performance that will transform the reader. The hero is the poet as performer; the quest is to cross the gap between *I* and *you*. "What I assume you shall assume" – that transaction is the plot of "Song of Myself."

The distinction between story and strategy, between narrative and performative, has many implications. In this essay I can pursue only one: the way making the hero a performer subverts the poem's most grandiose claims, for Whitman, although the poem's creator as well as its hero, cannot finally determine the outcome of the performance plot. That depends on *you*, the readers "*up* there." In the poem *I* may seem to possess the power to roam freely through all of space and time, but in fact he has to keep coming back to his readers. He may try in the poem's second stanza to pose as a loafer "at my ease," but in fact he is working constantly to fetch his readers to him. We in the audience can choose to attend to the performance on its own terms, and admire or censure, in any case be amazed by Whitman's egotism, his delight in himself, the sureness with which he exhibits that self to us. Whitman's cocky aplomb, his apparent adequacy to any occasion, even the occasion the poem creates of appearing naked before a crowd of strangers, is the absolute center of his performance. On the other hand, if we notice how dramatically and tirelessly he keeps thrusting himself at the audience, we might decide that deeper than his self-possession is an utter need for us, that the self he celebrates is not the pretext, the occasion for the performance, but instead exactly what the textual performance is trying to bring into existence. He explicitly gives his readers the power to *be* "Walt Whitman," but implicit in his preoccupation with holding their attention is the idea that it is actually the readers who have the power to *create* "Walt Whitman." At times Whitman can himself admit this dependency. At most times, of course, he asserts his godlike sovereignty: "I exist as I am, that is enough, / If no other in the world be aware I sit content, / . . . One world is aware, and by far the largest to me, and that is myself" (1855, 44). Yet there is too much that such an assertion cannot account for, including Whitman's need to "exist as he is" in public. He comes closer to telling the truth about his rhetorical situation, his dependence on the awareness of others, when he says: "These are the thoughts of all men in all ages and lands, they are not original with me, / If they are not yours as much as mine they are nothing or next to nothing" (1855, 41). Since the "thoughts" revolve around the greatness of the self, it clearly follows that unless *you* celebrate that self too, the self itself is nothing or the next thing to it.

Without *you*, I am enough; without *you*, I am nothing: This contradiction is what makes Whitman's performative stance so hard to pin down. We can say that consistently he steps to the front of the poem to address his readers directly, but at those moments he speaks in many different tones of voice. He can be aggressive, taunting *your* assumptions: "Have you felt so proud to get at the meaning of poems?"; "Have you outstript the rest? Are you the President? / It is a trifle. . . ." Or he can seriously ask for *your* opinions: "I wish I could translate the hints about the dead young men and women, / . . . What do you think has become of the young and old men?" He can be nurturing: "Undrape . . . . you are not guilty to me, nor stale nor discarded." He can be threatening: "Encompass worlds but never try to encompass me, / I crowd your noisiest talk by looking toward you." He can be ingratiating: "This hour I tell things in confidence, / I might not tell everybody but I will tell you." It is also unclear how participatory the performance is. He regularly says that we must learn to celebrate our selves too: "All I mark as my own you shall offset it with your own." And he can define himself simply as our representative: "It is you talking just as much as myself. . . . I act as the tongue of you." But then there are moments when he asserts himself as our savior and master, and defines our selves merely as the extension of his will: "You there, impotent, loose in the knees, open your scarfed chops till I blow grit within you, / . . . I do not ask who you are . . . . that is not important to me, / You can do nothing and be nothing but what I will infold you."[7] Is he up on stage to be the mirror of our selves, or are we in the audience to serve as the mirror of his self?

That question is one readers can best settle for themselves, and will perhaps answer differently at different points in the poem or on different readings of it. The related question I want to explore concerns the way Whitman changes the largest terms of the performance in "Song of Myself." At times he specifically depicts the rhetorical situation as a very public one. For example, the poem's peroration, the last eleven sections, begins with a dramatic signal that the performance is moving into its concluding act:

> . . . A call in the midst of the crowd,
> My own voice, orotund sweeping and final.
>
> (1855, 73)

This trope identifies the poem's *I* as a kind of orator and the *you* as a crowd, a mass audience. In the poem's most striking figuration of the relationship between *I* and *you*, however, they meet privately, as two people, and the orotund call drops into a caressing whisper:

> Listener up there! Here you . . . . what have you to confide to me?
> Look in my face while I snuff the sidle of evening,
> Talk honestly, for no one else hears you, and I stay only a minute longer.
>
> (1855, 85)

Each of these passages is typical of a number of others. At one extreme the *you* of "Song of Myself" is the plural pronoun and refers to the American reading public, which Whitman addresses oratorically, democratically, impersonally. But if public oratory is one analogue for the kind of performance he is engaged in, seduction is another: At this extreme, *you* is the singular pronoun and refers to the solitary reader whom Whitman addresses personally, intimately, erotically. The date with *you* that he makes at the very end – "I stop some where waiting for you" – offers the prospect of a regenerate society, a new heaven and a new earth, and a chance at emotional fulfillment, a lover's rendezvous.

Watching Whitman perform in "Song of Myself" can be as disconcerting as watching Madonna on stage for the way it forces us to realize how much blurring there is between realms we might wish to keep distinct. There is probably always some sexual content in the public relationships between orators or entertainers and audiences, and some performative self-consciousness, some rhetoric, even in our moments of greatest intimacy. Certainly a major source of Whitman's power over our attention is his confessional breaching of the line most people draw between public and private, which is what he meant by saying "I remove the veil" (1855, 45), and which is what happens when he simultaneously seduces a crowd of strangers and puts on a show for a prospective lover. Where Whitman is large enough to contain contradictions, it would be a mistake for the critic to insist on resolving them too neatly. Betsy Erkkila rightly refers to this mixture of public and private as "Whitman's ever-shifting and shifty relationship with the *you* of the reader."[8] C. Carroll Hollis insightfully notes how Whitman's mode of address exploits an ambiguity peculiar to English as a language: that the same pronoun can be used as a singular or plural one: "The secret of Whitman's poetic maneuver here is that it [*you*] is *both* or *either.*"[9] In "Song of Myself," *you* is both an individual and a crowd, and the performance is both a public and a private one. Yet if we keep the focus on Whitman's own imagination, we should be able to say which alternative predominates. In terms of the hopes, the ambitions, and desires that he invested in his poetry, was he writing mainly for a crowd of strangers or a lover?

What Whitman himself says about *you* can help us only up to a point. I've already quoted his favorite formulation; it was appended to the first *you* that appeared in this essay: "And would fetch you whoever you are flush with myself." "Whoever you are" is as sweeping as that call in the midst of the crowd, and is the only way to describe *you* consistent with his program to "accept nothing which all cannot have their counterpart of on the same terms" (1855, 48). For the most part, Whitman does define his readership this democratically. As part of his strategy in "Song of Myself," for example, he writes his own appreciative audience right into the poem itself. In what would become the forty-seventh of the poem's fifty-two sections, he pictures the way he and his "voice" and "words" have become part of the daily lives of the young mechanic, the woodman, the farm boy, fishermen and seamen, the hunter, the driver, the young and the old mothers, the girl and the wife (1855, 82). As an indication of whom he meant by *you,* although dominated by young men who work with their hands, this group of common men and women is consistent with such formulations as "you whoever you are" or "each man and each woman of you" (1855, 80).

The enthusiasm with which he imagines this audience responding to his poetry is a crucial aspect of the faith on which the whole vision of "Song of Myself" rests: that the greatness inherent in each man or woman's self will instantly recognize itself in Whitman's prophetic summons to greatness. Thus he was not bragging just on his own behalf, but on everybody's, when he wrote Emerson, in the public letter that he placed as an appendix to the second (1856) edition of *Leaves of Grass:*

A few years, and the average call for my Poems is ten or twenty thousand copies – more, quite likely. Why should I hurry or compromise? In poems or speeches I say the word or two that has got to be said, adhere to the body, step with the countless common footsteps, and remind every man and woman of something.   (1856, 346)

Numbers like these make *you* a very plural pronoun. An average yearly sale of over 20,000 copies would have made him the best-selling American poet of his time,[10] but these were appropriate numbers for him to be thinking in, given his democratic desire to speak the "word en masse" (1855, 47). And he was prepared to stake more than his faith in the common man and woman on such numbers. He was apparently prepared to let popularity be the measure of his greatness as a poet. The last line of the Preface to the first edition of *Leaves of Grass* asserts that "The proof of a poet is that his country absorbs him as affectionately as he has absorbed it" (1855, 24).

If Whitman believed in letting the majority rule this way on the issue of his own aesthetic achievement, his faith was sorely tested by the country's total failure to reciprocate his affection. Although he told Emerson (and every other reader of the 1856 *Leaves*) that the thousand copies of the 1855 edition had "readily sold" (1856, 346), he knew that his book's actual first year's sales had been closer to a dozen. Even most of the people to whom he had sent complimentary copies either ignored or condemned it. The truth about the book's reception is reflected in his decision to redefine the proof of a poet; much of the 1855 preface is recast in the 1856 *Leaves* as "Poem of Many in One," where Whitman now says: "The proof of a poet shall be sternly deferred till his country absorbs him as affectionately as he has absorbed it" (1856, 195).[11] There is a good deal of evidence to show that he wanted and expected *Leaves* to be quickly and widely popular, and that he was severely disappointed by its failure. Despite all such signs, however, I think we must wonder how he could have believed what he predicted about his own popularity.

It is not hard to understand why Whitman, who knew a lot about advertising, would want to mislead Emerson (and others) about how well his poetry was selling. But it is very hard to understand how he could have misled himself so spectacularly. Although in 1855 "Walt Whitman" was a new poet, Walter Whitman was no young man. As a thirty-six-year-old veteran of American journalism who had also published a temperance novel, he was an experienced man of letters. As someone who had edited newspapers well enough to increase their subscription lists, he was thoroughly acquainted with the prevailing appetites and expectations of the contemporary reading public. If the *you* of his poem is the average American reader of 1855, then "Song of Myself" was an almost complete assault on all *your* assumptions – about poetry, about religion, about the body, about life. Whitman knew this. It is what puts the tension in the tense changes whenever he shifts his focus from the self he can already celebrate or the physical world he can already devour with his omnivorous lines to the other, the reader, whom he *would* fetch or who *shall* share his assumptions. For all its celebratory mood, there are passages in the poem that indicate plainly, if obliquely, how deep was the gap between his and his potential readers' assumptions across which the performance had to carry; there is, for example, the passage about living "awhile with the animals" because "They do not make me sick discussing their duty to God, / . . . not one is demented with the mania of owning things" (1855, 55, 56). How could Whitman have expected that Americans in 1855, who believed devoutly in owning things, and in God, would love his poetry?

Even more incredibly, to quote the question asked in the earliest English notice of Whitman's poems, "Is it possible that the most prudish nation in the world will adopt a poet whose indecencies stink in the nostrils?"[12] We need not agree with the judgments here – to me, there is nothing indecent about Whitman's poetry, and there may have been other nations as prudish as Victorian America. But this reviewer gets directly to the widest, deepest part of the gap between Whitman and his contemporary audience: his treatment of human sexuality. How could he have expected his culture to absorb his poems affectionately?

To me, this is the most perplexing of all the questions connected with Whitman's performance as an American poet. Perhaps he had temporarily lost touch with the reality of his literary and cultural situation; he might have been so wrapped up in the rapturous cosmic consciousness that the poem itself witnesses that he simply assumed his ecstasy would transport his audience with it into the new world – post-Christian, postcapitalist, post-cultural – he claims for the self. The idea of a poet so absorbed in his own vision, however, would have to ignore Whitman's persistent, strategically shrewd preoccupation with *you*. Perhaps he was simply running the kind of bluff advertisers and politicians run all the time: declaring that the people love something in the hope of convincing at least some of them to do so. But that idea has to ignore his evident despair in the late 1850s at his poetry's unpopularity; if it's hard to believe how in 1855 he could have expected his poems to become popular, when we note his mood in 1857 and 1858, it becomes impossible to doubt that he had had such expectations. On the other hand, it is possible that there was a division in his own mind about his ambitions. Consciously, he may have needed to believe he was addressing a mass audience that would absorb him affectionately, while unconsciously knowing that only a few readers could be so receptive, but because he could not bring himself to admit that he was addressing such a "singular" *you*, he used the fiction of a democratic performance to disguise his desires even from himself.

I can put this complicated thought more simply by saying that I am talking about the problem of Whitman's homosexuality. I don't mean that it is a problem for us, although I have some anxiety about finding the right way to discuss it. I mean that it was a problem for Whitman. It might seem hypercritical to argue that the least inhibited nineteenth-century American writer – the prophet of the body and its polymorphous pleasures – was seriously repressed himself, but I think that the testimony of Whitman's whole life and work points to that conclusion. He could write much more evocatively, for example, about the beauty of the male physique than about the female, but could never bring himself to acknowledge that his attraction to men was sexual. Given the cultural circumstances of his era, it would have been extraordinarily difficult to discuss such desires publicly. Under no circumstances could he have said they were "homosexual," since that word did not even come into the English language until after his death. But the circumstances of his own temperament made it necessary for him to disguise his sexual preferences even from himself. He found a number of terms to describe "the love of comrades." His favorite, "adhesiveness," he took from phrenology, where the term stood for one's capacity to enter into high-minded, platonic friendships, especially, but not exclusively, with members of the same sex.[13]

Although it seems clear enough to most modern readers that with such terms Whitman is often expressing homoerotic desires, he himself insisted, as R. M. Bucke put it in the study of Whitman that Whitman silently coauthored, that comradeship was "an exalted friendship, a love into which sex does not enter as an element."[14] The most egregious public instance of this denial is the reply to John Addington Symonds, who had written to ask if Whitman's "conception of Comradeship" included any "semi-sexual emotions and actions": "the possibility of such construction," Whitman wrote back, "is terrible"; any such "inferences" are "disavow'd" as "damnable."[15] We can prove that out loud and in public, Whitman denied his homosexuality. I think that this pattern of denial extended into his psychic life as well: that even to himself he did not want to admit the truth about his sexuality.

This particular repression would, I suggest, provide the basis for an explanation of how Whitman used *you* in his poetry. He knew that what he wrote would profoundly offend or alienate most contemporary readers, but he had to believe it was democratically addressed to them all; in what he wrote he was seeking a specific audience – an audience of men who, like himself, had unacknowledged homoerotic longings – but could never be this specific, not even in his own mind. According to Walter J. Ong, a writer's audience is always a fiction,[16] but we can be specific about the kind of fiction Whitman's conflicted desires made necessary. The universal "you whoever you are" was his substitute for the more singular *you* he sought to communicate with. Whitman and this *you* meet surreptitiously in the figure of the one person mentioned in "Song of Myself" who comes closest to attaining the status of a character: the twenty-ninth bather he describes in section eleven, the woman who has unacknowledged desires for the naked young men bathing in the river.

Given the nature of repression, there is little direct evidence to support this idea of a singular *you* disguised as a plural one. An exception is the way Whitman began one of the three reviews he wrote and printed anonymously in 1855 to promote *Leaves of Grass:* "Very devilish to some, and very divine to some, will appear the poet of these new poems."[17] This is one of the few places where Whitman segregates his potential audience into different kinds of people, only "some" of whom, clearly, are ever likely to be interested in sharing his assumptions. There is also the remarkable avowal of his ambitions – again, as much private as public – that Whitman made in a footnote to the preface he wrote in 1876 for *Two Rivulets.* "I meant LEAVES OF GRASS," the passage begins, "to be the Poem of Identity, (of *Yours*, whoever you are, now reading these lines)." He goes on, in a passage worth quoting in full, to admit the emotional dissatisfaction out of which his poetry sprung. In this passage, as in "Out of the Cradle Endlessly Rocking," Whitman makes the connection between his poetry and "the cries of unsatisfied love" (1860, 276), though here without the screening fiction of the broken-hearted bird:

> Something more may be added – for, while I am about it, I would make a full confession. I also sent LEAVES OF GRASS to arouse and set flowing in men's and women's hearts, young and old, (my present and future readers,) endless streams of living, pulsating love and friendship, directly from them to myself, now and ever. To this terrible, irrepressible yearning, (surely more or less down underneath in most human souls,) – this never-satisfied appetite for sympathy, and this boundless offering of sympathy – this universal democratic comradeship – this old, eternal, yet ever-new interchange of adhesiveness, so fitly emblematic of America – I have given in that book, undisguisedly, declaredly, the openest expression. . . . Poetic literature has long been the formal and conventional tender of art and beauty merely, and of a narrow, constipated,

special amativeness. I say, the subtlest, sweetest, surest tie between me and Him or Her, who, in the pages of *Calamus* and other pieces realizes me – though we never see each other, or though ages and ages hence – must, in this way, be personal affection. And those – be they few, or be they many – are at any rate *my readers,* in a sense that belongs not, and can never belong, to better, prouder poems.[18]

This is just about as full a confession as any writer is likely to give us about the merely human longings that can provoke someone to publish the self. Even here Whitman's characteristic defenses are on display. He keeps trying to convert the unsettling realities of private desire – terrible yearning, never-satisfied appetite – into the more acceptable generalizations of public politics – emblematic of America, democratic comradeship. And he is still trying to keep *you* from coming too clearly into focus and so says "Him or Her" – although the idea of "comradeship" has already excluded or at least marginalized "Her." But what Whitman does so honestly in this passage is to debunk the myth of creation that a poem like "Song of Myself" seeks to assert. There his poetry is described as the overflowing of a self already full with the cosmos, as when his own voice prods him to poetic speech: "Walt, you understand enough . . . why don't you let it out then?" (1855, 51). Here, however, the figure he implicitly uses for himself is not the overflowing fountain but the parched hollow, the empty vessel. The admission that literary performance is the quest for love, friendship, and sympathy helps us appreciate how literally we should be prepared to take a word like "affectionately" when Whitman uses it to define the relationship between a poet and his culture, or how literally Whitman means it when he says that he wants to "fetch" his reader "flush" with himself.

I hasten to add that it would be a mistake to take such conceptions too literally. We are still dealing with the make-believe world of performance, where fantasies remain fantasies even when they are "acted" out. In the actual world, I've said, Whitman could not even acknowledge having such desires, much less realize them. When he talks about having his desires "realized" by the reader of his poems, he is talking about an imaginative reality. In that world *I* and *you* can meet. This might seem to be a very frustrating, impersonal way to look for "personal affection," but in our age of the celebrity interview we have a vast amount of testimony from actors, actresses, and other performers about how being in the center of the stage and of an audience's attention can feel like being loved. What pushes performers onto the stage is often the need to get from a crowd of strangers what they cannot get from the people in their private lives. Seen this way, perhaps Whitman's tireless self-promotion – the reviews he wrote anonymously, the pictures he posed for, the news items he planted with editors, and so on[19] – seems less offensive.

We need to make a crucial distinction, though, between the imaginative performance a real performer engages in and the imaginative performance Whitman only *imagined*. Although he was deeply interested in all forms of performance, especially oratory and opera, and although at several points in his life he seems seriously to have considered attempting a career as an orator, especially in 1850–1 (before the first two editions of *Leaves of Grass*) and in 1857–8 (after those editions had failed so disastrously), in fact he lived out his fascination with performance the same way he lived out his sexual desires – vicariously. By writing about being in front of an audience, he made the relationship between *I* and *you* both more intimate (because reading is a private affair) and more impersonal (because, as he put it, "we never see each other"). Because the ambitions governing the performance were at once intimate and repressed, this indirect, mediated relationship with an other suited him much better than a more literal kind of public appearance could have done.[20]

Walter Whitman's transformation in the mid-1850s into the "Walt Whitman" who springs forth from the pages of *Leaves of Grass* is one of the great aesthetic miracles in American literary history. It will never be possible to explain such a transformation completely. But we can begin to account for the particular way "Song of Myself" addresses its audience with the idea that Whitman transferred his erotic longings to the realm of literary performance, where he could express them by disguising the *you* he wanted to court as the common reader of his time. This would help explain, for instance, how he could write what he had to know would be "devilish" to most readers in 1855 while nonetheless believing that it would be "affectionately absorbed" by them. Real popularity would have served Whitman in many ways, but the mere fiction that he was writing to be popular was equally valuable. That it was the fiction of being popular he needed would explain why, unlike Ralph Waldo Emerson or Mark Twain (to cite two other writers equally preoccupied with performing), Whitman would not make the compromises with or concessions to his audience's values that would have made real popularity at all possible.

I think this idea can also help us appreciate the performative rhythms of "Song of Myself." The way Whitman commingles public with private, politics with sexuality, the way *you* at times refers to a crowd of listeners and at others to a solitary reader, the way the poet's tone of voice runs the gamut from the stridency of the orator to the tenderness of the suitor – all of this is consistent with the notion of Whitman's divided rhetorical ambitions and the need to keep the division hidden from himself. "Song of Myself" as a little "r" romantic quest for love has to appear in the guise of a big "R" Romantic cultural manifesto. Whitman can advance toward intimacy with *you* as a singular reader only so far before needing to pull back to the psychically safer terms of a public relationship with *you* as his democratic audience.

David Leverenz is one of the few commentators to talk about what it feels like to be *you*, to articulate the emotional experience of reading "Song of Myself." For him that experience is similarly ambivalent: "I like [Whitman's] bold brag about my hidden strength of self, even when he claims to be my tongue. I welcome his call to 'fetch' me 'flush with myself,' so long as 'myself' includes me as well as him, and so long as his 'I' evokes a vaguely arrogant spirit rather than a specifically desiring body. My resistance leaps into consciousness when he gets too physical with me."21 I know what he means – there are moments when Whitman crowds me too closely – but on the whole, in my reading of it, "Song of Myself" is well served by the balance it maintains between oratory and seduction. When Whitman personalizes *you* as a singular reader we can feel the intensity of his concern with us, but whenever this begins to feel threatening, the poem allows us to step back into the safety of being part of a crowd. I think this balance is one reason why, with most readers, "Song of Myself" is his most successful performance poem. The same needs, however, that pushed Whitman up onto the stage he created in that poem led him to try to get still closer to the reader. The poem that immediately follows "Song of Myself" in the 1855 *Leaves,* for example, begins:

> Come closer to me,
> Push close my lovers and take the best I possess,
> Yield closer and closer and give me the best you possess.
>
> This is unfinished business with me. . . . how is it with you?
> I was chilled with the cold types and cylinder and wet paper between us.
>
> I pass so poorly with paper and types. . . . I must pass with the contact
>   of bodies and souls.

(1855, 87)

By thus struggling to erase the distance between *I* and *you* that the written word made possible, Whitman is making demands of the reading process and on the reader that most people find impossible to understand, much less accept. At the center of the most significant new poem in the 1856 *Leaves of Grass* is again an encounter between *I* and *you*, but now the relationship is carried to an extreme beyond which not even Whitman could subsequently go.

The poem, eventually titled "Crossing Brooklyn Ferry," was called "Sun-Down Poem" in 1856. The encounter it dramatizes occurs between Whitman and the readers or reader (I'll discuss the difference) of the future, "of a generation, or ever so many generations hence" (1856, 212). That Whitman moves his audience into the future is an oblique indication of how badly the 1855 *Leaves* had done with the contemporary reading public. Once Whitman evokes this future audience, he writes about it in the present tense while writing about himself in the past: "Just as you stand and lean on the rail . . . I stood" (1856, 213). The grammatical gimmick displays the same lovely insouciance as many of Whitman's most nonchalant refusals to worry about death: Even when he exists only in the past tense, he's still very much alive to his readers. This is Whitman's characteristic redefinition of the trope of poetic immortality: It is not in art per se that he can transcend death, but in art as the means by which he reaches an audience that is always being generationally renewed; he doesn't live in the poem, but in the minds of that audience. Yet the poem also suggests that Whitman had another reason for projecting his readers into the future, and that there was something besides immortality that he wanted from an audience.

If Whitman's deepest desire was for eternal fame, then the best referent for *you* in a phrase like "you who peruse me" (1856, 220) would naturally be plural: the largest possible number of readers. This is what *you* stands for at the beginning: "Crowds of men and women" on the ferry with Whitman become "you men and women" of the future, who will ride the ferry as he did (1856, 211, 212). In the course of the poem, though, both *I* and *you* advance out of these crowds toward each other – "Closer yet I approach you" (1856, 218) – until we get to a line like "It is not you alone, nor I alone" (1856, 218), which, although written in the negative, clearly implies two people, an *I* and a *you*. The poem's climax is the mystical communion of these two in the eternal present tense of the immediate reading of the poem; all falls away except *I* and *you*, who become a seamless *we:*

Now I am curious what sight can ever be more stately and admirable to me
　　than my mast-hemm'd Manhatta,
My river and sun-set, and my scallop-edged waves of flood tide,
The sea-gulls oscillating their bodies, the hay-boat in the twilight,
　　the belated lighter;
Curious what Gods can exceed these that clasp me by the hand, and with voices
　　I love call me promptly and loudly by my nighest name as I approach,

Curious what is more subtle than this which ties me to the woman or man
   that looks in my face,
Which fuses me into you now, and pours my meaning into you.

We understand, then, do we not?
What I promised without mentioning it, have you not accepted?
What the study could not teach – what the preaching could not accomplish
   is accomplished, is it not?
What the push of reading could not start is started by me personally, is it not?

(1856, 218–19)

Such absolute communion, such transcendence of all signs of otherness –
even the words and the reading through which the meeting takes place – is
the extreme beyond which Whitman could not go in his attempt to express
his ideal relationship with his reader. But although he couldn't go beyond it,
he arrived at the same extreme again in the well-known assertion he makes
in "So Long!," the poem he put last in the third, 1860, edition of Leaves of
Grass; "So Long!," which he used to close the performance in every subsequent edition of Leaves, expresses the relationship in still more intimate
terms:

My songs cease – I abandon them,
From behind the screen where I hid, I advance personally.

This is no book,
Who touches this, touches a man,
(Is it night? Are we here alone?)
It is I you hold, and who holds you,
I spring from the pages into your arms – decease calls me forth.

O how your fingers drowse me!
Your breath falls around me like dew – your pulse lulls the tympans
   of my ears,
I feel immerged from head to foot.
Delicious – enough.

(1860, 455)

While I think most readers are intrigued by these two passages, I expect
they probably decline to play the part of imaginary lover that Whitman
writes for them in both. They remain readers holding a book, mystified and
– if they think about it seriously – uncomfortable with the idea of suddenly
finding a strange man in their arms. But I think these passages reveal how
Whitman sought love or, more accurately, erotic satisfaction in the realm of
art, where his private imaginings became public performances of these per-

sonal encounters. And although they indicate this desire with almost embarrassing nakedness, I think these passages also confirm what I've been saying about his need to disguise as well as sublimate that quest. For example, they both describe encounters in the dark: What "*So Long!*" seems to require as a precondition for meeting the reader, that it is "night," "Crossing Brooklyn Ferry" helps us appreciate. Though thematically a point of the poem is that all time, time present and time future, is one, it nonetheless carefully tracks the passage of the time between sundown (when the poem begins) and night (when *we* come together). Exactly as *I* and *you* move closer to that moment when *I* am fused into *you*, so does the light disappear; the scene becomes "dimmer and dimmer" (1856, 215), until all that can be seen are "the fires from the foundry chimneys burning high and glaringly into the night" (1856, 215).

If the darkness is essential to hide the very encounter that Whitman is about to express, it is also appropriately what makes it possible to see the fires flaming forth, for throughout Whitman's early poetry, outflaming fires are a favorite image of the desires that he admits are hard to acknowledge. As he puts it in the first poem of the 1860 *Leaves*, talking specifically about "the ideal of manly love": "I will therefore let flame from me the burning fires that were threatening to consume me, / I will lift what has too long kept down those smouldering fires" (1860, 11). What in fact forms the immediate bond between the *I* and *you* who merge on the ferry in the "wild red and yellow light" of the flames (1856, 215) are the passions and feelings that Whitman calls "the dark patches" that are usually hidden in shame: "guile, anger, lust, hot wishes I dared not speak" (1856, 217). By confessing these desires without guilt in himself and identifying them in his reader without judgment, Whitman makes these "dark patches" the common ground on which he and his reader meet. They are not exactly unrepressed, however; they remain in wordlessness, the poetic equivalent of impenetrable darkness. The hot wishes remain unspoken, and what the reader "accepts" remains "unmentioned."

The other and most remarkable "screen" to the encounter between *I* and *you* in both these passages is death. "Decease calls me forth," Whitman writes in "*So Long!*" It is not a living man who steps in front of his songs to hold and be held by the reader, but a dead one – which makes the embrace at once more mystical and considerably less erotic. The passage both revels in bodily sensuality – arms, fingers, breath, pulse, delicious – and *disembodies* the poetic self. Even at this extreme of intimacy, alone in the dark with *you*, Whitman is talking about something that can only happen imaginatively, not physically. This is equally true about the union with the reader he stages in "Crossing Brooklyn Ferry." "I project myself," he notes at the start (1856, 215), establishing what the poem's distribution of verb tenses also underlines: He draws nearer to the reader only as a kind of holy spirit, a self that no longer possesses the body in which it stood by the ferry's rail. Again the diction is physical – fuse into, pour into, push – but the encounter is strictly metaphysical.

If we look again at "Song of Myself," we see the same pattern even there. As I said, throughout the poem he is continually moving closer to and farther from the reader; at the end he stops and makes a date – "I stop some where waiting for you" – but again, only after he has died and presided over his own bodily dissolution. The most explicit instance of this pattern occurs in the poem he put at the end of the "Calamus" sequence, where in the first two lines Whitman goes from being "Full of life" to dead, and in the next two the reader gets pushed into the distant future – at least "a century hence." *I* and *you* actually become lovers in this poem, but only in the poem – because *I* "seeking you" am dead, and *you* are "you, yet unborn":

When you read these, I, that was visible, am become invisible;
Now it is you, compact, visible, realizing my poems, seeking me,
Fancying how happy you were, if I could be with you, and become your lover;
Be it as if I were with you. Be not too certain but I am now with you.

(1860, 378)

"*As if* " – these are the two words that govern Whitman's relationship with his reader. One of Whitman's most impressive achievements as the poet of common reality is his ability to dispense almost entirely with metaphor. This metaphor, however, was the one that as a performer he could not do without. "As if" *I* and *you* were alone together is what enables him simultaneously to express and repress the longings that governed the dynamics of his literary performance.

The "Calamus" sequence is the most significant addition to *Leaves of Grass* in the 1860 edition. I don't have space to discuss the sequence in any detail, but I should mention the way it constitutes the last movement in Whitman's attempt to redefine the nature of poetic performance. (As Ezra Greenspan has noted, in most of the poems he wrote after 1860 Whitman is in "retreat from this reader-in-the-text strategy."[22]) Like "Song of Myself" and "Crossing Brooklyn Ferry," the "Calamus" poems as a group are very illocutionary, very much organized as a performance for a *you* the poems keep coming back to. By writing and publishing these poems, Whitman is moving in the direction of his private desires – "To tell the secret of my nights and days" (1860, 342) – and away from the values or assumptions he could expect his larger culture to share. He still cannot admit this into consciousness, and so he treats "the need of comrades" (1860, 342) and the secret love of strangers (1860, 362) as a political rather than a sexual theme: "The dependence of Liberty shall be lovers, / The continuance of Equality shall be comrades" (1860, 351). As he put it in prose in 1876, "the special meaning of the *Calamus* cluster . . . mainly resides in its political significance."[23] But of all Whitman's poems, these come closest to appealing directly to a singular *you*.

Even here he cannot escape his mixed emotions, and as Betsy Erkkila has noted, throughout the sequence *you* refers to everything from "America and democracy" to "an exclusive group" to "an intimate lover."[24] "Whoever You Are Holding Me Now in Hand," the third poem in the sequence, begins with Whitman's familiar assertion of equal opportunity, a universal *you*, but then quickly sets up a specific entrance requirement to the rest of the poems: "Who is he that would become my follower? / Who would sign himself a candidate for my affections? Are you he?" (1860, 345). The forty-five poems in "Calamus" move back and forth from the front of the stage where Whitman can address the reader directly, and variously define that reader in general and in very particular terms, but I think the tendency of the whole sequence is made manifest in the forty-first poem, which leaves the mass audience behind: "Among the men and women, the multitude, I perceive one picking me out by secret and divine signs, / . . . Some are baffled – But that one is not – that one knows me" (1860, 376). This passage brings the tension between his private needs and the public performance in which he sought to satisfy them right up to the surface of the poetry. Either the love of comrades is what knits the multitude together, or it is what distinguishes the few from that multitude, but it cannot be both.

To fix this squarely on the tension that I've suggested inheres in the performance itself: Either he is telling "the thoughts of all men in all ages and lands," as he put it in "Song of Myself" (1855, 41), or he is making "secret and divine signs" that only one other will know how to interpret. Of course, in terms of what I've tried to say about the psychic dynamic of Whitman's performance, it was both – in the sense that he was writing for a restricted *you* but had to see it himself as a universal one. In the first three editions of *Leaves*, between 1855 and 1860, he moved steadily further from defining the relationship between *I* and *you* as the democratic prophet speaking oratorically to the crowd and closer to enacting it as a private affair, as two lovers alone in the dark. But even as he came closer to identifying *you* this specifically, and closer to an explicit account of what "fetch you flush with myself" might mean, he projected *you* into the future. When he makes that strange leap in "*So Long!*" – "I spring from these pages into your arms" – he is, as the very last line of *Leaves of Grass* continued to say from 1860 until the final edition of 1892, "as one disembodied, triumphant, dead." In terms of what I'm saying about how he imagined the encounter with his reader, the first of those three adjectives may be the most important. We can say that seeking *you* through poetry is one means to triumph over death. We can also say, however, that seeking *you* through poetry was not unlike death: As "Walt Whitman" he is a "disembodied" lover.

NOTES

1 *Walt Whitman's Leaves of Grass: The First (1855) Edition,* ed. Malcolm Cowley (New York: Viking, 1959), p. 74. Subsequent references to Whitman's poetry will be cited in parentheses in text. Because one of my concerns is to trace changes in Whitman's performance as he enacted them during the 1850s, and not with his subsequent revisions, I quote in every case from the earliest version of a poem. All references to the first edition of *Leaves of Grass* will be to Cowley's widely available reprinting of it, cited as 1855, followed by the page number. All references to the second edition will be to the original issue: *Leaves of Grass* (Brooklyn, 1856), cited as 1856, followed by the page number. All references to the third edition will be to Roy Harvey Pearce's modern facsimile reprinting – *Leaves of Grass, By Walt Whitman: Facsimile Edition of the 1860 Text,* ed. Pearce (Ithaca, N.Y.: Cornell University Press, 1961) – cited as 1860, followed by the page number.
2 Hollis, *Language and Style in Leaves of Grass* (Baton Rouge: Louisiana State University Press, 1983), p. 98.
3 See especially the chapter called "Speech Acts" (*Language and Style,* pp. 65–123). "Illocutionary" is John Searle's term.
4 *Walt Whitman and the American Reader* (Cambridge: Cambridge University Press, 1990), p. 196. Hollis and Greenspan have done the most interesting recent work on the role of the reader in Whitman's poetry; my analysis of that topic, I think, complements theirs.
5 *Walt Whitman: Notebooks and Unpublished Prose Manuscripts,* ed. Edward F. Grier, 6 vols; 1: *Family Notebooks and Autobiography: Brooklyn and New York* (New York: New York University Press, 1984), p. 202.
6 "Whitman's New Man" in *Walt Whitman: Walt Whitman's Autograph Revision of the Analysis of Leaves of Grass (For Dr. R. M. Bucke's Walt Whitman),* text notes by Stephen Railton (New York: New York University Press, 1974), pp. 24–5.
7 Four dots (. . . .) are Whitman's markers in the 1855 text; three dots (. . .) indicate my ellipses. The quotations in this paragraph are, respectively, from pages 26, 45, 30, 51, 43, 43, 82, and 70.
8 Erkkila, *Whitman: The Political Poet* (New York: Oxford University Press, 1989), p. 182; she goes on to survey the various antecedents for *you* that can be found in the "Calamus" poems.

156,498

LIBRARY
College of St. Francis
JOLIET, ILLINOIS

9   Hollis, *Language and Style,* p. 94.

10 During Whitman's career, the best-selling American poet was Longfellow. According to William Charvat, Longfellow's most popular book of verse – *Hiawatha,* also published in 1855 – sold just over 50,000 copies in thirteen years (see Charvat, *The Profession of Authorship in America, 1800–1870,* ed. Matthew J. Bruccoli [n.p.: Ohio State University Press, 1968], p. 140).

11 In 1882 Whitman reprinted the 1855 preface in *Specimen Days and Collect;* one of the revisions he made at that time was to leave out the "proof of a poet" idea entirely (see *Walt Whitman: Leaves of Grass, Comprehensive Reader's Edition,* ed. Harold W. Blodgett and Sculley Bradley [New York: New York University Press, 1965], p. 729).

12 From the (London) *Critic,* April 1, 1856; quoted in *Walt Whitman: The Critical Heritage,* ed. Milton Hindus (New York: Barnes & Noble, 1971), p. 56.

13 See Michael Lynch, "'Here Is Adhesiveness': From Friendship to Homosexuality," *Victorian Studies* 29 (1985):67–96.

14 Bucke, *Walt Whitman,* p. 86.

15 Justin Kaplan does a good job telling the story of this exchange, and prints both Symonds's and Whitman's letters, in his biography: *Walt Whitman: A Life* (Toronto: Bantam Books, 1982), pp. 45–8.

16 Ong, "The Writer's Audience Is Always a Fiction," *PMLA* 90 (1975):9–21.

17 From the *Brooklyn Daily Times;* reprinted in *Walt Whitman: The Critical Heritage,* p. 45.

18 *Leaves of Grass, Comprehensive Reader's Edition,* p. 751.

19 Edward F. Grier, for example, lists almost fifty items of what he refers to as Whitman's "self-advertisements" in his edition of Whitman's notebooks and adds that "a close reading of the gossip columns of newspapers in New York, Washington, Philadelphia, and Camden . . . would probably turn up a large number of items [Whitman] planted": *Walt Whitman: Notebooks and Unpublished Prose Manuscripts,* 1, p. 333.

20 Hollis, on the other hand, argues that even as a poet, Whitman was an "orator manqué," who would have preferred to address his culture orally but who was temperamentally unsuited to such a performance, and so turned to writing by default (see *Language and Style in Leaves of Grass,* pp. 79ff. and 227).

21 Leverenz, *Manhood and the American Renaissance* (Ithaca, N.Y.: Cornell University Press, 1989), p. 31.

22 Greenspan, *Walt Whitman and the American Reader,* p. 221. For good accounts of the way Whitman's poetry changed after 1860, see the entire last chapter of Greenspan's book. See also Hollis, *Language and Style in Leaves of Grass,* passim.

23 Whitman, "Preface 1876," in *Comprehensive Reader's Edition,* p. 751.

24 Erkkila, *Whitman: The Political Poet,* pp. 182–3.

3

M. WYNN THOMAS

Fratricide and Brotherly Love: Whitman and the Civil War

"Must not worry about George, for I hope the worst is over – must keep up a stout heart."[1] This jotting from Whitman's notebooks early in 1863 is a vivid reminder of the person around whom, for Whitman and his family, the whole of the Civil War seemed to revolve for the full four years of its duration. A great deal of attention has by now been paid to everyone and everything else that was of central concern to Whitman at this time. His fierce commitment to the Union cause; his boundless admiration for Lincoln; above all, his tender yet invigorating care for the sick soldiers in general and the complex passion of his attachment to a few individuals in particular – all these matters have been extensively studied, not only for the insights they offer into Whitman's character but also for the light they throw on his poetry. By contrast, Whitman's wartime connection with his younger brother George (who was thirty-two when he entered the army, to the poet's forty-two) has been treated as at best a relatively minor matter of merely biographical interest. On closer examination, however, this fraternal relationship begins to assume much greater significance. Indeed, it could be argued that it was at least partly through George that Whitman was led to an intimate understanding of the real, hidden nature of the war, and that it was around George that Whitman was able (perhaps unconsciously) to arrange several of those imaginative configurations that articulated his hopes and anxieties and that supplied the deep structure of his war poetry.

For the Whitman family the Civil War literally began and ended with soldier George; for them he was the measure of the conflict. Six days after the rebels fired on the flag at Fort Sumter, George was one of the first to volunteer for active service, initially joining the Brooklyn 13th Regiment before reenlisting with the 51st New York Volunteers when his original 100-day term expired. Four years later, at the grand Victory Review in Washington, Whitman watched the parade with a pride doubtlessly intensified by relief that his younger brother had not only come safely through some of the fiercest campaigns of the war, but had also recently survived several months' incarceration in one of the notorious southern military prisons. Moreover George's war record had been a distinguished one, and his courage in the field had won him repeated promotion. Whitman's admiration of him extended to the regiment as a whole, and he carefully chronicled its battle honors. But this appreciation of what the veterans had suffered, and had achieved through the stubborn strength of their long endurance, was only one aspect of the complex insight Whitman had gained into the conditions of war through his close identification with his soldier-brother.

From the beginning, George was implicated (unwittingly, of course) in Whitman's work of creating in poetry a propagandist iconography for the Union cause. What Walt liked to think of as a "national uprising and volunteering" – namely, the frenzy of indignantly patriotic activity that immediately followed the firing on Fort Sumter – passed into *Drum-Taps* in the form of "First O Songs for a Prelude." There he showed "[t]he blood of [New York] city up – arm'd! arm'd! the cry everywhere," and the series of verbal snapshots he proudly displayed to back up his bellicose claims included one of "The tearful parting, the mother kisses her son, the son kisses his mother, / (Loth is the mother to part, yet not a word does she speak to detain him)."[2] This minor melodramatic detail, probably based on George's own departure, matters, however, only for what it more generally signifies – a spontaneous unanimity of support in New York for the Union effort. Whitman's hysterical delight at this was proportionate to his previous despair at the city's selfish pursuit, before Sumter, of its mercenary commercial goals. Its change of heart (short-lived though it turned out to be) was typified for him by George's enlistment. And although "First O Songs" depicts a city in the grip of an enlistment fever that sweeps across occupations and ignores social classes, the emphasis is nevertheless on "The mechanics arming, (the trowel, the jack-plane, the blacksmith's hammer, tost aside with precipitation)" (*Leaves of Grass, CRE* 280). This was in keeping with Walt's deepest political conviction, his abiding belief (which the war was profoundly to confirm) that the true custodian of his visionary democracy was not the ruling élite but the working class, of which his brother was a representative member.

Although there is much heatedly aggressive talk in "First O Songs" and in the other poems in *Drum-Taps* that relate to the early phases of the war, there is scarcely a mention of the enemy. This is no accident. Whitman's feelings about the South were so mixed and so complicated that he found it much easier to construct a positive rhetoric (in favor of union, democracy, liberty etc.) than a negative rhetoric. Two poems in particular – "Virginia –

The West" and "The Centenarian's Story" – represent interesting attempts to deal with the problem, and in both cases the figure of George Washington is crucial. The former poem constructs a tableau in which Virginia is depicted as "The noble sire fallen on evil days" who, in an amnesiac state of senile dementia, raises "The insane knife toward the Mother of All" (*Leaves of Grass, CRE* 293). She calmly rebukes him by reminding him that it was he who once famously supplied the greatest of all the defenders of her liberty, namely, George Washington. This tableau bears a curious resemblance to relations within Whitman's own family – as if, in creating the figure of the "sire," the poet had conflated his deceased father (moody, irascible, sporadically violent) with his oldest brother, Jesse, who eventually had to be committed to an insane asylum because of his increasingly violent attacks on his mother. What is really important, though, is that by figuring the North–South conflict as an internecine family drama, Whitman was able both to discount southern claims to independence and to make its "rebellion" seem a betrayal of its own history and of that "true self" symbolized by Washington. This was, of course, a propaganda ploy that ran directly counter to the South's image of itself. Confederates specifically saw themselves as the true heirs of the Revolutionary tradition, and found "an inspiring analogy between the struggle of the Confederacy and that of Revolutionary America under the generalship of Lee's great hero, Washington."[3]

The founding president of the United States is again the key figure in "The Centenarian's Story," a narrative poem set in Washington Park, Brooklyn, where an ancient veteran of the war against the British for independence watches young soldiers drilling before setting off for the front. Involuntarily the old man remembers the battle for Brooklyn, when the brigade of Virginia and Maryland, under the supreme command of Washington, marched out to meet the enemy, only to be decimated by murderous artillery (*Leaves of Grass: CRE,* 297). For Whitman the story is a nexus of meanings: The tragic irony is that southerners are about to march to their death once more, this time at the hands of fellow Americans who fight in the name of that very liberty that the South had so bloodily helped win. The North may, however, have to suffer defeat, like Washington himself, before final victory is won, and must therefore resolutely set its heart, like him, against the idea of capitulation. Thus, in both poems, Whitman creates images of "the enemy" in which feelings of pity, sympathy, and condemnation commingle, and in both cases George Washington is the crucial common denominator between North and South, a historically connecting figure who brings out the tragic absurdity of the conflict. The full name of Whitman's brother was George Washington Whitman, and it is difficult to believe that this fact didn't resonate in Walt's mind at some level when he was writing the two poems. What is at least possible is that his mixed feelings about fighting the South found expression in an unconscious association of the two George Washingtons. This may have helped him feel that the North, in the person of his soldier-brother, was setting out not to attack an enemy, but rather to liberate the South in the name of its true, libertarian, historical self.

What is certain is that Walt believed that the Union army, whose formation was so joyously celebrated in "First O Songs," would be a revolutionary body – revolutionary in the sense that, unlike all the armies of history, it would be thoroughly democratic in spirit and in structure. When reality struck home, it therefore struck with a revelatory force that eventually dictated the vision, the terms, and the pattern of Whitman's war poetry. As the relevant passages in *Specimen Days* show, he blamed the debacle at First Bull Run (July 21, 1861) entirely on the officers, and in concluding that the northern armies consisted of superb fighting men with abominable leaders, he may have been eagerly building on information given by George, some of whose early letters contained similarly aggrieved sentiments.[4]

When Walt experienced this criminal incompetence for himself after moving to Washington, he was quick to inform his prospective publisher, James Redpath, that "[t]he officers should almost invariably rise from the ranks – there is an absolute want of democratic spirit in the present system & officers – it is the feudal spirit exclusively."[5] In fact, George did gradually win promotion in precisely this way, rising from private to acting lieutenant colonel of his regiment by dint of proven courage and recognized qualities of natural leadership. Walt, though, continued to be possessed by the desire to produce a revolutionary book that would "push forward the very big & needed truth, that our national military system needs shifting, revolutionizing & made to tally with democracy, the people" (*Correspondence* I, 171). In a way, *Drum-Taps* was that book, undemonstratively egalitarian in language and in outlook, and bearing quiet testimony to the pure democracy of courage and of suffering Whitman believed he'd been privileged to witness in the hospitals.

Walt's journey to the hospitals started in December 1862, when he was aroused from the lethargy that had seized him virtually since the war began, by a newspaper report the family in Brooklyn thought might possibly be a garbled account of a serious injury sustained by George during the recent fighting. Whitman immediately traveled down to Washington and then on to Falmouth camp, where he met his brother, who, it transpired, had suffered only a superficial flesh wound six days earlier during the savage battle for Fredericksburg. As the surviving notebooks show, it was during this short visit to the front that Whitman collected the basic material for several of the best poems in *Drum-Taps*. It was also around this time that a pattern of reactions to the war began to form in his mind, a pattern that was to serve as the template for many of his future wartime experiences.

While Walt was searching for George, his mother received a letter from her soldier-son assuring her of his safety, "although I had the side of my jaw slightly scraped with a peice [sic] of shell which burst at my feet" (*Civil War Letters*, 75). It was to this letter Whitman alluded in a note he sent his mother after returning from Falmouth camp to Washington: "Mother, how much you must have suffered, all that week, till George's letter came – and all the rest must too. As to me, I know I put in about three days of the greatest suffering I ever experienced in my life" (*Correspondence* I, 58). Even after allowing for the exaggerated tones of familial concern that mark all Walt's correspondence with his mother, these sentences still strike one as basically genuine. The sincerity of the sentiments expressed seems to be confirmed by the pleas made in the postscript to the same letter: "Jeff must write oftener, and put in a few lines from mother, even if it is only two lines – then in the next letter a few lines from Mat, and so on. You have no idea how letters from home cheer one up in camp, and dissipate home sickness" (*Correspondence* I, 59). These pleas are all the more striking when one realizes that during the preceding few months, when Walt was still at home in Brooklyn, George had repeatedly, and fruitlessly, begged his family to be better correspondents. Indeed, the last of these notes home was written either on or about the day Walt actually arrived in Falmouth camp: "Mother why dont you write to a fellow I have not had a letter from you in a long time" (*Civil War Letters*, 77).

His arrival at the front brought home to Whitman what, in these circumstances, a letter really meant and what a vast psychological distance it had to cross. He realized, with a shock that galvanized his whole being and irrevocably altered his imagination, that the soldiers and civilians lived worlds apart from each other, separated by a fearful gulf of unknowing. Thereafter, much of his work for the remainder of the war consisted of attempts to connect these worlds – to build bridges, open lines of communication, establish lifelines – through his regular reports to the newspapers, by means of the poems he wrote, and, of course, via the innumerable letters he sent on behalf of the wounded and the dead. These famous letters lie at the heart of his enterprise and are a kind of synecdoche of all his wartime writings. His war poems became, in turn, his letters to the world, just as Emily Dickinson's poems were hers. Yet, even before he went in search of George, Whitman already knew the anguish of being totally in the dark about what was really happening in that other world of the soldier. Some members of his immediate family, particularly his emotionally unstable sister Hannah, tended to become hysterical under the strain of such uncertainty. Her letters sometimes grew shrill with anxiety: "Mother, will you *be sure* and send me word the minute you hear that he is safe. I am like you, I cannot see a bit of peace till I hear" (*Correspondence,* I, 220n73). By traveling to Falmouth, Whitman completed his bipolar education. He now had both a combatant's and a noncombatant's experience of receiving letters.

On August 11, 1863, Whitman put his own nagging fears in writing: "I sent Jeff a letter on Sunday, I suppose he got at the office – I feel so anxious to hear from George, one cannot help feeling uneasy, although these days sometimes it cannot help being long intervals without one's hearing from friends in the army" (*Correspondence* I, 130). By suggestive coincidence, he had only the previous day sent a poignant yet carefully composed letter to Mr. and Mrs. S. B. Haskell informing them of the death of their son Erastus. In the accidental juxtaposition of these two letters, an important connection may stand revealed. It may well be that Whitman's self-assumed duties as secretary to the wounded were unconsciously informed by those worries about George that were themselves dramatically focused in the acts of sending and receiving a letter.

It is worth noting that Whitman began the habit of writing letters home on behalf of the soldiers as soon as he first arrived in Falmouth camp and found that George was alive and well. The professional writer had discovered his wartime vocation as amateur amanuensis. His quiet discovery of the depth of experience locked away in the muteness and inarticulateness of these soldiers corresponded to his more famous, dramatic discovery in the same camp of the heap of amputated limbs outside the Lacy House. Indeed, the tearing of youngsters violently away from their families produced a sort of psychological amputation, as Whitman was to realize later in the hospitals. With reference to both kinds of maiming, physical and psychic, Walt discovered that the reality of the war continued to be unspoken because it was felt to be unspeakable and therefore remained unimaginable to the outside world. Whitman immediately set about breaking this taboo of silence, as this piece he sent to the *New York Times* shows:

> I do a good deal of this, of course, writing all kinds, including love-letters. Many sick and wounded soldiers have not written home to parents, brothers, sisters, and even wives, for one reason or another, for a long, long time. Some are poor writers, some cannot get paper and envelopes; many have an aversion to writing because they dread to worry the folks at home – the facts about

them are so sad to tell. I always encourage the men to write, and promptly write for them.[6]

Indeed, George Whitman himself confessed in a letter to his mother that "I have often thought when I have been in a pretty hot place, how glad I was that none of you at home, knew anything about it" (*Civil War Letters,* 78). This feeling existed in tension, though, with a worry that "you would frett and worry about not hearing from me, and I have often thought, I would give almost anything to let you know that I was all right" (*Civil War Letters,* 120).

Such contrary impulses – to conceal and to disclose – were, of course, felt unbearably acutely by Walt when he had sad news of suffering or of death to communicate. He resolved the problem, as both his letters and his poems show, by telling the truth within what a modern psychiatrist might call a "holding environment." In other words, he tried whenever possible to set potentially demeaning and humanly devastating suffering in a redeeming context, emphasizing the transfiguring courage of the sufferer, the love and care that attended him. "The Wound-Dresser" is his great epic achievement in this vein – "Bearing the bandages, water and sponge, / Straight and swift to my wounded I go" (*Leaves of Grass CRE,* 310). The poem is almost a conscious tour-de-force of sympathy, almost a tall tale of hyperbolic charity: "[I] Cleanse the [foot] with a gnawing and putrid gangrene, so sickening, so offensive, / While the attendant stands behind aside me holding the tray and pail." To emphasize the extravagant, histrionic element in this writing is not, however, to question, but rather to affirm, the authenticity of the experience.

What Whitman here reveals is what he has to conceal in his letters, namely, the psychic economy of his acts of sympathy – the heavy price in internal strain he has to pay for remaining "faithful, I do not give out": "I dress with impassive hand, (yet deep in my breast a fire, a burning flame)." Accounts by other observers confirm that in the hospitals a mounting hysteria frequently underlay a surface calm that could sometimes appear brutal in character. The heartlessness of the field surgeons as they snatched the knife from between their teeth to despatch yet more limbs was punctuated, said a contemporary observer, by the reaction of the occasional surgeon who, "having been long at work, would put down the knife, exclaiming that his hand had grown unsteady, and that this was too much for human endurance – not seldom hysterical tears streaming down his face" (*The Blue and the Gray,* 791).

The semiliterateness of many of the ordinary soldiers, which made them ill at ease with the written word, was another factor preventing their experiences from finding an effective voice. But if they needed a scribe, they also needed an interpreter – someone who could faithfully translate the reality of their situation into terms distant noncombatants could comprehend imaginatively as well as intellectually. Whitman's genius for doing this was inseparable from the humility of spirit with which he sought to adapt himself to the situation of the men – "With hinged knees returning I enter the doors, (while for you up there, / Whoever you are, follow without noise and be of strong heart." And yet, in spite of the heroic service he rendered, Whitman could not but remain centrally divided in feeling about his role as scribe. In *Drum-Taps,* the powerful cross-currents of feeling Whitman associated with the sending and the receiving of wartime letters – feelings in which his own and his family's anxieties about George merged with his secretarial work in the hospitals – are most clearly apparent in "Come Up from the Fields Father."

"O mother," Whitman wrote in August 1863, "what would we [have] done if it had been otherwise – if [George] had met the fate of so many we know – if he had been killed or badly hurt in some of those battles – I get thinking about it sometimes, & it works upon me so I have to stop & turn my mind on something else" (*Correspondence* I, 137). In "Come Up from the Fields," Whitman does indeed live out precisely such an anxiety fantasy in imagination, while at the same time putting himself in the place of those parents to whom he had sent news of their sons' serious injuries and even of their death (*Leaves of Grass CRE,* 302–3). The striking feature of the poem is the dramatic use made within it of two voices – the voice of the actual family receiving the letter and the voice of the observer who sympathetically watches their stunned reaction. There is already a suggestion of such a divide in the opening two lines of the poem: "Come up from the fields father, here's a letter from our Pete, / And come to the front door mother, here's a letter from thy dear son."

As the poem develops the two voices grow more distinct, yet are carefully coordinated, and they, of course, precisely correspond to the dual relationship in which Whitman himself stands to the imagined scene. He is both the imaginary sender of the letter and the imagined recipient of it, being both the brother who received news in Brooklyn of George's injuries at the front and the person who later wrote innumerable letters from Washington hospitals on behalf of the soldiers. Indeed, the shock of premonition first enters the poem at the very point the mother realizes "O this is not our son's writing, yet his name is sign'd, / O a strange hand writes for our dear son, O

stricken mother's soul!" In context, that "strange hand" signifies the impersonal forces that have commandeered the soldier's life and that coldly govern his affairs at a remote distance from the fertile family farm in Ohio,
"Where apples ripe in the orchards hang and grapes on the trellis'd vines."
This impression is reinforced by the sense given of the totally separate,
unsynchronized lives lived by soldiers and civilians, who inhabit entirely
different zones of experience: "While they stand at home at the door he is
dead already, / The only son is dead."

The poem concludes with a sensitive awareness of how the profound need
of the bereaved to mourn is damagingly frustrated by the absence of the
dead body: "In the midnight waking, weeping, longing with one deep longing, / O that she might withdraw unnoticed, silent from life escape and
withdraw, / To follow, to seek, to be with her dear dead son." As several
powerful poems in *Drum-Taps* show, Whitman undertook in the hospitals
to be not only a "psychological nurse" to the wounded (in Jerome Loving's
excellent phrase) but also a surrogate mourner of the dead – one who took
it on himself to do what the relatives could not do: to remember the dead
man in the very presence of his corpse. It is Whitman's psychologically
perceptive understanding of the human need to do this that turns "Vigil
Strange," for instance, into a poem *about* mourning as well as a poem *of*
mourning.

During the war, Whitman many times took it on himself to inform parents that their son had died and that he had been witness to that dying. In its
pathos, therefore, the letter sent on August 10, 1863, to Mr. and Mrs. S. B.
Haskell is typical of many over which he labored and anguished. But a short
time earlier he had implored them to write to their son, who was critically ill
with typhoid fever, and he had even gone so far as to "enclose you an
envelope to send your letter to Erastus – put a stamp on it, & write soon"
(*Correspondence* I, 119). Now he ended his sadly graphic account of Erastus's final decline with the following explanation:

> I write to you this letter, because I would do something at least in his memory
> – his fate was a hard one, to die so – He is one of the thousands of our
> unknown American young men in the ranks about whom there is no record or
> fame, no fuss made about their dying so unknown, but I find in them the real
> precious & royal ones of this land, giving themselves up, aye even their young
> and precious lives, in their country's cause.   (*Correspondence* I, 129)

These comments lay bare one of the deepest compulsions behind Whitman's
wartime activities, namely, his passionate determination to record the
achievements and sufferings of the "unknown" soldier and, wherever pos-

sible, to restore to those soldiers at least a trace of that personal identity that had almost been obliterated by the new techniques of mass warfare. And here once again it was his concern for George that had been the means of initiating Whitman into a revelatory understanding of the unprecedented scale and terrifyingly modern character of the Civil War.

When Whitman first arrived in Washington posthaste from home in search of George, he hadn't the slightest idea where he might be. There were, he discovered, upward of fifty hospitals in the vicinity, each of which treated thousands of soldiers. Had he not stumbled, by the purest chance, on old friends who could tell him where he was likely to find his brother, he might well have failed entirely to locate him. A few months later, by which time he was a veteran of the wards, he reflected indirectly on what might have been under the ironically laconic heading of "hospital perplexity":

> To add to other troubles, amid the confusion of this great army of sick, it is almost impossible for a stranger to find any friend or relative, unless he has the patient's specific address to start upon. Besides the directory printed in the newspapers here, there are one or two general directories of the hospitals kept at provost's headquarters, but they are nothing like complete; they are never up to date, and, as things are, with the daily streams of coming and going and changing, cannot be. I have known cases, for instance such as a farmer coming here from northern New York to find a wounded brother, faithfully hunting round for a week, and then compell'd to leave and go home without getting any trace of him. When he got home he found a letter from the brother giving the right address. (*Prose Works* I, 69)

Having himself been very fortunate to escape this demoralizing extreme of disorientation in December 1862, he was able to make his way fairly directly to George in camp at Falmouth. There he saw several bodies, each of which was covered by an identical brown woolen blanket. When he came to re-create this episode in "A Sight in Camp," he deliberately turned what had been an unexpected, unnerving encounter into a dignified ceremony of recognition (*Leaves of Grass CRE*, 306–7). (One of the least appreciated aspects of *Drum-Taps* is the ritualistic and liturgical character of so much of the poetry; no wonder Whitman could refer to himself as writing "psalms of the dead," the "sacred" texts of his secular faith.) Instinctively in the poem he reverts to the ancient triadic pattern that for millennia, and through the myths and legends of many cultures, has signified a process of understanding that culminates in transcendent illumination. When he first lifts the blanket, he sees the gaunt face of an elderly man that leaves him wondering, "Who are you my dear comrade?" Next, he uncovers the face of a "child" and inquires, "Who are you sweet boy with cheeks yet blooming?" In both cases, he is therefore baffled in his urgent wish to bestow a fully humanizing individual identity on these dead forms. "Then to the third," and this time it is "a face nor child nor old," but rather a union of these opposites: "Young man I think I know you – I think this face is the face of the Christ himself, / Dead and divine and brother of all, and here again he lies." Whitman, we know, was not an orthodox Christian, and it will not do to read this line as routinely pious. What seems to happen is that in this final attempt – the third, as required by the ancient symbolism of numbers – Whitman finds a "name" that can give human meaning even to the irreducibly anonymous suffering and death that man visits upon his fellows. This is an occurrence best understood, perhaps, in relation to the instances of "displaced Christianity," along with the "plethora of very unmodern superstitions, talismans, wonders, miracles, relics, legends and rumors" that, as Paul Fussell has shown, was a feature of the soldiers' psychological reaction to that other "triumph of modern industrialism, materialism, and mechanism," the First World War.[7]

Whitman found this wholesale anonymity of the dead very disturbing. He returned to the subject repeatedly in *Specimen Days* after the war, noting, for instance, that in one particular war cemetery only eighty-five of the bodies were identified. It is against this background that a poem like "Vigil Strange" cries out to be read. Then it can perhaps be appreciated that the emotional impulse behind the poem is partly the desire to ensure that the battlefield dead are individually recognized, remembered, and mourned: "Then on the earth partially reclining sat by your side leaning my chin in my hands, / Passing sweet hours, immortal and mystic hours with you dearest comrade – not a tear, not a word, / Vigil of silence, love and death, vigil for you my son and my soldier" (*Leaves of Grass CRE*, 303–5). It's noteworthy that in draft form the poem referred to the dead comrade in the third-person singular, so that in altering it to the second-person singular, Whitman increased both the sense of mystery and the sense of intimacy, as Edward Grier remarked in his edition of the notebook (*Notebooks* II, 611–13). Both versions are, in fact, highly significant because taken together they offer another example of that dual perspective that was noted in "Come Up from the Fields." Whitman both felt drawn toward a rapt immersion in the soldiers' experience (as expressed in the printed version of "Vigil Strange") and impelled to mediate their experience to the civilian world (hence the style of report of the original draft form).

The poetry of *Drum-Taps* is strongly marked by this quality of double vision. So, for instance, the entranced and entrancing little poem "Bivouac on a Mountain Side," in which Whitman loses himself in what he sees, is contrasted with "Cavalry Crossing a Ford" (*Leaves of Grass CRE,* 300). The former opens with "I see before me now a traveling army halting"; the latter, however, deliberately omits any mention of personal sight/vision – "A line in long array where they wind betwixt green islands." In this interesting version of a pastoral, the (civilian) reader is brought into the poem to be the observer of the scene: "Behold the silvery river, in it the splashing horses loitering stop to drink, / Behold the brown-faced men, each group, each person a picture, the negligent rest on the saddles."

It has generally been accepted that "Vigil Strange" was very loosely based on an actual story, or perhaps several stories, Whitman had heard veterans tell. But one other possible source is also worth considering. When he had moved to Washington directly after first finding George in Falmouth camp, Whitman sent a letter home to his mother in which he particularly mentioned the name of George's cook, Tom: "Tom thinks all the world of George – when he heard he was wounded, on the day of the battle, he left every thing, got across the river, and went hunting for George through the field, through thick and thin" (*Correspondence* I, 60). It seems very possible that other accounts Whitman may later have heard of soldiers scouring the battlefields for their wounded or dead comrades struck a particularly deep chord in him precisely because of this incident, about which he was told during his first, impressionable experience of life at the front. Here again, Whitman's close relationship with one very special soldier – his brother, George – sensitized his imagination and prepared it to respond acutely to certain kinds of war experience.

Very shortly after arriving in Washington from Falmouth camp, Whitman began his unofficial visits to the hospitals, and so inaugurated a routine that lasted for most of the remaining two and a half years of the war. In his letter of Saturday, Jan. 3, 1863, he explained to his sister-in-law Martha why he had first gone into the wards. A note had come from Brooklyn boys asking him to visit them in the Campbell hospital. There he found about 100 sick and wounded soldiers lying in the one long, whitewashed shed. "One young man was very much prostrated, and groaning with pain. I stopt and tried to comfort him. He was very sick. I found he had not had any medical attention since he was brought there – among so many he had been overlooked" (*Correspondence* I, 63). What Whitman had once more discovered, but this time in a new setting, was the dangerously depersonalizing scale of operations during this war. His time thereafter was to be spent combatting this sinister and genuinely life-threatening aspect of the hospital scene. As he realized a few days after this first visit, the life of the youngster he'd befriended had indeed been hanging in the balance, not for want of medical care only, but also for want of solicitously individualizing attention. Had he remained but a day or two longer without such encouragement, Whitman was convinced he would have lost heart entirely, and with it he would undoubtedly have lost his life.

Several of the great *Drum-Taps* poems enact a psychically healing process of bestowing a kind of identity on some poor unknown through a glance of sympathetic human recognition. The key word in Whitman's wartime vocabulary to describe such an event is "sight." It is a word he first began to use deliberately in his Falmouth camp notes at a time when, it seems, he was considering preparing a book of wartime "sights." The pictorial, even picturesque, associations of the word were, however, subordinated from the very outset to the new meanings that accumulated around it as Whitman used it in a new, highly charged context. It came to stand for epiphany – for those rare moments of spiritual insight granted to Whitman, when the hidden inner meaning of the war seemed to be revealed to him. It also came to stand for the perfectly focused glance that was the gift of such insight.

The word occurs in a pivotal position in "A March in the Ranks," a poem that opens with a soldier's baffled sense of being at the mercy of immense forces bent on inscrutable ends (*Leaves of Grass CRE,* 305–6). It is one of the passages where Whitman best suggests the impersonality of this war and the impossibility of the soldiers knowing where they were, both literally and metaphorically speaking: "A march in the ranks hard-prest, and the road unknown, / A route through a heavy wood with muffled steps in the darkness." This opening captures the bewildering speed with which the northern armies traversed the country, that impetus of modern warfare that is again registered in "As Toilsome I Wander'd Virginia's Woods": "Mortally wounded he and buried on the retreat, (easily all could I understand,) / The halt of a mid-day hour, when up! no time to lose – yet this sign left" (*Leaves of Grass CRE,* 307). As George tellingly wrote, "I believe I last wrote home from Lowell, but a fellow has to change about so often in this country, its [sic] hard work to remember where he was two days ago" (*Civil War Letters,* 93). It is therefore appropriate that no place names are ever mentioned in *Drum-Taps.* The action takes place in vividly realized yet carefully unspecified locations, thus creating a physical landscape that corresponds to the mental landscape of the soldiers. Indeed, the correlation between the general numbing of the mind and the weariness of the legs is suggested in the central lines from "An Army Corps on the March": "The swarming ranks press on and on, the dense brigades press on, / Glittering dimly, toiling under the sun – the dust-cover'd men, / In columns rise and fall to the undulations of the ground" (*Leaves of Grass CRE,* 301). Under such circumstances of forced marching, the halts became a mental event of striking character and assumed a heightened, hallucinatory, almost psychedelic quality.

When the army stops in "A March in the Ranks" the speaker stumbles, as it were, on an old church in a clearing, and "[e]ntering but for a minute I see a sight beyond all the pictures and poems ever made." At first everything is shadowy and vague, until, that is, he is able to see "At my feet more distinctly a soldier, a mere lad, in danger of bleeding to death, (he is shot in the abdomen,) / I staunch the blood temporarily, (the youngster's face is white as a lily,) / Then before I depart I sweep my eyes o'er the scene fain to absorb it all." Through this second glance, he is able to distinguish clearly the "faces, varieties, postures" of the various separate individuals who on first glance had merely constituted one dark, undifferentiated mass. His recognition of the individual soldier has therefore resulted in a transformation of the whole scene. Shadows have been resolved into flesh and blood. Not only have his eyes become used to the gloom, his inner eye of the imagination has also readjusted, so that it is once more capable of register-ing the real, piteously human scale of this extensive scene of suffering. By concentrating on the individual youngster at his feet, the speaker has been able to get the whole picture into focus and can view it in its proper colors and perspective. This, in poetic microcosm, is precisely what Whitman spent his time doing in the hospitals.

Lastly, before again being propelled onward and away, the speaker bends "to the dying lad, his eyes open, a half-smile gives he me, / Then the eyes close, calmly close, and I speed forth to the darkness." In his writings about the war, Whitman insisted almost obsessively that he was as much the consoled as the consoler in his work of caring for the dying. There was in him a kind of repetition compulsion, which seems partly to have stemmed from the need to overcome his fear of death by witnessing, time and again, the inspiring calm with which the soldiers faced their end. Another element in the obsession, however, may have been Whitman's need to prepare him-self mentally to deal with the probable news of George's death. "I suppose it is idle to say I think George's chances are very good for coming out of this campaign safe," he wrote his brother in May 1864, "yet at present it seems to me so – but it is indeed idle to say so, for no one can tell what a day may bring forth" (*Correspondence* I, 225). He proceeded to fortify Jeff by draw-ing on his hospital experiences: "then one finds, as I have the past year, that our feelings & imaginations make a thousand times too much of the whole matter – Of the many I have seen die, or known of, the past year, I have not seen or heard of *one* who met death with any terror."

So concerned was Walt in June 1864 that George might be one of the casualties brought to Washington that he refused to return home to Brooklyn, although his health had by then broken down. In the event, George survived the war – and outlived his brother – to die eventually in 1902. It was with mingled relief and pride, therefore, that Walt watched the great Washington review that preceded demobilization. He recorded the emotional occasion in a poem: "How solemn as one by one, / As the ranks returning worn and sweaty, as the men file by where I stand, / As the faces the masks appear, as I glance at the faces studying the masks" (*Leaves of Grass CRE,* 321–2). By that mention of "masks" Whitman overtly meant to indicate that it is always the indwelling spirit that constitutes essential identity, and not external features and manners: "How solemn the thought of my whispering soul to each in the ranks, and to you, / I see behind each mask that wonder a kindred soul, / O the bullet could never kill what you really are, dear friend, / Nor the bayonet stab what you really are." But the poem is also about Whitman's pride in the unique intimacy of his knowledge of the soldiers' life: If they present only a mask to public (civilian) scrutiny, to him they show a different, private face. "Easily all could I understand," he wrote in "As Toilsome I Wander'd," meaning that he was skilled, through hospital experience, at deciphering the coded meanings, the "signs," of this closed society.

But could he really understand all? Could he truly penetrate the mask? Was he genuinely one of them? The agonizing answer to these questions was "no," as Whitman realized when, on December 26, 1864, his brother's trunk was opened – George being by then an inmate of one of the notorious military prisons of the South. The trunk had just arrived and had "stood some hours before we felt inclined to open it." Eventually his mother and brother Eddy nerved themselves for the task and were confronted by papers, a diary, a revolver, photographs, and countless other private knickknacks that reminded them painfully of George, from whom they had not heard for almost three months: "whether living or dead, we know not." That evening Whitman settled down to read the diary, and found it contained the barest records of George's movements, along with a list of the campaigns in which he had participated:

> I can realize clearly that by calling upon even a tithe of the myriads of living & actual facts, which go along with, & fill up this dry list of times & places, it would outvie all the romances in the world, & most of the famous histories & biographies to boot. It does not need calling in play the imagination to see that in such a record as this, lies folded a perfect poem of the war, comprehending all its phases, its passions, the fierce tug of the secessionists the interminable

fibre of the national union, all the special hues and characteristic forms &
pictures of the actual battles, with colors flying, rifles snapping cannon thun-
dering, grape whirling, armies struggling ships at sea or bombarding shore
batteries, skirmishes in woods, great pitched battles, & all the profound scenes
of individual death, courage, endurance & superbest hardihood & splendid
muscular wrestle of a newer larger race of human giants, with all furious
passions aroused on one side, & the sternness of the unalterable determination
on the other.   (*Notebooks* II, 745–6)

The paradox is clear. These are the sights that Whitman had not seen but
George presumably had. In this respect, Walt had, after all, been able to
follow George only so far: far enough to see what the war was really like,
but not far enough to get to the heart of the soldier's experiences. But these
are also the scenes that Whitman, the artist, can convincingly conjure into
being by unfolding the perfect poems of the war, whereas the soldier simply
records a "dry list of times and places." In fact, it was in part the very
artistic sensibility that enabled Whitman to mediate aspects of the war to
the civilian world that also set Whitman apart from the mental world of
George and other soldiers – a world of frequently prosaic, practical effort.
To set passages from George's letters alongside broadly corresponding experiences in Walt's poetry is to discover differences between the two that vary
from the comic to the tragic. So, for instance, George's yearnings for home
take the form of touchingly simple memories: "I often think that I can
imagine just what you are all doing at home and ile bet now, that Mother is
makeing pies I think Mat is putting up shirt bosoms like the deuce so as to
get through before dinner I guess Sis is down stairs helping Mother mix the
dough, Walt [then still at home] is up stairs writing, Jeff is down town at the
Office, Jess is pealing potatoes for dinner, and Tobias has gone down cellar
for a scuttle of coal, Bunkum I guess is around somewhere looking for a
good chance to go sogering" (*Civil War Letters,* 71). Contrast that picture
with Whitman's haunted and haunting account, in "By the Bivouac's Fitful
Flame," of the way the ghosts of home throng the minds of soldiers in the
field: "While wind in procession thoughts, O tender and wondrous
thoughts, / Of life and death, of home and the past and loved, and of those
that are far away; / A solemn and slow procession there as I sit on the
ground, / By the bivouac's fitful flame" (*Leaves of Grass CRE,* 301).

To put it crudely: George's work was to produce results, Walt's was to
produce meanings. They were very different indeed in their temperaments
and in their gifts. And the same difference manifested itself, to varying
degrees, in Whitman's dealings with most of the soldiers he so lovingly
tended in the hospitals. "Adieu O soldier," Whitman wrote in a poem that

captures this difference poignantly, "You of the rude campaigning, (which we shared)." The painful truth was that he never could fully share in the "rudeness" of such campaigning, as the second verse paragraph tacitly admits: "Adieu dear comrade, / Your mission is fulfill'd – but I, more warlike, / Myself and this contentious soul of mine, / Still on our own campaigning bound" (*Leaves of Grass CRE,* 325). Walt's campaigns were, of course, examples of what Blake called mental warfare – episodes in the politics of the spirit and attempts to change human society by transforming human consciousness. Although over a three-year period the soldiers he tended in the hospitals had been regularly recruited by Whitman for his campaigns, they themselves had no awareness of this and very little understanding of what he was about.

Implicit in Whitman's portrayals of men at war and in the military hospitals was the view that they constituted an alternative and superior society, the redeemed society of his visionary America. By contrast, the civilian society of actual wartime America was for him "the world of gain and appearance and mirth" he stigmatized in "The Wound Dresser." His deep mistrust of the power of money in the booming capitalist society of the North led him to emphasize that a different "currency" circulated in the hospitals – a currency of love and affection symbolized, as he explained in *Specimen Days,* both by the little gifts he brought the men and the caresses he exchanged with them: "Another thing became clear to me – while *cash* is not amiss to bring up the rear, tact and magnetic sympathy and unction are, and ever will be, sovereign still" (*Prose Works* I, 82). *Drum-Taps* is, therefore, a book that sought to replace the cash nexus that was coming to dominate existing northern society with a network of intimate, comradely relationships.

Whitman's dream was that, once returned to civilian life, the soldiers would proceed to infuse it with a new, comradely spirit. However, what actually happened was well exemplified by what became of George in the months following demobilization. He sank part of his army savings into speculative building, only to find that the construction industry was already controlled by the New York bosses. This disappointment evidently left its mark on him, for his mother complained that her son's "wartime generosity had shrunken to insensitive frugality" (*Civil War Letters,* 28). Perhaps intuiting at heart that this would, after all, be the dispiriting course of postwar society, Walt chose not to return to Brooklyn with his brother but to remain in Washington, where he continued to visit those increasingly forgotten soldiers who had been left behind in the hospitals. So Walt and George went the separate ways dictated by their different temperaments, with the latter never realizing the contribution he had inadvertently made to his brother's baffling poetry. But that he had indeed contributed is finally confirmed by the line about the Civil War that Whitman added to "Song of Myself": "Battles, the horrors of fratricidal war, the fever of doubtful news, the fitful events" (*Leaves of Grass CRE*, 32). It was "the fever of doubtful news" about George that had so inflamed Walt's imagination in December 1862, and the outcome was a moving poetry of palimpsest in which brotherly love was overwritten by, yet never obliterated by, "the horrors of fratricidal war."

NOTES

1   Edward F. Grier, ed., *Notebooks and Unpublished Prose Manuscripts*, 6 vols. (New York: New York University Press, 1984), vol. II, p. 548. Subsequent references to this edition will be cited parenthetically in the text as *Notebooks*.
2   *Leaves of Grass: Comprehensive Reader's Edition*, ed. Harold W. Blodgett and Sculley Bradley (New York: New York University Press, 1965), p. 281. All subsequent references to this edition will be cited in the text parenthetically as *Leaves of Grass, CRE*.
3   Henry Steele Commager, ed., *The Blue and the Gray* (New York: Fairfax Press, 1982 edition), pp. xxix–xxx. Subsequent references to this book will be cited parenthetically in the text as *The Blue and the Gray*.
4   For instance, his comment in a letter to his mother following the battle of First Fredericksburg (December 13, 1862): "I am pretty well satisfied that as yet we have had no one to command the Army of the Potomac that was a match for Lee, and it seems to me that in all the fights I have been in since we have been in the Potomac army (except the battle of South Mountain) we have been most terribly outgeneraled, the men fight as well as men can fight, and I firmly believe that all we want, is some one competent to lead, to finish up this work in short order." Jerome M. Loving, ed., *Civil War Letters of George Washington Whitman* (Durham, N.C.: Duke University Press, 1975), p. 80. All subsequent references to this book will be cited parenthetically in the text as *Civil War Letters*.
5   Edwin Haviland Miller, ed., *Walt Whitman: The Correspondence* (New York: New York University Press, 1961), I, 171. All subsequent references to this edition will be cited parenthetically in the text as *Correspondence*.
6   Walt Whitman, *Prose Works 1892,* ed. Floyd Stovall, 2 vols. (New York: New York University Press, 1963), I, p. 38n. All subsequent references to this work will be cited parenthetically in the text as *Prose Works*.
7   Paul Fussell, *The Great War and Modern Poetry* (Oxford: Oxford University Press, 1977), p. 115.

4

JAMES PERRIN WARREN

Reading Whitman's Postwar Poetry

Two significant problems face the student who wishes to read beyond Whitman's stunning achievements in "Song of Myself," "The Sleepers," "Crossing Brooklyn Ferry," "Out of the Cradle Endlessly Rocking," "As I Ebb'd with the Ocean of Life," and "When Lilacs Last in the Dooryard Bloom'd." The first problem concerns the clear changes in Whitman's voice and style in the post–Civil War poems. Where Emerson rather quizzically praised the 1855 *Leaves of Grass* as a "strange mixture of the *Bhagavad-Gita* and the *New York Herald,*" most twentieth-century critics remark disapprovingly of the abstract, archaic vocabulary and conventional poetic form of the late poetry.[1] Though Whitman is often considered America's greatest poet, he is accorded greatness on the strength of the first ten years of his career.

The second problem is perhaps even more critical and relates to the shape of Whitman's career. If the prewar style represents Whitman at his best, then the twenty-seven years of his postwar writing should be read as a story of decline and failure. But this tragic narrative in fact mixes two plots – one concerning Whitman's life of illness and depression, particularly in the 1870s; the other concerning the majority of his public years as a writer, including the three postwar editions of *Leaves,* the so-called Deathbed Edition of 1891–2, and the voluminous prose of *Democratic Vistas, Specimen Days,* and *Prose Works 1892.*[2] Modern critics appear willing to take the poet at his word when he writes, in "A Backward Glance O'er Travel'd Roads," that *Leaves of Grass* is "an attempt, from first to last, to put *a Person,* a human being (myself, in the latter half of the Nineteenth Century, in America,) freely, fully and truly on record" (*CRE,* 573–4). But they waver, at the very least, in accepting Whitman's stated preference for the 1891–2 edition: "As there are now several editions of L. of G., different texts and dates, I wish to say that I prefer and recommend this present one, complete, for future printing."[3] In effect, critics tend to view Whitman either as a gifted *naif,* a poet who is unaware of his own gifts and accomplishments, or as a moral coward intent on preserving and promoting his

45

fragile reputation. For all of these reasons, modern readers tend to promote a particular edition of *Leaves* as what Whitman called "the *true* Leaves of Grass" (*Corr.* 1: 44), and the 1855 edition has enjoyed the most attention since Malcolm Cowley's popular paperback edition appeared in 1959.

The problems of style and criticism are, of course, closely connected to one another, and they must be treated in just that close connection. The critical narrative of decline exercises such power over readers of Whitman's poetry that they are often unable to separate their reading of the poetry from their reading of the poet's career/life. In its most extreme form, the privileging of the critical narrative could obscure Whitman's post–Civil War poetry to such an extent that it would be unread, lost. Fortunately, however, Whitman's writing provides several means of avoiding such losses, for it reveals at least two distinct models of stylistic change.

I

The first model could be called "revolutionary," and the primary example of the style appears in the sudden, unexpected publication of the first *Leaves of Grass* in 1855. The poems Whitman published from 1838 to 1850 are mainly exercises in iambic tetrameter quatrains, with rhymed second and fourth lines. Archaisms and conventional poetic formulas dominate the diction, especially in the earliest poems, whereas in poems like "Song for Certain Congressmen" and "Blood-Money" Whitman strives to create a blend of the poetic and the vernacular.[4] With very little warning, then, the 1855 *Leaves* marks an abrupt departure from Whitman's previous style and an absolute discontinuity with the traditions of English verse.

The poetics of discontinuity and Whitman's revolutionary style are perhaps most apparent in the first words of the 1855 volume:

> America does not repel the past or what it has produced under its forms or amid other politics or the idea of castes or the old religions . . . . accepts the lesson with calmness . . . is not so impatient as has been supposed that the slough still sticks to opinions and manners and literature while the life which served its requirements has passed into the new life of the new forms . . . perceives that the corpse is slowly borne from the eating and sleeping rooms of the house . . . perceives that it waits a little while in the door . . . that it was fittest for its days . . . that its action has descended to the stalwart and well-shaped heir who approaches . . . and that he shall be fittest for his days.
>
> (CRE, 711)

This opening pronouncement of literary and cultural independence is not as revolutionary as it first seems. Though Whitman pronounces the traditions of English literature a corpse, lingering in the doorway of American culture, he also acknowledges the corpse as having produced the "stalwart and wellshaped heir" of America. The rhetoric of the passage balances patience and impatience, continuity and discontinuity, by creating a family resemblance between the corpse and the wellshaped heir.

It could be argued that the identity of the corpse is not so specific as I have asserted, but later in the 1855 Preface, Whitman makes the identification likely:

> The English language befriends the grand American expression. . . . it is brawny enough and limber and full enough. On the tough stock of a race who through all change of circumstance was never without the idea of political liberty, which is the animus of all liberty, it has attracted the terms of daintier and gayer and subtler and more elegant tongues. It is the powerful language of resistance . . . it is the dialect of common sense. It is the speech of the proud and melancholy races and of all who aspire. It is the chosen tongue to express growth faith self-esteem freedom justice equality friendliness amplitude prudence decision and courage. It is the medium that shall well nigh express the inexpressible.   (CRE, 729–30)

Whitman reads the English language as a direct expression of the English spirit – "a race who through all change of circumstance was never without the idea of political liberty." Like the opening paragraph of the Preface, this passage seeks to accept the past without being dominated by it. Hence Whitman's parallel clauses ambiguously praise "it," which could refer to the English language or to the "grand American expression." The passage mixes the two in the same way that it mixes linguistics and ethnology, implying that the political liberty of American democracy is inherited along with the "chosen tongue" of English. Whitman's revolutionary vision of the "grand American expression" owes a clear debt to the "befriending" role of the English language. Moreover, Whitman freely acknowledges that debt, even though he also calls "it" the "powerful language of resistance."

The model of revolutionary style reveals a more varied and complex sense of Whitman's relationship to tradition than the totalizing critical narrative suggests. If the opening paragraph of the 1855 Preface can be read as an Oedipal and cultural fantasy of independence, it also presents an undeniable kinship between corpse and heir. Likewise, if the "grand American expression" is the "chosen tongue" that will "well nigh express the inexpressible," it is also "befriended" by the English language and draws on the heritage of English language and culture. Nor is this mixed sense of the revolutionary style confined to the Preface. "Song of Myself," although utterly revolutionary in style and theme, also pays ample tribute to the past; thus Whitman writes with near contempt of past religions in Section 41, while in Section 43 he figures himself as participating in past religious rites.[5]

The second model of stylistic change, already implicit in the first, could be called "evolutionary." Examples of this model abound in the poet's postwar essays, prefaces, and poems. In the 1872 Preface to "As a Strong Bird on Pinions Free," Whitman employs the figure of "some colossal drama" to portray the cultural role of the United States in the world:

> To me, the United States are important because, in this colossal drama, they are unquestionably designated for the leading parts, for many a century to come. In them History and Humanity seem to seek to culminate. Our broad areas are even now the busy theatre of plots, passions, interests, and suspended problems, compared to which the intrigues of the past of Europe, the wars of dynasties, the scope of kings and kingdoms, and even the development of peoples, as hitherto, exhibit scales of measurement comparatively narrow and trivial. And on these areas of ours, as on a stage, sooner or later, something like an *eclaircissement* of all the past civilization of Europe and Asia is probably to be evolved.   (*CRE*, 742)

The passage restates many of the ideas advanced in the 1855 Preface: America is figured as the principal actor in the world's cultural drama, and the plot Whitman proposes is progressive, leading to an *eclaircissement*. Just as important as the ideas, however, is the style of the passage. In the 1855 Preface, Whitman resists the dependence of American culture on past cultures, past languages. In the 1872 Preface, he acknowledges the influence of the past by placing it within an evolutionary scheme: "an *eclaircissement* of all the past civilization of Europe and Asia is probably to be evolved." Both the figuration and the visionary narrative make American culture the culmination and necessary outcome of *all* past civilizations, though Whitman hedges at the end of the passage, moving from "unquestionably designated for the leading parts" to "probably to be evolved." Within the poet's evolutionary vocabulary, his real doubts concerning American culture are ultimately a measure of possibility for evolutionary change. Thus the "plots, passions, interests, and suspended problems" of the present render all of "the past of Europe . . . comparatively narrow and trivial." But if that apparent contrast echoes the Oedipal tone of the 1855 Preface, the word *eclaircissement* binds American English to the "past of Europe," both in the French language and in the history of the English language. For Whitman's use of the foreign term harks back to its initial borrowing in the seventeenth century and to its common usage in eighteenth-century English (*OED*). Moreover, Whitman's projected *eclaircissement* will clarify the *past*, not the present or future. The "colossal drama" features, therefore, a variety of combinatory rhetorical strategies.

The hallmark of Whitman's combinatory strategies and evolutionary style is the continuity between past and present. Continuity does not preclude significant and palpable change, nor does it represent an obstacle to Whitman's progressivist view of language and culture. Rather, the theory of evolution gives Whitman a scientific metaphor for understanding how the history of Western civilization has resulted in the "colossal drama" of the United States. Moreover, the theory of evolution allows Whitman to figure his own changing poetic style and the resulting poems as "something like an *eclaircissement*" of all his past work.

If the 1872 Preface suggests that the theory of evolution plays a role in Whitman's understanding of cultural history, the 1876 Preface to *Leaves of Grass* and *Two Rivulets* points to a parallel role in figuring the postwar poems and their "new" style. The 1876 Preface distinguishes between the "first and main Volume, LEAVES OF GRASS" (*CRE*, 746), and the "special chants of Death and Immortality," which are supposed to "stamp the coloring-finish of all, present and past" (747). In an extensive, seven-paragraph note on the "special chants," Whitman focuses on the 1871 book *Passage to India* as providing that "coloring-finish":

> PASSAGE TO INDIA. – As in some ancient legend-play, to close the plot and the hero's career, there is a farewell gathering on ship's deck and on shore, a loosing of hawsers and ties, a spreading of sails to the wind – a starting out on unknown seas, to fetch up no one knows whither – to return no more – And the curtain falls, and there is the end of it – So I have reserv'd that Poem, with its cluster, to finish and explain much that, without them, would not be explain'd, and to take leave, and escape for good, from all that has preceded them. (Then probably *Passage to India*, and its cluster, are but freer vent and fuller expression to what, from the first, and so on throughout, more or less lurks in my writings, underneath every page, every line, every where.)   (747)

The image of the "legend-play" recalls the "colossal drama" of the 1872 Preface, and as in that earlier passage, Whitman here combines the gestures of farewell and starting out. But in the 1876 Preface, the mixed gestures figure Whitman's sense of his own poetry. *Passage to India* is supposed to play a double role in the shipboard drama Whitman imagines: First, it must "finish and explain" the previous poems; second, it must "take leave, and escape for good, from all that preceded them." In Whitman's evolutionary figurations, the 1871 collection plays the same role in the poet's career that America plays in cultural history – that of "something like an *eclaircisse-*

ment," a role that merges continuity and significant change. Later in the note, therefore, Whitman writes that *Passage to India* is "based on those convictions of perpetuity and conservation which, enveloping all precedents, make the unseen Soul govern absolutely at last" (748).

2

Whitman's "convictions of perpetuity and conservation" find clear parallels in popular versions of evolutionary theory that were current in postwar America. One such version is contained in the popular axiom "Ontogeny recapitulates phylogeny," propounded and popularized by Ernst Haeckel.[6] Whitman's phrase, "enveloping all precedents," is another formulation of Haeckel's famous sentence. But more important than Haeckel's possible influence on Whitman's ideas concerning evolution is the currency of evolutionary ideas in the decades following the publication of Darwin's *Origin of Species* in 1859. Whitman was acquainted with two of the most important popularizers, Edward L. Youmans and John Fiske, and he was familiar with Youmans's important periodical, *Popular Science Monthly,* published by Appleton and described as "the most influential scientific magazine of the age."[7] The sources of Whitman's ideas are less important than the poet's strategy of corroborating his own views by means of popular scientific theories.

That strategy is abundantly clear in Whitman's postwar prose writings, from *Democratic Vistas* (1871) to "A Backward Glance O'er Travel'd Roads" (1888). In the 1876 Preface, for instance, he asserts that "without being a Scientist, I have thoroughly adopted the conclusions of the great Savans and Experimentalists of our time, and of the last hundred years, and they have interiorly tinged the chyle of all my verse, for purposes beyond" (*CRE,* 754). And he delineates the "purposes beyond" as "the greatest office of Scientism, in my opinion, and of future Poetry also, to free from fables, crudities and superstitions, and launch forth in renewed Faith and Scope a hundred fold" (755). Whitman's "convictions of perpetuity and conservation" thus apply to his vision of combining "the unseen Soul," evolution, and poetry.

The combinatory strategy is particularly clear in the essay "Darwinism – (Then Furthermore)," first published in *Two Rivulets* under the title "Origins – Darwinism – (Then Furthermore)" and reprinted in the "Notes Left Over" section of *Specimen Days & Collect* in 1882. The 1876 title suggests the three-part structure of the short essay. Whitman begins by opposing the two theories of human origins – divine and developmental – and then suggests that "out of them is not a third theory, the real one, or suggesting the real one, to arise" (*PW*, 2: 524). Similarly, in the paragraph devoted to "Darwinism," Whitman begins by praising the "all-devouring claims" of evolutionary theory and then concludes that "the Evolution theory" is "but one of many theories, many thoughts, of profoundest value – and re-adjusting and differentiating much, yet leaving the divine secrets just as inexplicable and unreachable as before – may-be more so" (524). In the third section of the essay, Whitman escapes his circular underminings by proposing that "only the priests and poets of the modern, at least as exalted as any in the past, fully absorbing and appreciating the results of the past, in the commonalty of all humanity, all time, (the main results already, for there is perhaps nothing more, or at any rate not much, strictly new, only more important modern combinations, and new relative adjustments,) must in-deed recast the old metal, the already achiev'd material, into and through new moulds, current forms" (524–5). Poetry is the "then furthermore" that resolves the opposition between religious and scientific theories of origins. And it does so by adapting the "main results" of the past to "modern combinations," recasting old metal into current forms. As in the Prefaces of 1872 and 1876, Whitman's rhetoric stresses continuity in combination with change.

For many readers, the problem with Whitman's rhetorical resolution of the debate over human origins is that it does not so much resolve the contradiction as evade it. But that rhetorical strategy is characteristic of Whitman in all his phases. Moreover, in the 1888 conversation with Traubel about Youmans, Whitman describes the strategy in somewhat surprising terms: "I like the scientific spirit – the holding off, the being sure but not too sure, the willingness to surrender ideas when the evidence is against them: this is ultimately fine – it always keeps the way open – always gives life, thought, affection, the whole man, a chance to try over again after a mistake – after a wrong guess" (*WWWC*, 1: 101). Whitman's idea of the "scientific spirit" emphasizes the provisional, undogmatic assertion of truths, rather than an absolute, totalizing version of "the" truth. For that reason, he can tell Traubel that "I always put the two together: Emerson, Darwin" because they both possess "the style of all the greatest sages . . . the modesty – the readiness to yield, to see what they might have excuses for not seeing. All modern science is saturated with the same spirit, and in this exists its excuse for being" (*WWWC*, 2: 517).

The concurrence of the scientific spirit and Whitman's characteristic rhet-oric has as much to do with the evolution of language as it does with the language of evolution. Whitman had been a student of language theories since the early 1850s, and his studies coincided with the establishment of comparative philology as a new science. Popular versions of current language theories emphasized developmental models of linguistic change and, perhaps more important, drew a strict connection between the form of a language and the spirit of the people speaking that language. Thus, for example, a popularizer like Baron Bunsen, whose *Outlines of the Philosophy of Universal History* Whitman studied, could assert that the families of languages correspond to stages of spiritual development.[8] Whitman is merely summarizing contemporary notions of language, then, when he writes in *Rambles Among Words:*

> The Japhetites embrace the noblest antique and later races – the Brahminic Indians, the Persians, Medians, Greeks, Romans and European peoples – theirs those noble and highly developed languages, the Sanskrit, Zend, Persian, Hellenic, Latin, Germanic, Keltic, Teutonic. In the Vedas of the Indians, especially the hymns of the Rig-Veda, and in the Zend-Avesta of the Persians – primeval documents of the Iranic world – we see the germs of all we call Europe. Here were the beginnings of the cultures of the occidental world. Science was born in that mind, the intuition of nature, the instinct for political organization and that direct practical normal conduct of life and affairs.
>
> From this mind, too flowered out the grandest and most spiritual of languages. The Japhetic or Iranic tongues are termed by the master-philologers the Organic Group, to distinguish them from the Agglutinative and Inorganic speech-floors that underlie them in the Geology of Language. They alone have reached the altitude of free intellectual individuality and organism. To them belongs the splendid plasticity of Sanskrit, Greek, German, English! Such are the primeval lines in the genesis of the English language. And so it is that sounds and structures – words and forms – that were heard along the Ganges, five thousand years ago – words heard in Benares and Delhi, in Persia and Greece – are now scaling the Rocky Mountains of the Western world!
>
> (*NUPM*, V: 1653)

In these two paragraphs, Whitman openly celebrates the ethnocentric assumptions of many nineteenth-century "master-philologers." In the poet's version of Indo-European linguistics, the English language is the latest flowering forth of the "noblest antique and later races." But if Whitman makes great claims for the English language, especially in America, he also finds in the "primeval documents" of India and Persia the "germs of all we call Europe," and he ends the second paragraph by connecting past and present through language. Whitman's vision of language, in *Rambles Among Words,* is much like his idea of poetry as the "then furthermore" in the 1876 essay, for in both texts he employs a combinatory strategy to accommodate both continuity and change.

The evolution of language and the language of evolution are more deeply connected, in the middle of the nineteenth century, than by mere word play. The boundaries separating disciplines like philology, biology, anatomy, and ethnology are fluid at best and often nonexistent. So, for instance, John Fiske's first important publication concerning evolutionary theory is a review article, "The Evolution of Language," that appears in the October 1863 issue of *The North American Review.*[9] The article presents a detailed, well-informed summary of German language theory, and Fiske employs Herbert Spencer's *First Principles* (1862) to argue that languages evolve according to the same principles that govern organic evolution. Fiske concludes that the three morphological classes of languages – Monosyllabic, Agglutinative, Inflectional – are "three successive epochs of linguistic development" (446), and that linguistic progress corresponds to social and spiritual progress (449–50). But the essay is less interesting for its conclusions, which are commonplaces of midcentury language theory, than for its method. Fiske combines philology, ethnology, and evolutionary theory in order to present "new uniformities" between "apparently disconnected phenomena," even prophesying the day that "science and religion will be in complete accord" (450).[10]

Fiske's review article is a fair example of the "scientific spirit" Whitman praised in his conversation with Traubel. The method combines data from disparate yet connected disciplines within an argumentative framework that focuses on patterns implying natural origins and developmental principles. Moreover, the rhetorical spirit underlying the method is quasi-objective and undogmatic. In the 1873 article on "Agassiz and Darwinism," Fiske describes that spirit in terms Whitman could certainly appreciate:

> For the direct grappling with that complicated array of theorems which the genius of such men as Darwin and Spencer and their companions has established on a firm basis of observation and deduction, Prof. Agassiz seems in these lectures hardly better qualified than a child is qualified for improving the methods of the integral calculus. These questions have begun to occupy earnest thinkers since the period when his mind acquired that rigidity which prevents the revising of one's opinions. The marvellous flexibility of thought with which Sir Charles Lyell so gracefully abandoned his antiquated position, Prof. Agassiz is never likely to show. This is largely because Lyell has always been a thinker of purely scientific habit, while Agassiz has long been accustomed to making profoundly dark metaphysical phrases do the work which properly belongs to observation and deduction.[11]

If Whitman's evolutionary style finds definite parallels in the rhetoric of popular science, it also marks itself as a "then furthermore" to the debate between religion and science. Because Whitman conceives of literature as the reconciler of opposed ideas, he can claim, in the 1876 Preface, to remain loyal to "Modern Science" and yet recognize "a higher flight, a higher fact, the Eternal Soul of Man" (*CRE,* 755). Immediately following these contradictory claims, Whitman focuses on his own style as a means of reconciling contradictions:

> In certain parts, in these flights, or attempting to depict or suggest them, I have not been afraid of the charge of obscurity, in either of my Two Volumes – because human thought, poetry or melody, must leave dim escapes and outlets – must possess a certain fluid, aerial character, akin to space itself, obscure to those of little or no imagination, but indispensable to the highest purposes. Poetic style, when address'd to the Soul, is less definite form, outline, sculpture, and becomes vista, music, half-tints, and even less than half-tints. True, it may be architecture; but again it may be the forest wild-wood, or the best effects thereof, at twilight, the waving oaks and cedars in the wind, and the impalpable odor.   (755)

The rhetoric of this description is much like that of the other prose passages I have presented. Whitman's rhetoric leaves "dim escapes and outlets" everywhere, especially when it addresses the soul, either as an abstract entity or as a more concretely realized identity. The description of "poetic style" does not, however, merely detail the obscure, ethereal, aerial – that is, poetically conventional and potentially exhausted. Whitman's combinatory strategy is at work even here, for his description includes the sculptural and architectural at the same time that it makes such "definite form" less important than the barely visible forms or "best effects" of a twilight natural scene. The passage therefore enacts the poetic style it describes, for the last two sentences begin with definite and material images but move toward progressively indefinite and, in context, spiritual images. So the passage is itself "address'd to the Soul" of the reader.

3

The prose works I have been discussing point inevitably to "Passage to India" as a proof text for reading Whitman's postwar poetry. Whitman himself pointed in the same direction, since he noted to Traubel that "there's more of me, the essential ultimate me, in that than in any of the poems. There is no philosophy, consistent or inconsistent, in that poem . . . but the burden of it is evolution – the one thing escaping the other – the unfolding of cosmic purposes" (*WWWC,* 1: 156–57). Despite Whitman's old-age assessment (the conversation with Traubel is dated May 15, 1888), "Passage to India" has not received critical praise in the last twenty years. The most influential interpretation of the poem, Arthur Golden's "Passage to Less Than India: Structure and Meaning in Whitman's 'Passage to India,'" exercises special authority because Golden examines the manuscript versions of the poem, showing that Whitman used three previously unpublished, independent poems in three important sections of "Passage."[12] Golden's thesis is that "Passage" does not form an artistic unity because Whitman is unable to integrate the disparate elements of the poem: "Whitman . . . was for the most part unsuccessful in his attempt to hold together themes whose implications to the poem as a whole he had apparently not fully thought out" (1095).[13]

Golden's method of argumentation blends genetic and formal approaches: Multiple sources lead to a poem lacking formal and thematic unity. Some readers would reject a genetic approach out of hand; after all, they might argue, the origin of a poem does not necessarily tell us anything about the poem itself, and the search for origins is in any case a vexed enterprise. Although a dose of poststructuralist skepticism is healthy, the genetic and formal approaches can be countered on their own ground. An important and unacknowledged source for the poem, the notebook *The Soul's Procession,* suggests that Whitman's plans for a long poem "based on those convictions of perpetuity and conservation" were more coherent and focused than the "patchwork" metaphor allows. It also indicates that the poet planned the form and style of the poem as counterparts to the theme.[14]

The thematic coherence of the poem is suggested by the notebook's title. Whitman focuses on the analogy between "the long chain of endless development & growth in the physical world" and "in the ethereal world an endless spiritual procession of growth" (*NUPM,* 4: 1391–2). On most of the notebook pages, Whitman clusters images to be developed, including "the latest versions of the truths of Modern Science – Astronomy, Geology, Ethnology or History," "the growths of the earth," and "leading points in *History* as of the different races & empires – wars some few Characters" (1392). He also shows that he is quite aware of the epic sweep of the project, noting that "the best plan will be (staccato) to make a staccato strain of picture-verses or groups . . . in strong florid poetry" (1392). The musical term, denoting a disconnected or detached succession of notes, is a telling analogy for Whitman's nine-section poem, whereas the self-description "strong florid poetry" suggests that the poet consciously adopted an extravagant style. The term "florid," in fact, may have a musical meaning in addition to the common sense of "excessively ornate." The word is a synonym for "figurate," and both terms were used as early as the eighteenth century to mean "running in rapid figures, divisions, or passages" (*OED*). Thus the notebook, which dates from 1869–70, indicates that Whitman had a clear sense of purpose and method in his initial attempts to write a major poem on "evolution." It also outlines the basic movement of "Passage to India," from material progress to spiritual progress, a passage from the material realm to "more than India" (224).

In "Passage to India," Whitman employs science and technology as corroborating analogies for the poetic and spiritual "flight" or passage of the poem. This is why Whitman opens the poem by "singing my days, / Singing the great achievements of the present" (1–2) but then immediately qualifies the present with the past:

> Yet first to sound, and ever sound, the cry with thee O soul,
> The Past! the Past! the Past!
>
> The Past – the dark unfathom'd retrospect!
> The teeming gulf – the sleepers and the shadows!
> The past – the infinite greatness of the past!
> For what is the present after all but a growth out of the past?
> (As a projectile form'd, impell'd, passing a certain line, still keeps on,
> So the present, utterly form'd, impell'd by the past.)
>
> (8–15)

The image of the present as "but a growth out of the past" signals the evolutionary theme of the poem, a theme that echoes the combinatory strategies of *Rambles Among Words,* the later prefaces, and "Darwinism – (Then Furthermore)." Section 1 presents a combination of two principal themes: the spiritual continuity between past and present and the material or scientific progress of the modern world.

Whitman's combinatory strategy in Section 1 helps to explain the inclusion of the "Not you alone proud truths of the world" passage in Section 2. Golden's textual expertise notwithstanding, I would argue that Whitman does not simply "patch" the manuscript into the poem, for the "proud truths" passage develops a specific aspect of the past:

> Passage O soul to India!
> Eclaircise the myths Asiatic, the primitive fables.
>
> Not you alone proud truths of the world,
> Nor you alone ye facts of modern science,
> But myths and fables of eld, Asia's, Africa's fables,
> The far-darting beams of the spirit, the unloos'd dreams,
> The deep diving bibles and legends,

The daring plots of the poets, the elder religions;
O you temples fairer than lilies pour'd over by the rising sun!
O you fables spurning the known, eluding the hold of the known,
    mounting to heaven!
You lofty and dazzling towers, pinnacled, red as roses, burnish'd with
    gold!
Towers of fables immortal fashion'd from mortal dreams!
You too I welcome and fully the same as the rest!
You too with joy I sing.

(16–29)

Section 2 focuses particularly on the "myths and fables of eld" because they are the remains of "elder religions." Literary and religious writings play a role at least equal to that of science in clarifying the relationship between spirit and matter. Indeed, the three-part structure of "Darwinism – (Then Furthermore)" suggests that religious literature is Whitman's privileged means of producing that *eclaircissement*. A passage from *Democratic Vistas* (1871) confirms that suggestion:

> The altitude of literature and poetry has always been religion – and always will be. The Indian Vedas, the Nackas of Zoroaster, the Talmud of the Jews, the Old Testament, the Gospel of Christ and his disciples, Plato's works, the Koran of Mohammed, the Edda of Snorro, and so on toward our own day, to Swedenborg, and to the invaluable contributions of Leibnitz, Kant and Hegel – these, with such poems only in which, (while singing well of persons and events, of the passions of man, and the shows of the material universe,) the religious tone, the consciousness of mystery, the recognition of the future, of the unknown, of Deity over and under all, and of the divine purpose, are never absent, but indirectly give tone to all – exhibit literature's real heights and elevations, towering up like the great mountains of the earth.
>
> (*PW*, 2: 417–18)

The image of religious literature "towering up" parallels that of the "towers of fables immortal" (27). In Whitman's combinatory strategy, "Passage to India" is an attempt to "sing well of persons and events, of the passions of man, and the shows of the material universe," while still developing a "religious tone" that colors all of the poem's materials.

The first two sections of "Passage" thus establish a double theme of connections – between the past and the present, and between a spiritual literature and a "material universe." The theme is developed through the dynamic image of change, figured as a passage from one state to another – or, as Whitman later told Traubel, "the one thing escaping the other." The combined passage is delineated in the last two stanzas of Section 2:

> Passage to India!
> Lo, soul, seest thou not God's purpose from the first?
> The earth to be spann'd, connected by network,
> The races, neighbors, to marry and be given in marriage,
> The oceans to be cross'd, the distant brought near,
> The lands to be welded together.
>
> A worship new I sing,
> You captains, voyagers, explorers, yours,
> You engineers, you architects, machinists, yours,
> You, not for trade or transportation only,
> But in God's name, and for thy sake O soul.
>
> (30–40)

The "worship new" is more than what one influential critic has called "a return to earlier, more innocent intuitions," for the first two sections of the poem insist that we read the present as the "growth out of the past."[15] That is, "Passage to India" seeks to transform the material achievements of "trade or transportation" into emblems of the spiritual progress of human-kind, which has been "God's purpose from the first." And it is through this poetic transformation that Whitman attempts to close the gap between spirit and matter.

The four stanzas of Section 2 suggest Whitman's awareness of that gap, but they also enact his combinatory transformations on the level of style. The four stanzas appear to alternate between addresses to the soul and addresses to "modern science," and the alternations emphasize the gap between the two. Whitman accents the gap further in his manner of direct address, using the plural and modern "you" for science and its proponents, the singular and archaic "thou" for the soul. But the "proud truths" stanza complicates this initial description, for it effects a passage between present and past, matter and spirit. By addressing the "facts of modern science" by the archaic "ye," Whitman rhetorically combines the present and the past. And in a subtle reversal, he creates a similar combination by addressing the "towers of fables immortal" by the modern "you." The combination of archaic and modern diction thus respects the distance between past religions and present sciences, but at the same time it brings "the distant . . . near." Similarly, the third and fourth stanzas project the "worship new" into an undefined future, but the poet bequeathes that new religion to the makers of material progress – "in God's name, and for thy sake O soul."

The evolutionary theme and form of Sections 1 and 2 reveal a coherent strategy underlying the apparent "patchwork" of Whitman's postwar style. Golden sharply criticizes Section 3, in which Whitman presents "of tableaus twain" (42), as "a dreadful succession of clichés reinforced with exclamatory flourishes," and he lists a series of phrases that, when isolated, sound flat and lifeless (1101). But these are not the only dictional elements at work in the section. The imagery of the Suez Canal scene is so general as to seem ill-imagined ("the strange landscape, the pure sky, the level sand in the distance," 45), but the stanza treating the Pacific Railroad features some of Whitman's most effective geographical imagery, including eleven place names in ten lines (50–9). In addition, the poet presents specific features of the imagined scene: "the buttes," "larkspur and wild onions," "sage-deserts," "the great desert," and "the alkaline plains" (53–60). And these dictional elements are marshaled in a clausal catalog that is both visionary and realistic, featuring a speaker who is both detached and engaged by the scene he describes.

On another formal level, Whitman's awareness of the gap between material and spiritual progress clarifies the apparent confusion of temporal sequence in the middle sections of the poem. Section 4 focuses on "a ceaseless thought, a varied train" (74), running "along all history" (72) and giving rise to "the plans, the voyages again, the expeditions" (75). The imagery of struggling sea captains and dead sailors (69) directly echoes *The Soul's Procession,* which identifies the "ceaseless thought" as "The idea – after carrying the Soul through all experiences tableaux Situations Sufferings heroism *Especially* AT SEA wrecks storms picture of a ship in a storm at sea / – then The Soul stalks on by itself" (*NUPM,* 4: 1390–1). The "ceaseless thought" is thus the dynamic soul itself, which in the notebook Whitman figures as "a sufficient solitary ship by itself" (1391). When the poet proclaims "man's long probation fill'd, / Thou rondure of the world at last accomplish'd" (79–80), then, he is speaking directly of the material progress of nations, the technological progress of trade and transportation.

The material progress of the present yields, in Section 5, to the spiritual progress of the past. The movement from Section 4 to Section 5 thus repeats the movement we have seen in Sections 1 and 2. In Section 5, the poet concentrates on the "teeming spiritual darkness" (83), repeating the image of the past as "the teeming gulf – the sleepers and the shadows" (11). The darkness resides in the human soul; therefore, Whitman's expansive rhetoric figures the mythic origins of the human race in conjunction with its spiritual explorations:

> Down from the gardens of Asia descending radiating,
> Adam and Eve appear, then their myriad progeny after them,
> Wandering, yearning, curious, with restless explorations,
> With questionings, baffled, formless, feverish, with never-happy hearts,

With that sad incessant refrain, *Wherefore unsatisfied soul?* and
Whither O mocking life?

(88–92)

This poignant stanza matches the dynamism of the soul with a lack of clear
spiritual direction, and in both diction and tone it echoes the opening of
"The Sleepers," the dark twin of "Song of Myself." Whitman recognizes the
soul's inherent need to explore and change, but he balances that optimistic
sense with the darker "restless explorations" the soul pursues. He even
questions his own soul in wondering who can properly answer the "sad
incessant refrain" (93–100). As in the 1855 poems, however, Whitman
answers his own doubts with the alchemy of words:

After the seas are all cross'd, (as they seem already cross'd,)
After the great captains and engineers have accomplish'd their work,
After the noble inventors, after the scientists, the chemist,
   the geologist, ethnologist,
Finally shall come the poet worthy that name,
The true son of God shall come singing his songs.

Then not your deeds only O voyagers, O scientists and inventors,
   shall be justified,
All these hearts as of fretted children shall be sooth'd,
All affection shall be fully responded to, the secret shall be told,
All these separations and gaps shall be taken up and hook'd
   and link'd together,
The whole earth, this cold, impassive, voiceless earth, shall be
   completely justified,
Trinitas divine shall be gloriously accomplish'd and compacted
   by the true son of God, the poet,
(He shall indeed pass the straits and conquer the mountains,
He shall double the cape of Good Hope to some purpose,)
Nature and Man shall be disjoin'd and diffused no more,
The true son of God shall absolutely fuse them.

(101–15)

The two stanzas strongly recall Section 23 of "Song of Myself," in which
Whitman cries out, "Hurrah for positive science!" in order to assert that the
works of the lexicographer, the chemist, the mariner, and the geologist are
the means by which the poet enters "an area of my dwelling" (485–92). In
the first stanza, the poet is figured as the spiritual result of material progress.
Whitman's combinatory rhetoric creates an evolutionary narrative, but it
withholds the arrival of the poet with the repeated "shall." That word,
occurring in every line, governs the parallel clauses of the second stanza, just

as the strategy of deferring the poet's arrival governs the shift from dark questions to hopeful answers. Finally, Whitman's rhetoric of deferral parallels his notion of the "scientific spirit" as "the holding off, the being sure but not too sure" (*WWWC*, 1: 101).

In Section 6, the poet shifts from the rhetoric of deferral to the rhetoric of present accomplishment. But Whitman is no longer treating technological achievements; instead, the figure of the poet in Section 5 prepares for the union of the material and the spiritual in the present:

> Year at whose wide-flung door I sing!
> Year of the purpose accomplish'd!
> Year of the marriage of continents, climates and oceans!
> (No mere doge of Venice now wedding the Adriatic,)
> I see O year in you the vast terraqueous globe given and giving all,
> Europe to Asia, Africa join'd, and they to the New World,
> The lands, geographies, dancing before you, holding a festival garland,
> As brides and bridegrooms hand in hand.
>
> (116–23)

Here Whitman's rhetoric of performance transforms the deferred marriage of Section 2 ("The races, neighbors, to marry and be given in marriage," 33) into an accomplished fact. That sense of material accomplishment leads, in turn, to a catalog of historical scenes presented to the poet's own soul. As in Section 5, Whitman combines doubts and losses of the past with the overwhelmingly optimistic figure of growth. Thus he asserts that he sees "the retrospect brought forward" (127), cataloging the "flowing literatures, tremendous epics, religions, castes" (134) of the past in order to focus on the figure of Columbus as the "chief histrion" (152), the voyager whose apparent failure gives birth to America. The catalog rhetoric effects several passages – from past to present, from Old World to New World, from the failure of the material voyager to the fulfillment by the spiritual voyager. Section 6 performs the marriage of the present and past by spiritualizing the present and its accomplishments, figuring the present as the inevitable "growth out of the past." Thus the section ends with the image of a seed that has lain "unreck'd for centuries in the ground" (162) and that now "sprouts, blooms, / And fills the earth with use and beauty" (163–4).

The evolutionary style of the first six sections leads to a moment of potential closure at the end of Section 6. After all, Whitman has negotiated several important passages, and it would be fair to suggest that he end the poem. But the very premise of the poem is a "ceaseless thought" of evolution, both material and spiritual, and in the last three sections of the poem

Whitman meditates on the ceaselessness of his evolutionary ideas. He does so by turning away from the "Rondure" of the world and his orbic sense of history in order to focus on the ceaseless nature of the soul. This is, as I suggested earlier, the plan announced in *The Soul's Procession*, especially in the last lines of the notebook: "intimate the procession continuing *for ever* / most of it through regions & experiences unknown / – and still from stage to stage / From life to life, higher & higher / From orb to orb continuous the journey" (1393). Because the poet and soul leave behind the material universe, there is no concrete, material focus in the last three sections, though the language combines abstractions with concrete, dynamic diction. It is as if Sections 7–9 constitute Whitman's "then furthermore" to the poem, launching him and his soul on a voyage toward God, the "Elder Brother" (222).

The structure of the last three sections repeats patterns established in Sections 1–6. In Section 7, the poet calls for the soul to join him in "the voyage of his mind's return" (171), and this return to "wisdom's birth" (173) signals a renewal of poetic energy. In Section 8, the stanzas form a truly staccato procession, emphasizing the dynamic quality of the soul and of the poet's creative spirit. Whitman returns, in this section, to some of the same doubts and questions that he raised in Section 5, but the "ceaseless thought" continually aims at the "thought of God" (206) as the goal of the voyage. At the end of Section 8, the "Elder Brother" is found, and "the Younger melts in fondness in his arms" (223). Once again, however, Whitman refuses to accept a perfectly acceptable closure. Instead, he insists on "Passage to more than India!" (224), shifting from the rhetoric of performance to the rhetoric of deferral. Thus Section 9 figures the "aged fierce enigmas" (230) and "strangling problems" (231) as the shores to which the poet and the soul are voyaging. And in a final shift, Whitman accepts the passage as an answer in itself. No other answer provides the dynamic, shifting figure of poet/soul with a sense of truth, for the only truth Whitman can accept is the dynamic shifting of continuous change:

> O my brave soul!
> O farther farther sail!
> O daring joy, but safe! are they not all the seas of God?
> O farther, farther, farther sail!
>
> (252–5)

Whitman's combinatory strategy is evident even here, for in the penultimate line of the poem he allows a deep whisper of doubt to invade his exclamatory rhetoric, just before the "then furthermore" of the constantly evolving soul takes him beyond his final question. And that dynamic combining is, finally, the deepest affirmation of Whitman's brave soul.

NOTES

1 Emerson's assessment is quoted by F. B. Sanborn in "Walt Whitman Recognized" (September 4, 1871), *Literary Studies and Criticism,* ed. Kenneth W. Cameron (Hartford, Conn.: Transcendental Books, 1980), p. 307.

   The negative view of Whitman's late poetry is pervasive. For a list of representative critics from the 1950s to the 1980s, see my *Walt Whitman's Language Experiment* (University Park: Pennsylvania State University, 1990), p. 194n. A younger generation of Whitman scholars has largely followed the critical narrative established by the older generation. See, for example, George Hutchinson, *The Ecstatic Whitman* (Columbus: Ohio State University Press, 1986); M. Jimmie Killingsworth, *Whitman's Poetry of the Body* (Chapel Hill: University of North Carolina Press, 1989); Ezra Greenspan, *Walt Whitman and the American Reader* (Cambridge: Cambridge University Press, 1990); Michael Moon, *Disseminating Whitman* (Cambridge, Mass.: Harvard University Press, 1991); Mark Bauerlein, *Whitman and the American Idiom* (Baton Rouge: Louisiana State University Press, 1992). Despite the wide range of critical approaches represented here, all of these writers subscribe to some version of the dominant narrative.

2 My references to Whitman's writings are to the following standard editions: For prefaces and poems, *Leaves of Grass: Comprehensive Reader's Edition,* ed. Harold W. Blodgett and Sculley Bradley (New York: New York University Press, 1965; prefaces are cited by page number, poems by line number; the abbreviated citation is *CRE.* The letters are quoted from *The Correspondence,* ed. Edwin Haviland Miller (New York: New York University Press, 1961–77) and are cited as *Corr.,* with volume and page numbers. Unless otherwise noted, the manuscript materials are quoted from *Notebooks and Unpublished Prose Manuscripts,* ed. Edward F. Grier (New York: New York University Press, 1984), and are cited as *NUPM,* with volume and page numbers. Other prose works are cited from *Prose Works 1892,* ed. Floyd Stovall (New York: New York University Press, 1964), and are cited as *PW,* with volume and page numbers. The other standard source for Whitman's words is Horace Traubel, *With Walt Whitman in Camden,* 7 vols. (1908–83) [with various publishers], cited as *WWWC,* with volume and page numbers.

3 The quotation appears on the copyright page of the 1891–2 *Leaves,* from which I quote.

4 See *The Complete Poems,* ed. Francis Murphy (Harmondsworth: Penguin, 1975), pp. 631–72.

5 For a different and compelling argument concerning Whitman's interest in the European revolutions of 1848 and their effect on the style of *Leaves of Grass,* see Larry Reynolds, *European Revolutions and the American Literary Renaissance* (New Haven, Conn.: Yale University Press, 1988), pp. 125–52. Reynolds offers a particularly laudatory reading of "Resurgemus," which, it should be noted, is the

earliest of the twelve poems gathered in the 1855 *Leaves*. Reynolds's narrative of the poet's career parallels the standard plot of decline: In this case, the writer contrasts "Resurgemus" to the 1871 poem "O Star of France" and finds in the later poem the "inflated and strained" rhetoric of "labored occasional verse" (152).

6   Haeckel first makes the statement in his *Generelle Morphologie* (1866) and continues to repeat the idea throughout his career. A useful example of Haeckel's popularizing of evolutionary theories is the two-volume translation, *The Evolution of Man: A Popular Exposition of the Principal Points of Human Ontogeny and Phylogeny* (New York: D. Appleton and Co., 1897), which begins with an epigraph from the *Generelle Morphologie*: "Ontogeny is a brief and rapid recapitulation of Phylogeny" (1, p. 1).

7   The quotation is from Charles M. Haar, "E. L. Youmans: A Chapter in the Diffusion of Science in America," *Journal of the History of Ideas* 9 (1948):197. Haar's essay provides a concise account of Youmans's career as a popularizer of evolutionary theories, a career that saw him edit the "Scientific Miscellany" of the *Galaxy* from 1871 to 1874 and the *Popular Science Monthly* (earlier known as *Appleton's Journal of Popular Literature, Science, and Art*) from 1872 to his death in 1887 (Haar, "E. L. Youmans," pp. 193–213). Whitman's acquaintance with Youmans is documented in *NUPM* 1, pp. 206n, 248n; *NUPM* 2, p. 910 (this note refers to Youmans as "Ed. Appleton's weekly"); *WWWC* 1, p. 101.

8   For a detailed account of Whitman's studies, including a discussion of Bunsen and Maxmilian Schele de Vere, see *Walt Whitman's Language Experiment*, pp. 1–33.

9   *NAR* 97, pp. 411–50. Fiske reviews three books, by Max Müller, Ernest Renan, and Herbert Spencer, and he cites nearly a dozen more philological texts in arguing for an evolutionary principle of linguistic change.

10   Nor is Fiske alone in searching for such a unified theory of knowledge. In *The Evolution of Man*, Haeckel also argues that comparative philology follows the same "phylogenetic" method and demonstrates the same fundamental unity of descent that characterize evolutionary theory (2, pp. 18–28).

11   *Popular Science Monthly* 3 (1873):704–5.

12   *PMLA* 88 (October 1973):1095–1103; the passages are lines 18–29 in Section 2 ("Not you alone proud truths of the world"); lines 81–115 in Section 5 ("O vast Rondure, swimming in space"); and lines 182–223 in Section 8 ("With laugh and many a kiss"). The two main manuscript sources of the poem are presented in two articles by Fredson Bowers: "The Manuscript of Whitman's 'Passage to India,'" *Modern Philology* 51 (1953):102–17; "The Earliest Manuscript of Whitman's 'Passage to India' and Its Notebook," *Bulletin of the New York Public Library* 61 (1957):319–52.

13   Golden supports his thesis in four ways. First, he argues that the principal theme of the poem is scientific or material progress, symbolized in Section 1 by the three "great achievements of the present" (p. 2) – the Suez Canal, the transcontinental railroad, and the transatlantic cable. But if these achievements of the present are to be the focus of the poem, the addition of sections treating the past, such as the "Not you alone proud truths of the world" passage in Section 2, damages the thematic coherence of the poem. Second, the added

passages tend to disrupt the temporal order of the poem. For instance, Section 4 announces that the "rondure of the world" is "at last accomplish'd" (p. 85), but in the "O vast Rondure" addition to Section 5 Whitman "moves abruptly from accomplishment in sections 1–4 to the anticipation of that same accomplishment in section 5, back again to accomplishment in section 6, which had probably followed section 4 before the addition of 'O vast Rondure'" (p. 1098). Third, Golden notes that "Passage" does not develop all three of the "achievements of the present," since by Section 3 Whitman drops the image of the transatlantic cable in order to present the "tableaus twain" of the canal and railroad (p. 1100). Finally, Golden criticizes the archaisms, clichés, and exclamatory rhetoric of the poem, seeing in Whitman's "patchwork" style a synecdoche for the "patchwork" structure – or lack of structure – of the entire poem (p. 1101).

14   The notebook is in the Clifton Waller Barrett Collection of American Literature in the University of Virginia's Alderman Library. It is edited by Grier in *NUPM* 4:1390–4. Where my transcription differs from Grier's, I make a silent revision.

15   Stanley K. Coffman, Jr., "Form and Meaning in Whitman's 'Passage to India,'" *PMLA* 70 (June 1955):349; see Golden, "Passage to Less Than India," p. 1096.

5

DAVID S. REYNOLDS

Politics and Poetry: *Leaves of Grass* and the Social Crisis of the 1850s

The subject of Whitman and politics has often been considered, but the relationship between his shifting political loyalties, his maturation as a poet, and the larger national picture has yet to be discussed in detail. Scholars such as Newton Arvin and Betsy Erkkila have made connections between Whitman's democratic poetics and the tradition of Jeffersonian and Jacksonian republicanism.[1] Largely unexplored, however, are the significant changes in Whitman's literary voice that occurred in response to the shifting political climate of the 1846–55 period.

Many of the things we commonly associate with Whitman's poetry – its air of defiance, its radical egalitarianism, its unabashed individualism, its almost jingoistic Americanism – had been largely absent from his apprentice writings and appeared in his work only as social conditions worsened to the degree that he took on a self-appointed cultural rescue mission. "Of all nations," he wrote in the 1855 preface to *Leaves of Grass*, "the United States . . . most need poets."[2] When he wrote these anxious words, the phrase "the United States" was virtually an oxymoron. Sectional animosities had flared up in 1850 with the congressional debates over slavery and then had exploded into full view in 1854 with the passage of the Kansas–Nebraska Act, which repealed the Missouri Compromise and opened up the western territories to slavery. The states, soon to be at war, were hardly united.

Nor were the parties. The early 1850s witnessed one of the most momentous phenomena in American political history: the collapse of the party system. The Whig Party, weak for years, broke up in 1854 as a result of sectional quarrels over slavery, and Whitman's Democratic Party became strife-ridden as well. The party crisis aroused Whitman's wrath against the governmental authority figures he had once revered. The presidencies of Millard Fillmore, Franklin Pierce, and James Buchanan eroded his confidence in the executive office. This period was a time of egregious presidential incompetence, mainly because of these leaders' soft-spined compromises on the slavery issue. Whitman, once a faithful party politician who had respected the presidential office, regarded the three presidencies before Lincoln as "our topmost warning and shame."[3] The 1850s was also a decade of unprecedented political corruption, a time of vote buying, wire pulling, graft, and patronage on all levels of state and national government. Class divisions were growing at an alarming rate.

The social forces that drove Whitman to despair simultaneously opened up new vistas of self-empowerment. As authority figures collapsed, the individual self – sovereign, rich, complex – stood forth amid the ruin of the parties. Whitman's growing disillusionment with authority figures sparked his deep faith in common people and in the power of populist poetry. He had come to view American society as an ocean covered with the "scum" of politicians, below which lay the pure, deep waters of common humanity.

To some extent, his vision corresponded with that of the new political movements of the 1850s, particularly anarchism, Know-Nothingism, and the emerging Republican Party. But just as his vision of social collapse was almost uniquely grim, his strategies for renewal were far more broad-ranging than those of any of the individual movements. Into the vacuum created by the dissolution of the nation's political structure rushed Whitman's gargantuan "I," assimilating images from virtually every aspect of antebellum American culture in a poetic document of togetherness offered to a nation that seemed on the verge of unraveling. As Whitman wrote in a note preparatory to the 1855 preface: "We want satisfiers, joiners, lovers. – These heated, torn, distracted ages are to be compacted and made whole."[4] The healing of a divided nation, he had come to believe, could be best achieved through all-absorptive poetry.

Although Whitman had been involved in politics at least since the time he had electioneered for Martin Van Buren in 1840, his concern for national events did not have notable poetic results until the 1846–8 period, when he edited the *Brooklyn Daily Eagle,* the Democratic Party organ of Kings County.

Early in his editorship, he was very much a Democratic loyalist who had full faith in the party's leaders and in the soundness of the two-party system. America's parties and elections washed away all impurities, he wrote, so that "true Democracy has within itself a perpetual spring of health and purity."[5] He could express his party loyalty in unequivocal black-and-white terms: "[T]he struggles of those who have any faith in democracy at all, must be made *in the frame and limits of our own party.* . . . As far as the Democrats of Brooklyn are concerned, they recognize but two great political divisions – themselves, and the men who are not themselves. These are *all*. Those who work not for us, work against us."

His devotion to the Democratic president, James Polk, showed his willingness to conform to the party's hierarchy and structure. Polk, by acquiring huge new territories in the Southwest through financial dealings and war against Mexico, put into action the expansionist spirit of "manifest destiny." Whitman called Polk "a truly noble Magistrate, without fear and without reproach – whose name will shine with quiet brightness for years to come, in our most honored democratic galaxy!"[6] He placed Polk in the company of Andrew Jackson and Thomas Jefferson and praised the presidential office itself as "this Great Office," "the most sublime on earth," at a "towering height above all other human stations."

There was, however, the nagging problem of slavery in the territories. Like other antebellum presidents, Polk waffled on the slavery issue. When in the summer of 1846 he asked Congress for $2 million to negotiate with Mexico, a Democratic congressman from Pennsylvania, David Wilmot, proposed that the bill be passed only with the proviso that slavery be excluded from all newly acquired territories. Polk denounced the Wilmot Proviso as mischievous and foolish.

Whitman, in contrast, came out strongly and early for the Wilmot Proviso in the *Eagle*. Although he maintained his support of Polk's expansionist policies, the president's opposition to the Wilmot Proviso troubled him. Slowly, Whitman began to sour on the party that had nurtured him and to ponder the institution that would rip apart the parties and lead to war: slavery. Whitman was an antiextensionist: one opposed to the extension of slavery into the western territories. As was true of most antiextensionists, his main concern in 1847 was not the slaves themselves but rather the disruptions of American institutions posed by the South's apparent effort to put its own interests above those of the nation. Party conflict, he believed, was healthy and cleansing. Sectional conflict, by contrast, was not, since it upset the delicate balance between state and national interests.

Anything that threatened this balance was anathema to him. He vigorously denounced the opposing camps of proslavery southern fireeaters and northern abolitionists. Both, he insisted, threatened to rip apart the Union. When the South Carolina senate proposed to establish an independent government should the Wilmot Proviso become law, he wrote angrily: "Of all follies, the nullification and withdrawing-from-the union folly of a few hotheads at the South, has always appeared to us among the greatest."[7]

Abolitionism came under his constant attack for similar reasons. It is sometimes forgotten today that abolitionism – the movement for the immediate emancipation of slaves – was actually unpopular in the North. Like most northerners, Whitman could not accept abolitionists' proposed alternative to immediate emancipation: disunion, or the peaceful separation of the North and the South. He was not prepared to accept outbursts against the existing order, such as this one by William Lloyd Garrison:

> Accursed by the AMERICAN UNION, as a stupendous republican imposture! [. . .]
> Accursed be it, as a libel on democracy, and a bold assault on Christianity!
> Accursed be it, stained as it is with human blood, and supported by human sacrifices! [. . .]
> Accursed be it, for all the crimes it has committed at home – for seeking the utter extermination of the red men for its wildernesses, and for enslaving one-sixth of its teeming population!
> Accursed be it, for its hypocrisy, its falsehood, its impudence, its lust, its cruelty, its oppression![8]

Whitman was galled by such assaults on the American system. In an article titled "The Union, vs. Fanaticism" he blasted the abolitionists: "The effort to destroy our Constitution – the work of the wisest and purest statesmen ever assembled – and to dissolve the Union, is worthy only of a madman and a villain."[9] Calling the abolitionists "a few red-hot fanatics," an "angry-voiced and silly set," he wrote: "The abominable fanaticism of the Abolitionists has aroused the other side of the feeling – and thus retarded the very consummation desired by the Abolitionist faction."

Fearing extremes, he began tentatively testing out statements that balanced opposite views, as though rhetorical juxtaposition would dissolve social tensions. He was confronted with what he saw as extremists on both sides. The greatest balancing agent, he was coming to believe, could be poetry – poetry that took both sides while at the same time releasing the steam of curses. He began what would become a long-term strategy of his: resolving thorny political issues by linguistic fiat.

In a notebook dated 1847 there appeared his first truly "Whitmanesque" verses, beginning with the topic of slavery and moving on to curses:

> I am the poet of slaves, and of the masters of slaves, [. . .]
> I go with the slaves of the earth equally with the masters
> And I will stand between the masters and the slaves,
> Entering into both, so that both shall understand me alike.
>
> . . .
>
> I am a Curse:
> Sharper than serpent's eyes or wind of the ice-fields!

> O topple down Curse! topple more heavy than death!
> I am lurid with rage![10]

The first of these verses presents an "I" who, as a "poet," is able to "enter into" both slaves and their masters, identifying with both in such a way that the divisive slavery issue is imaginatively resolved. The second passage projects all the fire of those who curse (which for Whitman were usually ranting reformers) and funnels it through an "I" who, by becoming "a Curse," expresses a general rage without targeting specifically the American Union, as the extremists did.

Although Whitman steered a fairly moderate course on slavery in his *Eagle* editorials, his support of the Wilmot Proviso apparently got him into trouble with his conservative employer, William Van Anden, and by mid-January 1848 he had lost his job. In his three-month stint as writer for the New Orleans *Daily Crescent,* he steered clear of controversial political articles.

On his return North, the political issues he had temporarily evaded in New Orleans suddenly impinged on his consciousness. It was an election year, and there was great turmoil in both the Democratic and Whig parties. The Michigan senator, Lewis Cass, a weak party hack opposed to the Wilmot Proviso, had been chosen as the Democratic presidential candidate, and the Whigs had chosen the slaveholder Zachary Taylor, the military hero with little political record. The prospect of either of these colorless compromisers assuming power was too much to bear for antiextensionists who wanted to keep the territories free of slavery. In June, shortly after Whitman's return, a huge rally of Free Soilers was held in Manhattan's City Hall Park. Plans were laid out for a national antislavery convention to be held later that summer. The creation of a Free Soil Party was proposed. Its nominating convention was to open in Buffalo on August 9. Whitman was one of fifteen delegates from Brooklyn chosen to represent Kings County at the convention.

He participated in one of the most thrilling events of the era. The Buffalo Free Soil convention had all the intensity and excitement of a religious revival. For two days, about 20,000 people heard a dazzling array of speakers drive home their rallying points: "Free soil, free speech, free labor and free men!" and "No more slave states, no more slave territory and no more compromises with slavery anywhere!"

At the Buffalo convention Whitman got to hear many of the leading antislavery orators of the day, including the African-Americans Frederick Douglass, Charles Redmond, Henry Highland Garnet, Henry Bibb, and

Samuel Ringgold Ward. The presence of Douglass and the other African-Americans at the convention brings up the key question of race. Douglass left the convention dissatisfied because the rights of African-Americans were not considered. Within a month of the convention he was berating the Free Soil group because of its neglect of the racial issue. His complaint was justified. The Free Soil agenda, radical as it seemed to some, was in fact based on the racist presumption that whites must be preserved from association with African-Americans. The Buffalo platform stated that the western territories must be kept for "the hardy pioneers of our own land, and the oppressed and banished of other lands" – with no mention of African-Americans.[11]

The whites-only plan reflected not only a fear of economic competition from slave labor but also racial prejudice. David Wilmot, the congressman who had sparked the Free Soil movement, called his measure the "White Man's Proviso," declaring, "I would preserve for free white labor a fair country, a rich inheritance, where the sons of toil, of my own race and color, can live without the disgrace which association with Negro slavery brings upon free labor."[12] Most leading Free Soilers accepted this outlook.

Including Whitman. At this point in his career, he accepted the Free Soil program, even to the extent of not resisting its racial assumptions. The whole slavery issue, he had written in the *Eagle*, was "a question between *the grand body of white workingmen, the millions of mechanics, farmers and operatives of our country,* with their interests, on the one side – and the interests of the few thousand rich, 'polished,' and aristocratic owners of slaves at the south, on the other." "We call upon every mechanic [i.e., worker] of the north, east, and west," he continued, "to speak in a voice whose great reverberations shall tell to all quarters that the *workingmen* of the free United States, and their business, are not willing to be put on the level of negro slaves" (*UPP,* 1: 171, 172).

Whitman's views on race and slavery were in several ways like Lincoln's. Both criticized abolitionism, which they feared threatened the Union. Both were more concerned about preventing the spread of slavery than about getting rid of it. Both expressed doubt that the races could be successfully integrated. In some respects, Lincoln was more conservative than Whitman. In 1848 he refused to join the Free Soil Party and campaigned instead for the Whig Zachary Taylor. On the other hand, Whitman's attitudes toward race did not progress as far as Lincoln's over time. A combination of overwhelming national events and a deep-seated hatred of slavery would eventually impel Lincoln to take a quite radical stance after the second year of the Civil War.

Whitman followed a kind of arc around the center in his racial attitudes, starting fairly conservative, then becoming quite progressive (it was in this middle phase that the broadly democratic first edition of *Leaves of Grass* appeared), and finally settling into a deepened conservatism during and after the Civil War. One can only guess what his racial opinions were in childhood, although the vibrant presence of African-Americans in Brooklyn in the 1820s and his long-remembered friendship with an ex-slave named Mose suggest an openness to African-American culture. The rise of abolitionism in the 1830s seems to have pushed him, like others, to a fearful conservatism.

By the time Whitman wrote *Franklin Evans* (1842), he had imbibed certain prosouthern attitudes. He had his hero learn from a Virginia planter that slaves are "well taken care of – with shelter and food, and every necessary means of comfort" and that "they would be far more unhappy, if possessed of freedom," a hundred times less happy than poor whites in Europe.[13]

The rise of antiextensionism, culminating in the Buffalo Free Soil convention, pushed him in a more radical direction. A month after the convention he founded a newspaper, the Brooklyn *Freeman,* that championed the Free Soil cause. "Free Soilers! Radicals! Liberty Men!" he exhorted his readers. "All whose throats are not tough enough to swallow Taylor or Cass! Come up and subscribe for the *Daily Freeman!*" "Our doctrine is the doctrine laid down in the Buffalo convention," he announced. He warned readers against voting for any candidate who would add to the Union "a single inch of *slave land,* whether in the form of state or territory," and he strongly endorsed the Free Soil slate of Van Buren and Adams.[14] But he pointed out that the large majority of southerners were decent. It was the small fraction of rich plantation owners who had to be fought tooth and nail to prevent them from spreading slavery to the territories.

Neither the paper nor the Free Soil Party, however, had a happy fate. Shortly after the first edition was published, a disastrous fire destroyed the *Freeman* office at 110 Orange Street and much of downtown Brooklyn as well. By the time Whitman resumed publication in November, the Free Soil ticket had been roundly defeated in the presidential election. Zachary Taylor was swept into office. Whitman continued to edit his paper until the following September, when, to his dismay, it was taken over by Hunker Democrats. Free Soil enthusiasm was fizzling. Economic necessity and the dampening of the antislavery cause made him turn his attention elsewhere.

He was jarred back into political action in early 1850 by events on the national scene. The acquisition of 850,000 square miles of western land and the population explosion in California in the wake of the gold rush made the issue of slavery in the territories a tense one once more. A seeming solution to the problem appeared in the compromise measures forged by the Whig senators Henry Clay and Daniel Webster. According to the compromise, California would be admitted to the Union a free state, but there would be no legal restrictions on slavery in Utah and New Mexico. To satisfy the South, a stringent fugitive slave law would be enforced by which recaptured slaves would not be allowed jury trial and those who aided them would be subject to a $1,000 fine or six months in jail.

Whitman saw that the compromise threatened the political health of the American republic. Conflict over principles between opposing parties, he had long believed, was essential to the nation's health. But now principles and party differences were being tossed into a gray middle ground of compromise. He was prophetic. The two-party system, which had emerged in the year of his birth and had nurtured him, was on the verge of extinction.

Whitman tried to stir things up. He published four poems between March and June that represented a whole new tone and style for him. These were angry, agitated poems, erupting with rebellious ideas and occasionally straining beyond normal rhythms toward free verse.

The first poem, "Dough-Face Song," showed that his main concern about the slavery issue was that the tepid atmosphere of compromise was snuffing out all sense of principle among party leaders. Adopting the popular epithet "doughface," referring to malleable northerners who were like dough in the hands of southern slaveowners, he wrote sarcastically: "We are all docile dough-faces, / They knead us with the fist, / They, the dashing southern lords, / We labor as they list" (EPF, 44). Evasion and moral flabbiness, he pointed out, could very well destroy the parties and possibly even the nation.

His animus was less against the South than against northerners like Daniel Webster who seemed to be betraying their past principles. Webster had once been an ardent critic of slavery and a supporter of the Wilmot Proviso but was now making conciliatory gestures to the South. His momentous speech before the Senate on March 7, 1850, brought the wrath of antislavery northerners down upon him. His support of a harsh fugitive slave law drove Whitman, like others, to a white fury. On March 22 there appeared in the *New York Tribune* Whitman's poem "Blood-Money," which compared supporters of the new law to Jesus' betrayer, Judas Iscariot. He kept up the attack on the compromisers in "Wounded in the House of Friends," published in the *Tribune* on June 14. Southern slaveowners, he declared, were far more admirable than northern doughfaces, whom he branded as "crawlers, lice of humanity – [. . .] / Muck-worms, creeping flat to the ground, / A dollar dearer to them than Christ's blessing" (*EPF,* 37).

Whitman was hardly alone in his use of poetry to express outrage over the compromise. Whittier and Longfellow, for example, wrote poems denouncing the apostate Webster. But their poems protesting the compromise were restrained and conventional in their imagery. Whitman's poems, in contrast, were blackly humorous, darkly ironic. Unlike the other poets, Whitman was beginning to absorb the wildly subversive political rhetoric that had been used by American reformers during the 1840s. Mikhail Bakhtin has suggested that truly indigenous, national forms of writing are produced by authors who absorb what Bakhtin calls *skaz,* a rough translation of which is "current idiom" or "national voice."[15] Whitman would develop a similar theory. Later dedicating himself to producing what he called "the idiomatic book of my land," he would write in 1856: "Great writers penetrate the idioms of their races, and use them with simplicity and power. The masters are they who embody the rude materials of the people and give them the best forms for the place and time."[16]

As I show in *Beneath the American Renaissance,* one such popular idiom in mid-nineteenth-century America was a subversive style that combined gothic images and fiercely antiauthoritarian rhetoric. This rhetoric had appeared in various genres during the turbulent 1840s: in the working-class speeches and editorials of Mike Walsh and other Tammany "slang-whangers"; in some of William Lloyd Garrison's speeches and writings; and in the novels of George Lippard and George Thompson, who furiously excoriated America's ruling class.[17] Lippard's *The Quaker City* (1845), America's best-selling novel previous to *Uncle Tom's Cabin,* was the quintessential example of the subversive style. Lippard portrayed elite types – bankers, lawyers, clergymen, editors – engaged in all kinds of debauchery and exploitive practices. More important than the details of the labyrinthine plot of *The Quaker City* was its style, which combined black humor, fierce egalitarianism, and sheer sensationalism.

It was this bizarre combination of stylistic features that characterized Whitman's political poems of the 1850s, as well as many of the political moments of his major poetry and his prose writings like "The Eighteenth Presidency!" and *Democratic Vistas.* The connection between Whitman and Lippard has not been previously made. It has not been remarked, for instance, that Lippard was one of the few popular American writers mentioned in Whitman's voluminous notebooks. In 1860, when he was a regular at Pfaff's restaurant, he discussed Lippard with the Philadelphia writer Charles D. Gardette, to whom he had sent a copy of the 1860 *Leaves of Grass*. Had Whitman's interest in Lippard been long-standing? Had he known Lippard's works in the 1840s?

There are strong indications that he had. There was a close parallel between Lippard's indictment of capital punishment in *The Quaker City* and three Whitman articles published shortly after the novel appeared. Astounded by the incongruity of Christian ministers endorsing death by hanging, Lippard sprinkled ironic commentary about the cruel "gibbet" throughout his novel and devoted long sections to his blackly humorous protagonist Devil-Bug, who cheers savagely at the sight of a gallows: "Hurrah! The gallows is livin' yet! Hurrah!"[18] Whitman picked up Lippard's ironic wording in his 1846 *Eagle* pieces "Hurrah for Hanging!" and "Hurrah for Choking Human Lives!" (*UPP*, 1: 97, 116). In an 1845 *Democratic Review* article, "A Dialogue," he made the Lippardian comment that every time he passed a church he saw a gallows frame and heard the words "Strangle and kill in the name of God!" (*UPP*, 1: 103). Several of Whitman's scribblings in his early notebooks also bear the impress of Lippard. The outlandish scene at the heart of *The Quaker City* in which Devil-Bug has a nightmarish vision of a skeleton-filled coffin propelled on the Schuykill River seems to be echoed in Whitman's equally strange jotting: "A coffin swimming buoyantly on the swift current of the river" (*NP*, 1: 131).

By using in "Dough-Face Song" and "House of Friends" dark political irony and words like "lice," "crawlers," and "muck-worms," Whitman was bringing the idiom of Lippard and other working-class reformers into poetry.

His most intense experiment in the Lippardian vein was "Resurgemus," the last poem of the 1850 group and only one of two pre-1855 poems – the other was the equally Lippardian "A Boston Ballad (1854) – absorbed into *Leaves of Grass*. The poem registers both excitement and frustration surrounding the European revolutions of 1848, which had led temporarily to the toppling of several authoritarian governments but which had subsequently been reversed. Whitman's message is that the revolutions may have been put down for the time being, but the spirit of revolt was very much alive in the heart of the people, who some day would rise up in anger again. Critics have tried to locate sources for the gothicized images of "Resurgemus," some pointing to Poe. But Poe was no revolutionary, and he avoided political commentary in his writings. A more likely source was Poe's radical friend Lippard. Just as Lippard had often portrayed workers as "slaves" victimized by lying, cheating upper-class figures, Whitman indicted social rulers as "liars" who were inflicting "numberless agonies, murders, lusts" on the people and "Worming from his simplicity the poor man's wages" (*CP*, 133). Just as Lippard had imagined an apocalyptic time when the shapes of the murdered oppressed classes would rise in an eerie, vindictive procession behind the upper classes, so Whitman describes ruling-class exploiters and warns:

> Yet behind all, lo, a Shape,
> Vague as the night, draped interminably, head front and form in scarlet folds,
> Whose face and eyes none may see,
> Out of its robes only this, the red robes, lifted by the arm,
> One finger pointed high over the top, like the head of a snake appears.

Unlike Lippard, however, Whitman moves beyond gothicized protest to a positive, hopeful image of restoration:

> Not a grave of the murdered for freedom but grows seed for freedom,
>   in its turn to bear seed,
> Which the winds carry afar and re-sow, and the rains and the snows nourish.
>
> (CP, 134)

In "Resurgemus" Whitman is using the popular subversive style but is also moving toward the kind of affirmation that would characterize his major poetry. Formerly a loyal Democrat writing straightforward journalese, he had been driven by national and world events to a cynical view of society expressed in a rebellious style. In his image of the seeds of freedom being carried by the winds and nourished by the rains, he was beginning to forge a humanistic, artistic reconstruction on the ruins of his shattered political beliefs. And for the first time in print, he was using a form that approximated free verse. The seeds of *Leaves of Grass* were sown in the political crisis of 1850.

As the crisis deepened, Whitman temporarily backed off from poetic protest. The death of Zachary Taylor from typhoid fever on July 9, 1850, and the accession to the presidency of Millard Fillmore crushed the hopes of former Free Soilers like Whitman. Fillmore shepherded the various measures of the omnibus bill through Congress. The official enactment of the compromise virtually killed off the Free Soil Party. The fate of the western territories seemed sealed by law. For the time being, Whitman surrendered political activism.

In the presidential election of 1852 he was drawn inevitably back into Free Soil politics, which made a dramatic resurgence because of growing sentiment against the fugitive slave law. In the campaign of 1852, the Democrats chose a dark horse, Franklin Pierce, an amiable but shallow man of uncertain opinions on slavery. Free Soilers feared that, if elected, he would give into proslavery forces – a prediction that proved accurate. His opponent, the pompous, aging General Winfield Scott, was also equivocal on slavery. Given this unsavory choice of candidates, Free Soilers reorganized as the Free Democratic Party. At their convention in Pittsburgh, the New Hampshire senator, John P. Hale, was seriously considered as the Free Democratic presidential candidate. Hale was reluctant to accept the nomination, since the chances for victory in November seemed slim. In his moment of indecision he received a letter from "Walter Whitman" of Brooklyn urging him to accept.

Whitman's letter to Hale is an important transitional document revealing his growing disgust with the established parties and his turn toward humanistic alternatives to the party system. His mentality was still, at this point, within the framework of the political process, for he expressed hope that under Hale "a real live Democratic party" would arise, "a renewed and vital party, fit to triumph over the effete and lethargic organization now so powerful and so unworthy."[19] Expressing his disillusion with the current parties, he asked Hale "to make personal addresses directly to the people, giving condensed embodiments of the principal ideas which distinguish our liberal faith from the drag-parties and their platforms." Whitman stressed that current legislators were out of touch with "the great mass of the common people." He confessed he did not know "the great men" of Washington. "But I know the people. I know well (for I am practically in New York,) the real heart of this mighty city – the tens of thousands of young men, the mechanics, the writers, &c. &c. In all this, under and behind all the bosh of the regular politicians, there burns, almost with fierceness, the divine fire which more or less, during all ages, has only waited a chance to leap forth and confound the calculations of tyrants, hunkers, and all their tribe."

Hale was his last hope for party renewal. Perhaps influenced by Whitman's flaming words, Hale did accept the Free Democrat nomination and campaigned enthusiastically in the fall. But the November election was dismal for the Free Democrats, who got just 5 percent of the national vote. Whitman's hopes for "a renewed and vital party" were dashed. Worse yet, the party to which he had once been loyal, the Democrats, had put into office Franklin Pierce. Under Pierce, the erstwhile party of Jackson, once the defender of common people, became widely viewed as the defender of slavery. The charming but pliable Pierce rapidly became the tool of proslavery forces within the party. On May 30, 1854, he signed into law a bill that overturned the Missouri Compromise by permitting settlers of the Kansas and Nebraska territories to decide for themselves about slavery.

The Democratic leadership for whom Whitman may have retained some residual respect suddenly seemed corrupt and beyond redemption. Surveying all antebellum presidents, Whitman would call Pierce "the worst of the lot"[20] (he made a similar statement about Pierce's equally malleable successor, James Buchanan). Like many other northerners, he seized on the fugitive slave law as a symbol of wrongheaded government intervention into the affairs of free society. For him as for other antislavery activists, the capture and retrieval of the slave Anthony Burns in Boston became the archetypal example of corrupt government.

Anthony Burns, the property of Charles T. Suttle of Alexandria, Virginia, had escaped from slavery on a Boston-bound ship early in 1854. On May 24 he was arrested by a federal marshal and confined in a Boston courthouse. After a week-long trial, the judge of probate, Edward G. Loring, ruled that he be taken back to Virginia. Several leading antislavery agitators, including Wendell Phillips and Theodore Parker, led a rally at which they championed Burns as a helpless martyr and impugned Loring and the fugitive slave law. Because most Bostonians were strongly opposed to Loring's decision, federal troops, a thousand strong with fifes and drums, were called in to conduct the chained Burns through the streets of Boston to the ship waiting to carry him back to captivity. The slow procession was performed amid jeering crowds and buildings draped in black. On one building an enormous American flag hung upside down. On another was suspended a black coffin inscribed "Liberty."

The seizure of Burns was an act of infamy among antislavery activists. At a huge rally in Framingham on July 4 (a day now celebrated only in irony by them), Henry David Thoreau gave his searing address "Slavery in Massachusetts," and William Lloyd Garrison burned copies of the Declaration of Independence and the Constitution as the crowd cheered grimly. The retrieval of Anthony Burns had driven many to view established American institutions with cynicism and disdain.

One such cynic was Whitman. Appalled by the Burns case, he wrote a poem, "A Boston Ballad," which was a vigorous, sarcastic protest against the way the state and federal authorities handled the Burns case. Significantly, Burns himself is not mentioned in the poem. Whitman's emphasis is on the federal government's tyrannical violation of the idea of liberty. Picturing the government-authorized troops ushering Burns through the Boston streets, he writes ironically:

Clear the way there Jonathan!
Way for the President's marshal! Way for the government cannon!
Way for the federal foot and dragoons . . . . and the phantoms afterward.

(CP, 135)

As in his political poems of 1850, he resorts to the blackly humorous, gothicized protest imagery popularized by George Lippard. The central scene of Lippard's *The Quaker City* had been the terrible procession through the streets of a modern city in which haughty social rulers led black and white slaves in chains; the procession went forward jauntily until suddenly there arose the phantoms of patriots and poor people who followed and haunted the rulers. Whitman uses a strikingly similar image in his bitter rendering of the Burns procession. He has the Boston soldiers suddenly surrounded by the phantoms of old patriots who had died for freedom and are now shocked by the betrayal of American ideals in the retrieval of Burns. The patriot ghosts groan miserably and tremble with anger at the horrid scene. The cynical narrator asks: "What troubles you, Yankee phantoms? What is all this chattering of bare gums? / Does the ague convulse your limbs? Do you mistake your crutches for firelocks, and level them?" He orders the helpless ghosts back to their graves and whispers to the Boston mayor to send someone immediately to England to exhume the bones of King George III, bring them to America, glue them together, and set up the king's skeleton as a centerpiece for "the President's marshal" and all "roarers from Congress" to worship.

Among the messages of "A Boston Ballad" is that political power in America has become so corrupt that it can be described only in savagely subversive language. Whitman's image of the rising patriot ghosts may derive specifically from Lippard, but the overall spirit of protest against corrupt institutions was part of a larger reform rhetoric seen in many activists of the day.

Whitman was adopting the spirit of agitation popularized by reformers who were trying to arouse the moral conscience of the nation. The Brooklyn preacher he most admired, Henry Ward Beecher, declared in an antislavery speech of 1851: "Agitation? What have we got to work with but agitation? Agitation is *the* thing in these days for any good."[21] The next year the abolitionist Wendell Phillips declared: "Only by unintermitted agitation can a people be kept sufficiently awake not to let liberty be smothered in material prosperity. . . . Republics exist only on the tenure of being constantly agitated."[22] And Whitman's correspondent and favorite speaker, John P.

Hale, told the Senate, "I glory in the name of agitator. I wish the country could be agitated vastly more than it is."[23]

Whitman came to think that he, above all, was the one chosen to agitate the country. "I think agitation the most important factor of all," he once declared, "– the most deeply important. To stir, to question, to suspect, to examine, to denounce!" (*WWC,* 5: 529). In the 1855 preface to *Leaves of Grass* he announced that in a morally slothful age the poet is best equipped to "make every word he speaks draw blood [. . .] he never stagnates" (*CP,* 9). In a draft of a later preface he stressed that his poetry was meant to be bracing, rough, violent, "sharp, full of danger, full of contradictions and offence."[24] Key lines in his poems echo this zestful tone: "I am he who walks the States with a barb'd tongue, questioning every one I meet"; "Let others praise eminent men and hold up peace, I hold up agitation and conflict" (*CP,* 470, 379) He would never give up the spirit of agitation he had shared with the antebellum reformers. "As circulation is to the air, so is agitation and a plentiful degree of speculative license to political and moral sanity," he wrote in *Democratic Vistas.* "*Vive,* the attack – the perennial assault!" (*PW,* 2: 383, 386).

Like the reformers, he was ready to use black humor and gothicized mudslinging to describe corrupt politicians. In his unpublished prose tract "The Eighteenth Presidency!" (1856) he spewed forth horrible epithets that suggested the profundity of his disgust with the powers that be. Political leaders he compared to lice, corpses, maggots, venereal sores. About the Pierce administration he wrote: "The President eats dirt and excrement for his daily meals, likes it, and tries to force it on The States. The cushions of the Presidency are nothing but filth and blood. The pavements of Congress are also bloody" (*CP,* 1310). This kind of reformist protest rhetoric runs as a sharp, needling voice through his poetry, as in "The Sleepers" (1855), where he writes, "I am oppressed. . . . I hate him that oppresses me, / I will either destroy him, or he shall release me," or in "Respondez!" (1856), in which he portrays a topsy-turvy society in which churches are filled with vermin, criminals take the place of judges, God is pronounced dead, and so on, for over seventy scathingly subversive lines (*CP,* 113).

He was appalled not only by the slavery issue but also by the growing corruption in government. Corruption in the 1850s became entrenched in American politics, especially in Whitman's New York. In 1852 the infamous board of aldermen known as the "Forty Thieves" took power in Manhattan. Manhattan's political shenanigans were emblematic of what was happening in the nation as a whole. As Mark W. Summers has shown, during the 1850s corruption was common in other cities up and down the Eastern seaboard and even in the federal government.[25] There was direct historical reference, then, for Whitman's venomous diatribes, as in the 1855 preface, where he impugned the "swarms of cringers, suckers, doughfaces, lice of politics, planners of sly involutions for their own preferment to city offices or state legislatures or the judiciary or congress or the presidency" (CP, 18).

Another alarming social phenomenon was the growing inequality between the rich and the poor. With the rise of market capitalism, class differences in America widened far more rapidly between 1825 and 1860 than either before or after this period. A powerful discourse on working-class protest accompanied these growing class divisions. Novels by George Lippard, George Thompson, and Ned Buntline depicted upper-crust figures like bankers and lawyers involved in nefarious schemes while poor people starved.

Whitman absorbed the language of working-class protest. Like the popular writers, he used in his journalism the word "upper ten" to describe the privileged few. In one notebook entry he denounced the "vast ganglions of bankers and merchant princes" (WWW, 57). In another he sounded just like Lippard or Thompson characterizing the grotesque rich: "I see an aristocrat / I see a smoucher grabbing the good dishes exclusively to himself and grinning at the starvation of others as if it were funny, / I gaze on the greedy hog."[26] His poem "The Sleepers" included a similar image: "The head of the moneymaker that plotted all day sleeps, / And the enraged and treacherous dispositions sleep" (CP, 108). In "Song of Myself" he repeated the oft-made charge that the "idle" rich cruelly appropriated the products of the hard-working poor:

> Many sweating and ploughing and thrashing, and then the chaff
> for payment receiving,
> A few idly owning, and they the wheat continually claiming.
>
> (CP, 76)

Among radical agitators of the day, it was the individualistic reformers of the 1850s whose language and spirit most closely approximated Whitman's. The early 1850s witnessed the great flowering of American anarchism. Not far from Whitman's birthplace on Long Island was established in 1851 the utopian community of Modern Times, led by a group of reformers who practiced the doctrine of Individual Sovereignty, by which every individual was pronounced the "absolute despot or sovereign" of his or her own life, without reference to outside laws or governments.[27] The leading anarchist, Stephen Pearl Andrews, advanced his doctrine in a widely read series of articles in the New York Tribune in 1852. Gleefully celebrating himself,

Andrews announced: "I claim individually to be my own nation. I take this opportunity to declare my national independence, and to notify all other potentates, that they may respect my sovereignty."[28] The publication of Thoreau's *Walden* in 1854 gave further impetus to this individualistic reform.

In a decade when government authority was proving to be corrupt, individual authority seemed paramount. All the individualistic reformers explicitly or implicitly paid homage in their writings to the great enunciator of self-reliance, Ralph Waldo Emerson. Whether or not Whitman read Emerson in the 1850s (he twice said he didn't), Emerson's ideas flooded the reformist air in a decade when the individual seemed far more worthy than the state. Whitman's celebration of himself in egotistical poetry was right in step with the times. Frequently in the 1855 and 1856 editions this timely individualism breaks forth: "I celebrate myself"; "Going where I list, my own master total and absolute"; "Each man to himself and each woman to herself" (*CP*, 27, 299, 366). Like the individualist reformers, he was impelled by chicanery among America's rulers to put the individual above the state. In "Song of the Broad-Axe" he imagines a society "Where outside authority enters always after inside authority, / Where the citizen is always the head and ideal, and President, Mayor, Governor and what not, are agents for pay" (*CP*, 335).

The most confidently assertive poetic persona in literature, then, arose during a decade when the "inside authority" of individuals was widely placed above the "outside authority" of government.

Subversive rhetoric aimed at social rulers; profound disgust with the party system; willing participation in the individualistic attitudes of the 1850s – all of these facets of Whitman fed into his rebelliousness as a poet and as a person. We are so accustomed, however, to think of Whitman as a revolutionary that we are liable to forget his conservative side. He warned: "Be radical – be radical – be not too damned radical" (*WWC*, 1: 223). Although he associated with reformers of all stripes and absorbed their subversive spirit, he adopted none of their programs for social change. He once declared, "I am somehow afraid of agitators, though I believe in agitation" (*WWC*, 1: 166). He had vehement arguments with his abolitionist friends, who, he later recalled, got "hot" with him for not espousing the abolitionist cause (*WWC*, 1: 363). He also shied away from joining the women's rights movement, the free love movement, and the labor movement, though he observed them all with interest.

What Whitman feared was what then was called "ultraism," or any form of extreme social activism that he thought might rip apart the social fabric. He shied away from movements that seemed to upset the balance between opposing views, and he tried mightily to restore that balance in his poetry. His poetic strategy was one of balance and equipoise by poetic fiat. The kind of balance he asserted in his 1847 notebook jotting – "I am the poet of slaves and of the masters of slaves" – became far more crucial with the disturbing occurrences of the 1850s, especially after the party collapse and the Kansas debacle. The poet was to be the balancer or equalizer of his land. "He is the arbiter of the diverse and he is the key," Whitman emphasizes in the 1855 preface. "He is the equalizer of his age and land . . . . he supplies what wants supplying and checks what wants checking" (CP, 9).

With the possibility of resolution through normal political channels now dead, all the more reason, he thought, to forge a new resolution in his poetry. Believing that the Union was imperiled, in the 1855 preface he hopefully affirmed "the union always surrounded by blatherers and always calm and impregnable" (CP, 8). He knew that southerners and northerners were virtually at each other's throats, so he made a point in his poems constantly to link the opposing sides. He proclaimed himself in "Song of Myself" "a southerner soon as a northerner [. . .] / At home on the hills of Vermont or in the woods of Maine or the Texan ranch" (CP, 42). When he directly addressed the issues of sectionalism and slavery in his poetry, he also found a middle ground. In the 1855 preface he assures his readers that the American poet shall "not be for the eastern states more than the western or the northern states more than the southern" (CP, 15). He writes of "slavery and the tremulous spreading hands to protect it, and the stern opposition to it which shall never cease till it ceases of the speaking of tongues and the moving of lips cease" (CP, 8). The first half of this statement gently embraces the southern view; the second half airs sharp antislavery anger but leaves open the possibility that it may be a very long time before slavery disappears – a gradualist view confirming Whitman's statement in an 1857 Daily Times article that slavery would probably disappear in a hundred years.[29]

Fearing the sectional controversies that threatened disunion, he represented the southern point of view in his poetry, as when he described the plantation with "the negroes at work in good health, the ground in all directions cover'd with pine straw" (CP, 321). Elsewhere he projected northerners' hatred of the fugitive slave law and gave voice to the widely trumpeted notion of Frederick Douglass and others that African-Americans were fully human. "Song of Myself" contains a long passage in which the "I" takes an escaped slave into his house and washes and feeds him, keeping his firelock ready at the door to fend off possible pursuers. In another passage he actually becomes "the hounded slave," with dogs and men in bloody pursuit. In a third he admires a magnificent African-American driver, climbing up with him and driving alongside of him. The poem later called "I Sing the Body Electric" presents a profoundly humanistic variation on the slave auction, as the "I" boasts how valuable his auctioned slave is: "There swells and jets his heart. . . . There all passions and desires..all reachings and aspirations: [. . .] / In him the start of populous states and rich republics" (CP, 123).

His poetry was not only a meeting place for disparate sectional attitudes but also a reflection of the leading ideas of the two parties that dominated the North's political scene in the mid-1850s, the Know-Nothings and the Republicans. Several of Whitman's central themes – extreme valuation of the common person, intense Americanism, a cleansing impulse – tie him to these parties.

Both the Know-Nothings and the Republicans, besides being opposed to slavery, presented themselves as fresh, populist alternatives to previous parties, which were viewed as rotten to the core. They grew with amazing rapidity in 1854 partly because, with the disappearance of the Whig Party and the proslavery apostasy of the Democrats, they advertised a fresh beginning, a new world of political purity in a time of overriding ugliness and corruption. As Alexander H. Stephens, who moved, like Whitman, from the Democratic Party to the Republican, wrote at the end of 1854: "Old parties, old names, old issues, and old organizations are passing away. A day of new things, new issues, new leaders, and new organizations are at hand."[30] Whitman caught the spirit of the time when he wrote in the first paragraph of the 1855 preface that America "has passed into the new life of the new forms" (CP, 5).

The old party leaders, insisted the Know-Nothings and Republicans, were grotesque representatives of a party system that had grown corrupt and detached from the people. Below the corruption of America's rulers lay the genuineness of average Americans, whose values should be the basis of political action. One Know-Nothing typically called for a leader who was "fresh from the loins of the people."[31] The two Republican presidential nominees of the 1850s – the hardy explorer John Frémont and the Illinois rail splitter Abraham Lincoln – epitomized this populist, antiparty impulse. In the 1856 race Frémont was pushed in Republican editorials as "a new man, fresh from the people and one of themselves." Among his supporters was Whitman, whose whole family abandoned the Democrats and turned Republican.

Whitman shared the new populist impulse. He had once been quite snobbish, as witnessed by his snide aspersions on the simple Long Island villagers in his 1840 letters to Abraham Leech. His sympathy for the masses had increased between 1846 and 1848 with the rise of the Free Soil movement, when the territorial dispute led him to praise publicly American working people, whose values he suddenly championed. But he had then still been very much within the framework of the party hierarchy, and he retained an almost sheepish veneration of the presidency and the party leadership. With the corruption and political collapse of the 1850s, however, his veneration for entrenched rulers disappeared and his respect for common people increased exponentially.

He espoused a dialectical mode of thinking that was new to him, one that lay behind the parties of the mid-1850s, involving fierce rejection of entrenched authority coupled with equally intense praise of simple artisan values. In a notebook entry he wrote: "I perceive all the corruption – [. . .] I know that underneath all this putridity of Presidents and Congressmen that has risen to the top, lie pure waters a thousand fathoms deep" (NP, 6: 2148). Eric Foner has shown that the Republican Party rose to prominence in large part because of its appeal to the ideology of free labor, epitomized in average workers such as independent shopkeepers, farmers, and artisans of all kinds, whose values were posed as preferable to those of exploitive moguls and politicians.[32] Whitman shared this outlook. His tract "The Eighteenth Presidency!" follows the Republican dialectic. In it he unsparingly attacks the powers that be and sings praise to "the true people, . . . mechanics, farmers, boatmen, manufactures, and the like." He hopes that some "healthy-bodied, middle-aged, beard-faced American blacksmith or boatman" would "come down from the West across the Alleghanies, and walk into the Presidency" (CP, 1308).

A similar dialectic runs through the early editions of *Leaves of Grass*. Eight years earlier, he had written in the *Eagle* that the presidency was the most sublime office on earth. Now his attitude was exactly reversed. The people, he stressed in the 1855 preface, should not take off their hats to presidents: It should be the other way around. The president would no longer be the poet's referee: Now the poet would be. The genius of the United States, he wrote, was not in presidents or legislatures but "always most in their common people," as it was better to be a poor free mechanic or farmer than "a bound booby and rogue in office" (CP, 18). His early poems are full of long catalogs of average people at work. The party collapse and the devaluation of authority figures, in other words, had fueled his ardent populism, just as it had helped give rise to the new party organizations.

He also shared with the new parties an intense Americanism that tended toward jingoism. It has often been thought that his nationalistic instinct derived from the Young America movement or from Emerson. But by the early 1850s the Young America movement had turned sour. Its intense Americanism, which had in the early 1840s engendered literary nationalism, had been swept up in the politics of expansionism, which by the 1850s was allied with the South and proslavery. Two great champions of Young America, John L. O'Sullivan and Stephen Douglas, had by the 1850s become defenders of the South. As for Emerson, it is certainly likely that he directly influenced the nationalistic stance of Whitman's poetry, despite Whitman's later denials to the contrary. It is important to note, however, that at the only two *documented* moments of Whitman's awareness of Emerson – in 1842 and 1847 – the Concord sage had no fertilizing effect on his imagination. It was only after Whitman had escaped the shackles of party and had experienced the political crisis of the 1850s that he gave literary form to the Americanism Emerson represented. The timing of Whitman's suddenly intense nationalism coincided exactly with the dominance of that most nationalistic of all political movements, the Know-Nothings.

After the collapse of the Whig Party in early 1854, the strongly pro-American Know-Nothings suddenly became the most powerful new party in the nation. The Know-Nothings (probably so named because they started as a secret order whose members professed ignorance of it) tapped into long-smoldering nativist sentiment in the North. As a result of developments abroad, especially the Irish potato famine, immigrants were arriving in America at a rate never known before or since. Between 1845 and 1855, 3 million foreigners swarmed to America's shores, peaking in 1854, when 427,833 arrived. This was the largest proportionate increase in the number of immigrants at any time in American history. The large majority were Roman Catholic. The Know-Nothings responded to a deep-seated fear that Catholic foreigners would infiltrate American institutions and possibly even take over the government. Since many foreigners, particularly the Irish, supported slavery, the Know-Nothings appealed to antislavery activists. They also incorporated defenders of the working class.

Above all, they were the party of intense, unabashed Americanism. "America for Americans" was their motto, the Star Spangled Banner was their emblem, and in 1855 the "American Party" became their public name.

Their success in the northern elections of 1854 and 1855 was stunning. They elected 8 governors, over 100 congressmen, mayors in three major cities, and thousands of other local officials.[33] They peaked in popularity in June 1855, the month before *Leaves of Grass* appeared, numbering about 1.5 million members.

Whitman later recalled that the Know-Nothings were "the great party of those days" (*WWC*, 3: 91). Although he said he did not join the organization (but then, what Know-Nothing would confess joining it?), he had a history of flirtation with nativism. In 1842 he had come out strongly against Bishop John Hughes on the issue of public funding for Catholic schools, an issue that came back with redoubled fury in the 1850s and fueled the Know-Nothing debate. The politician in the 1850s he most admired, John P. Hale, was an ardent nativist. Since the Know-Nothings in 1854 and early 1855 were championing his favorite causes – antislavery, temperance, rights for working people – he may have found the American Party appealing.

At any rate, the jingoistic moments in his early poetry smacked of nativism. In one poem he wrote, "America isolated I sing; / I say that works here made in the spirit of other lands, are so much poison to these States," adding, "Bards for my own land only I invoke."[34] In the first two editions of *Leaves of Grass*, at the peak of the nativist frenzy, he identified himself in his signature poem, "Song of Myself," as "Walt Whitman, an American" – changed later, in less nativist times, to "Walt Whitman, of Manhattan the son." Trying to key into the nativist readership, he began a self-review of his poetry by boasting, "An American bard at last!," redoubling the boast in another self-review: "No imitation – No foreigner – but a growth and idiom of America."[35]

If he was a nativist, though, he was one with a difference. His first woman reviewer, Fanny Fern, saw this when she called him "this glorious Native American" but specified that he was "no Catholic-baiting Know Nothing" (*NYD*, 147). On the one hand, he did adopt some attitudes of the Know-Nothings, to the extent that he would once say that America's digestion was strained by the "millions of ignorant foreigners" coming to its shores (*PW*, 2: 762). Sketching plans for a lecture to be given to a Protestant group, he sounded like a Know-Nothing when he wrote that Catholics were sufficiently numerous to put all American enterprises in their grasp (*WWW*, 41–2).

On the other hand, as was true of his attitude toward antislavery groups, he wanted to avoid extremes and in fact extended a friendly hand to foreigners in his poetry. In "Song of Myself" he announced himself "pleased with the native and pleased with the foreign" (*CP*, 62). In "Proto-Leaf" he wrote,

"See, in my poems immigrants continually coming and landing" (*LGV*, 2: 288). His claim elsewhere that his poetry does not separate "the white from the black, or the native from the immigrant just landed at the wharf" in fact has validity, as is evidenced particularly by his poetic paean to international friendship, "Salut au Monde!"[36] The American Party, although it stimulated his nationalism, became one more narrow political group he rejected.

Time would tell that he had good reason to do so. The American Party rapidly fell prey to the same sectional divisions that had killed off the Whigs. The ascendant Republicans meanwhile spent more energy on attacking the southern "slaveocracy" than on representing the interests of northern workers. Both the problems and the proposed solutions of the parties were addressed to specific, practical needs of the moment.

For Whitman, American's problem was far deeper than the immigrant explosion or the slave power. Corruption in America was not superficial or easily removed. It was, he wrote, "in the blood" (*NP*, 1: 862). His disgust with the political process was more profound than that of any other commentator of the 1850s. He wrote that the parties had become "empty flesh, putrid mouths, mumbling and squeaking the tones of these conventions, the politicians standing back in the shadow, telling lies" (*CP*, 1317). Those responsible for selecting America's leaders came "from political hearses, and from the coffins inside, and from the shrouds inside the coffins; from the tumors and abscesses of the land; from the skeletons and skulls in the vaults of the federal almshouses; from the running sores of the great cities" (*CP*, 1313).

The final effect of the dramatic political changes of the 1850s was to drive him beyond parties altogether. In his 1856 notebook the former party loyalist could proclaim himself "no[t] the particular representative of any one party – no tied and ticketed democrat, whig, abolitionist, republican, – no bawling spokesman of natives against foreigners" (*NP*, 6: 2117). The history of parties and reforms had shown him that the former led to institutionalized corruption, the latter to narrow views and sometimes wild fanaticism. He now reminded himself, "We want no *reforms*, no *institutions*, no *parties* – We want a *living principle* as nature has, under which nothing can go wrong – This must be vital through the United States" (*NP*, 1: 145). He had once believed that the American system would perpetually purify itself through party debates and periodic elections. But with the party system having collapsed in a morass of bad principle and outright knavery, he had to look elsewhere for purification and ennoblement.

He looked mainly to nature. Nature in *Leaves of Grass* becomes more than just a Wordsworthian or Emersonian source of spiritual inspiration (though it is that too). It is a cleansing solvent into which Whitman cast all the disagreeable aspects of American experience, to be made pure and healthy. At its best, American democracy itself was chiefly valuable to him for what he called its "cleansingness," its ability to simulate "Nature's stomach" with its "kosmical, antiseptic power" in casting out "morbific matter" through its election cycle and laws (*CP*, 949). But in the 1850s, elections and laws were of little help. Refreshing nature imagery was needed to show the unclean body politic how to renew itself. Politics must reorganize itself according to what he saw as the all-rectifying principle of nature. In his poem "To a President," he drove home this political meaning of nature when he warned American's chief executive: "You have not learn'd of Nature – of the politics of Nature you have not learn'd the great amplitude, rectitude, impartiality" (*CP*, 410).

The politics of nature. That, finally, is what he turned to. The sky, the sea, plants, trees, roots, buds, sunshine, animals, sex, the body, the infinite universe. None of these natural phenomena had figured much in his early poetry and fiction, but suddenly they seemed all-important. He dreamed of his nature-filled poetry having an immense impact on American life. "The poets I would have must be a power in the state, and an engrossing power in the state," he wrote in his notebook (*NP*, 1: 144). If America saw its problems and its people recast amid nature imagery, perhaps it would change. Sectional divisions could be repaired by an absorptive, poetic "I" who traveled joyously through all regions and who reveled in the cycles of nature. Corruption could be positively counteracted by a poetic re-creation of nature's beauties. The metaphors Whitman used to describe his mission were little less than messianic. *Leaves of Grass* was "the new Bible," to be read outdoors by everyone every season of the year. The poet was "the age transfigured." The proof of the poet was that his country absorbed him as affectionately as he absorbed it.

Wishful thinking, to be sure. And, as it turned out, deluded thinking. Whitman had nowhere near the immediate impact he dreamed of. In some ways, America's social problems even worsened over time. But *Leaves of Grass* still stands as a testament to Whitman's struggle to plant poetic seed on volcanic political soil.

NOTES

1 See Arvin, *Whitman* (New York: Macmillan, 1938), and Erkkila, *Whitman the Political Poet* (New York: Oxford University Press, 1989).
2 Whitman, *Complete Poetry and Collected Prose,* ed. Justin Kaplan (New York:

Library of America, 1982), p. 8. This volume is hereafter cited parenthetically in the text as *CP.*

3 *Prose Works 1892,* ed. Floyd Stovall (New York: New York University Press, 1961), 2, p. 429. This volume is hereafter cited parenthetically in the text as *PW.*

4 *Notebooks and Unpublished Prose Manuscripts,* ed. Edward F. Grier (New York: New York University Press, 1984), 1, p. 96. This volume is hereafter cited parenthetically in the text as *NP.*

5 Brooklyn *Daily Eagle,* November 7, 1846. The following quotation in this paragraph is from the *Eagle,* March 12, 1846.

6 Brooklyn *Daily Eagle,* June 12, 1846. The following quotations in this paragraph are from the *Eagle,* June 19, 1846, and June 22, 1846.

7 Brooklyn *Daily Eagle,* December 6, 1847.

8 *Selections from the Writings and Speeches of William Lloyd Garrison* (New York: Negro University Press, 1968), p. 119.

9 Brooklyn *Daily Eagle,* May 29, 1846. The following quotation in this paragraph is from the *Eagle,* November 7, 1846.

10 *Uncollected Poetry and Prose of Walt Whitman,* ed. Emory Holloway (Gloucester, Mass.: Peter Smith, 1972), 2, pp. 69, 73. This volume is hereafter cited parenthetically in the text as *UPP.*

11 Platform reprinted in Frederick J. Blue, *The Free Soilers: Third Party Politics, 1848–54* (Urbana: University of Illinois Press, 1973), p. 295.

12 *Congressional Globe,* 29th Congress, 2nd Session, Appendix, 317–18.

13 *Franklin Evans or The Inebriate,* in *The Early Poems and the Fiction,* ed. Thomas L. Brasher (New York: New York University Press, 1963), 2, p. 202. *The Early Poems and the Fiction* is hereafter cited parenthetically in the text as *EPF.*

14 Brooklyn *Freeman,* September 9, 1848.

15 For Bakhtin's theory of the absorption of cultural idioms into literature, see especially *The Dialogic Imagination: Four Essays by M. M. Bakhtin,* trans. Caryl Emerson and Michael Holquist (Austin: University of Texas Press, 1981) and *Bakhtin: Essays and Dialogues on His Work,* ed. Gary Saul Morson (Chicago: University of Chicago Press, 1986).

16 *Life Illustrated,* April 12, 1856, in Whitman, *New York Dissected: A Sheaf of Recently Discovered Newspaper Articles by the Author of Leaves of Grass* (New York: Rufus Rockwell Wilson, 1936), p. 59. This volume is hereafter cited parenthetically in the text as *NYD.*

17 *Beneath the American Renaissance: The Subversive Imagination in the Age of Emerson and Melville* (New York: Alfred A. Knopf, 1988).

18 *The Quaker City; or, The Monks of Monk Hall,* reprinted as *The Monks of Monk Hall,* ed. Leslie Fiedler (New York: Odyssey, 1970), p. 375.

19 Whitman, *The Correspondence,* ed. Edwin Haviland Miller (New York: New York University Press, 1969), 1, pp. 39–40.

20 Horace Traubel, *With Walt Whitman in Camden* (New York: Mitchell Kennerly, 1914), 3, p. 30. This volume is hereafter cited parenthetically in the text as *WWC.*

21 In Paxton Hibben, *Henry Ward Beecher: An American Portrait* (1927; rpt., New York: The Press of the Readers Club, 1942), p. 187.

22 *Speeches, Lectures, and Essays* (1884; rpt., New York: Negro University Press, 1968), pp. 52–3.

23 In Eric Foner, *Free Soil, Free Labor, Free Men: The Ideology of the Republican Party Before the Civil War* (New York: Oxford University Press, 1970), p. 112.

24 *Walt Whitman's Workshop: A Collection of Unpublished Prose Manuscripts,* ed. Clifton Joseph Furness (New York: Russell and Russell, 1964), p. 130. This volume is hereafter cited parenthetically in the text as *WWW.*

25 *The Plundering Generation: Corruption and the Crisis of the Union* (New York: Oxford University Press, 1987).

26 Uncollected manuscript fragment in Whitman, *Leaves of Grass: Comprehensive Reader's Edition,* ed. Harold Blodgett and Sculley Bradley (New York: New York University Press, 1965), p. 696.

27 See Madeleine B. Stern, *The Pantarch: A Biography of Stephen Pearl Andrews* (Austin: University of Texas Press, 1968), pp. 74–5.

28 *Love, Marriage, and The Sovereignty of the Individual* (1853; rpt., Boston: Benjamin R. Tucker, 1884), p. 65.

29 Brooklyn *Daily Times,* May 14, 1857.

30 In Richard M. Johnson and William M. Browne, *Life of Alexander H. Stephens* (Philadelphia, 1883), p. 286.

31 Quoted in Michael F. Holt, *The Political Crisis of the 1850s* (New York: Wiley, 1978), p. 176. The following quotation in this paragraph is from the same volume, p. 176.

32 Foner, *Free Soil.*

33 See Taylor Anbinder, *Nativism and Slavery: The Northern Know Nothings and The Politics of the 1850s* (New York: Oxford University Press, 1992).

34 The 1856 version of "By Blue Ontario's Shore," in Whitman, *Leaves of Grass: A Textual Variorum of the Printed Poems,* ed. Sculley Bradley et al. (New York: New York University Press, 1980), 1, p. 192. This volume is hereafter cited parenthetically in the text as *LGV.*

35 In *Re Walt Whitman,* ed. Horace L. Traubel, Richard Maurice Bucke, and Thomas B. Harned (Philadelphia: David McKay, 1893), pp. 13, 23.

36 *Ibid.,* p. 19.

6

EZRA GREENSPAN

Some Remarks on the Poetics of
"Participle-Loving Whitman"

I take my title from a stray observation thrown off by Randall Jarrell in the course of his scintillating defense of Whitman's poetics back in the 1950s, when Whitman was generally out of fashion in the New Criticism-dominated days of American literary criticism.[1] Jarrell spoke at the time of "participle-loving Whitman" in the course of his discussion of several of the most distinctive features he found in Whitman's verse. In this essay, I take up Jarrell's observation and expand on it as a way of making several fundamental points about the poetics of *Leaves of Grass*. In doing so, I hope that I am capturing something of Jarrell's concern for the connection between the spirit of Whitman's poetry and that of the age – whether the age be Whitman's or our own.

The first point I would like to make is perhaps the most basic: Whitman had a lifelong attachment to the grammatical form of the present participle. I can make this point most convincingly, Whitman-style, simply by cataloging. Consider the following list of titles of his poems: "Beginning My Studies," "The Ship Starting," "I Hear America Singing," "Starting from Paumanok," "Facing West from California's Shores," "Whoever You Are Holding Me Now in Hand," "These I Singing in Spring," "I Saw in Louisiana a Live-Oak Growing," "We Two Boys Together Clinging," "Crossing Brooklyn Ferry," "A Song of the Rolling Earth," "Out of the Cradle Endlessly Rocking," "Roaming in Thought," "Cavalry Crossing a Ford," "Ethiopia Saluting the Colors," "Chanting the Square Deific," "Pensive on Her Dead Gazing," " 'Going Somewhere.' "[2] These poems come from all periods of his long career and encompass all the modes of verse in which he wrote.

Or consider this brief – very brief, it can go on for pages – lexicon of Whitman participles, culled unsystematically from his poetry: "ascending"; "preluding"; "existing"; "spreading"; "cleaving"; "roaming"; "passing"; "flowing"; "grazing"; "singing"; "starting . . . spreading . . . carrying"; "eating, drinking and breeding"; "Storming, enjoying, planning, loving, cautioning, / Backing and filling, appearing and disappearing"; "leaping, reclining, embracing, arm-curving and tightening"; "The current rushing so swiftly and swimming with me far away"; "The earth expanding right hand and left hand"; "Embracing man, embracing all, proceed the three hundred and sixty-five resistlessly round the sun; / Embracing all, soothing, supporting, follow close three hundred and sixty-five offsets of the first, sure and necessary as they"; "Throwing myself on the sand, confronting the waves, / I, chanter of pains and joys, uniter of here and hereafter, / Taking all hints to use them, but swiftly leaping beyond them, / A reminiscence sing"; "Passing the visions, passing the night, / Passing, unloosing the hold of my comrades' hands, / Passing the song of the hermit bird and the tallying song of my soul." Take them singly or in series – they pervade Whitman's poetry throughout all phases of his career.

Or consider some of his poems' most typical "acts": his self "compassionating" with others in "Song of Myself"; his persona "Stepping with light feet, swiftly and noiselessly stepping and stopping, / Bending with open eyes over the shut eyes of sleepers, / Wandering and confused . . . / Pausing, gazing, bending, and stopping" as he sets off on his night tour in "The Sleepers"; the child in "Out of the Cradle Endlessly Rocking" "cautiously peering, absorbing, translating" as he prepares himself, through observation of the mockingbird, for his future role as poet; the comrade-poet of *Drum-Taps* "Resuming, marching, ever in darkness marching, on in the ranks, / The unknown road still marching"; the creator spider in "A Noiseless Patient Spider" "ever unreeling" and "ever tirelessly speeding" the filaments of its connective tissue and the poet following close by and "ceaselessly musing, venturing, throwing, seeking the spheres to connect them"; the central symbols of "When Lilacs Last in the Dooryard Bloom'd" set into life: "Ever-returning spring, trinity sure to me you bring, / Lilac blooming perennial and drooping star in the west, / And thought of him I love"; or even his well-rehearsed deathbed departure in "Good-bye My Fancy!" with his "heart-thud stopping" and his mortal existence "undoing, turning."

Such uses of participles occur throughout Whitman's poetry. Not only did Whitman use them frequently; he also used them consequentially. He used them, for example, as one of the basic building blocks of his poems. Constructing entire stanzas, even poems, out of regularly repeated present participles was, in fact, one of the most basic tools in Whitman's poetic repertoire. A representative instance of this practice can be found in this important stanza from "Song of Myself":

> What is commonest, cheapest, nearest, easiest, is Me,
> Me going in for my chances, spending for vast returns,

Adorning myself to bestow myself on the first that will take me,
Not asking the sky to come down to my good will,
Scattering it freely forever.

(41)

In this stanza, the parallelism is constructed from the regular repetition of the participial phrases. These phrases stand in relation not only to one another but ultimately to the "Me" whose potentiality to be – simply to be – is the subject of the stanza and one of the central ideas of the entire poem. The effect of the participial phrases, whose number in such a structural configuration is unlimited, is to carry the potentiality of the persona forward and onward, as it were, similarly without limitation.

This is the reason why, structurally considered, so many of Whitman's poems open immediately or nearly immediately with a participial expression, as in the following instances: "Sauntering the pavement or riding the country byroads here then are faces" ("Faces"), "Starting from fish-shaped Paumanok where I was born" ("Starting from Paumanok"), "Facing west from California's shores" ("Facing West from California's Shores"), "Singing my days" ("Passage to India"), and "Chanting the square deific, out of the One advancing, out of the sides" ("Chanting the Square Deific"). If one thinks of the opening words of a poem as immediately committing a writer to many of the most important choices that he or she has to make with regard to tone, diction, and content, then one can see that Whitman's tendency to open his poems with participles is one requiring a strong explanation. What seems clear to me is that Whitman often did so because he saw the poetic act basically as one of physical and intellectual mobility, which required of him the verbal necessity of pushing off immediately participially, as though from a springboard.

A similar rule applies to the unit of the line in Whitman's poetry. If English is a language with, linguistically speaking, a relatively stiff syntactical spine, one of the most inventive aspects of Whitman's poetry is the considerable freedom he took by inverting (and sometimes convoluting) the normal subject–predicate sequence of the language. One of the most effective patterns he used in this regard was to begin his verses with participles or participial phrases, which, given the relative mobility of their positional attachment to the nouns they modify, allowed him to loosen the leash of syntactical connection in his poetry. One fine instance of this occurs in Section 32 of "Song of Myself," where it structures the following stanza:

Myself moving forward then and now and forever,
Gathering and showing more always and with velocity,
Infinite and omnigenous, and the like of these among them,

Not too exclusive toward the reachers of my remembrancers,
Picking out here one that I love, and now go with him on brotherly terms.

(60)

In fact, as even a cursory reading will indicate, this stanza lacks grammatical completion, having not even the rudiments of an independent clausal structure. What it does have, though, is the operative word "myself" and its accompanying array of participial and adjectival extensions, which project its movement laterally and longitudinally. Whitman was fond of this long-flowing poetic syntax, with the subject (normally, in the first person) stated first and its capabilities left unfolding via a string of participles. Conversely, he was also fond of precisely the opposite structure, delaying the appearance of the subject "I" until the end of a long-flowing sequence of participial, prepositional, or clausal expressions, thus creating the context out of which his "I" will be born. The best instance of this is one of the finest sustained pieces of verse he ever wrote: the opening strophe of "Out of the Cradle Endlessly Rocking."

Such recurrent, lifelong use of present participles makes it clear that Whitman's manipulation of these modifiers was no incidental or arbitrary component of his poetics, or that Whitman was attracted to them simply for the sake of decoration or elaboration. Where they are most splendidly decorative in Whitman, as in the panoramic catalog of Section 3 of "Crossing Brooklyn Ferry," they are also powerfully functional. In fact, to express my thesis concerning their importance to Whitman more directly, I would say that they constitute an essential part of his poetics and that they reflect and express some of this poet's most fundamental ideas and beliefs about the status, value, and meaning of the two things that meant most to him: life and poetry.

Where did his practice of self-consciously utilizing present participles come from? It is as difficult to answer that question as it is to explain the origins of Whitman's free-verse poetics. My own belief is that the two matters probably have a common provenance. Whitman clearly did not use participles as a self-conscious poetic practice back in the 1840s, when he worked primarily as a newspaper journalist and wrote only a very occasional poem, intended usually for publication in the press. Those early poems are virtually always of a derivative, conventional nature and are as self-contained in their poetics as his *Leaves of Grass* poems tend to be limit-transcending. The new character of his 1850s poetry appears most clearly for the first time in a well-practiced, systematized form in a free-verse notebook poem (later called "Pictures") that most scholars attribute to the early

1850s, when Whitman was experimenting with the verse techniques that would reach full maturity only in the 1855 *Leaves of Grass*. That poem originates in the figuration of the mind as a picture gallery containing a limitless array of self-selected portraits, through which it takes its reader on a poet-guided tour. The language of the poem, perhaps for the first time in Whitman, is heavily figured in participles, whose purpose is to enliven the description of the contents of individual pictures, as of the "Hebrew prophets chanting"; Christ "bearing" the cross with "blood and sweat streaming down his face"; Columbus "setting sail from Spain"; a man (no doubt, a projected image of Whitman himself) "working his way through the crowds, observant and singing"; woodcutters "cutting down trees"; a blacksmith "leaning on his upright hammer"; Jefferson "compiling the Declaration of Independence"; Emerson "at the lecturer's desk lecturing"; an old black man "begging, humming hymn-tunes nasally all day to himself and receiving small gifts"; and loggers "guiding logs down a stream in the North."

Although the participles do not yet serve the unifying or organizational principles that they will often serve in Whitman's fully mature poetry, their recurrence is already an effective device in this poem, as Whitman presumably knew, for imbuing each of the individuals named with his or her particular activity. Having used present participles even in this rudimentary fashion, he had or would soon come to a self-conscious recognition of the fact that they allowed him to realize his kinetic vision of what, for lack of a better term, I would call "sprawl" – of life as ceaseless, unauthorized (except as self-authorized) motion; of experience as an ongoing process of self-propelled thrust out into the world; of his time and place as a fluid continuum transcending beginning and end points. A poet as "electric" as the young Whitman needed language charged, as it were, with the potential energy of verbals to convey his sense of the sprawling vitality of modern life that he felt when he passed down the streets and rivers of the city, which was already a favorite subject of his journalism throughout the 1840s.

By the time he began the composition of his 1855 *Leaves of Grass* poems, Whitman was ready to activate the trope of his "picture gallery" and to take it directly outdoors to America, an activity closer to what we today think of as that of the motion picture camera than to the activity of poetry. In this context, I think of Whitman as an early anticipator of the "kino-eye" (or "cinema-eye") concept of the revolutionary Soviet filmmaker Dziga Vertov. Allowing for the necessary situational and ideological differences between the poet of bourgeois, capitalistic democracy and the cinematographer of the years immediately following the Bolshevik Revolution, one can find in

Vertov's kino-eye writings and in such films as *The Man with a Movie Camera* a fascinating parallel to the Whitman of the first edition of *Leaves of Grass*. Here is Vertov elaborating on his idea of the camera as "a kin-eye, more perfect than the human eye, for the exploration of the chaos of visual phenomena that fills space":

> I am kino-eye, I am a mechanical eye. I, a machine, show you the world as only I can see it.
>
> Now and forever, I free myself from human immobility, I am in constant motion, I draw near, then away from objects, I crawl under, I climb onto them. I move apace with the muzzle of a galloping horse, I plunge full speed into a crowd, I outstrip running soldiers, I fall on my back, I ascend with an airplane, I plunge and soar together with plunging and soaring bodies. Now I, a camera, fling myself along their resultant, maneuvering in the chaos of movement, recording movement, starting with movements composed of the most complex combinations.
>
> Freed from the rule of sixteen-seventeen frames per second, free of the limits of time and space, I put together any given points in the universe, no matter where I've recorded them.
>
> My path leads to the creation of a fresh perception of the world. I decipher in a new way a world unknown to you.[3]

The heady freedom that led Vertov, like other young Soviet artists of the post-revolutionary 1920s, to "the creation of a fresh perception of the world" was analogous to the ideological challenge Whitman had set in the 1850s for himself and for his generation of new poets to "advance through all interpositions and coverings and turmoils and stratagems to first principles."[4] Analogous, too, was their commitment to make art the instrumentality of communicating their fresh senses of the vitality of experience and the means of transmitting them to their contemporary audiences. For both men, vision unhinged from fixed perspective, point of view liberated from tradition or authority, animated their commitments to a new art and presented their imaginations with profoundly demanding aesthetic, as well as political, challenges.

But where Vertov relied on the mechanical instrumentality of the camera to picture his surrounding world, Whitman passed through his environs with only his human eye (well supplemented, to be sure, by the full complement of his acute senses) performing the act of recording. A representative case of Whitman's eye in the act of recording its impressions is the splendid outdoor catalog, already referred to, in "Crossing Brooklyn Ferry," in which the poem's speaker expresses his impression of New York harbor:

I too many and many a time cross'd the river of old,
Watch'd the Twelfth-month sea-gulls, saw them high in the air *floating* with
    motionless wings, *oscillating* their bodies,
Saw how the *glistening* yellow lit up parts of their bodies and left the rest in
    strong shadow,
Saw the *slow-wheeling* circles and the gradual edging toward the south,
Saw the reflection of the summer sky in the water,
Had my eyes dazzled by the *shimmering* track of beams,
Look'd at the fine centrifugal spokes of light round the shape of my head in the
    sunlit water,
Look'd on the haze on the hills southward and south-westward,
Look'd on the vapor as it flew in fleeces tinged with violet,
Look'd toward the lower bay to notice the vessels *arriving,*
Saw their approach, saw aboard those that were near me,
Saw the white sails of schooners and sloops, saw the ships at anchor,
The sailors at work in the rigging or out astride the spars,
The round masts, the *swinging* motion of the hulls, the slender serpentine
    pennants,
The large and small steamers in motion, the pilots in their pilot-houses,
The white wake left by the passage, the quick tremulous whirl of the wheels,
The flags of all nations, the falling of them at sunset,
The scallop-edged waves in the twilight, the ladled cups, the frolicsome crests and
    glistening,
The stretch afar *growing* dimmer and dimmer, the gray walls of the granite
    storehouses by the docks,
On the river the shadowy group, the big steam-tug closely flank'd on each side by
    the barges, the hay-boat, the belated lighter,
On the *neighboring* shore the fires from the foundry chimneys *burning* high and
    glaringly into the night,
Casting their flicker of black contrasted with wild red and yellow light over the
    tops of houses, and down into the clefts of streets.[5]

(161–2; my emphasis)

With its potential for vitality, breadth, fullness, and variety, this was the
kind of spectacle that both excited Whitman's sensibility and challenged his
imagination to construct its fitting verbal representation. With the scene's
center not clearly defined – it can be said to be nowhere or everywhere – as
often happens in Whitman, the real weight of the scene transfers from the
object viewed (the scene on the river as viewed during a ferry crossing) to
the subject viewer (the "I"). Given the slipperiness not only of this transfer-
ral but also of relations throughout the entire poem, one can appreciate the
sense behind the question that students typically ask in reading "Crossing
Brooklyn Ferry": "What has this poem got to do with either Brooklyn or the

Brooklyn ferry?" My own answer is that the poem has very little to do with this or any other location, considered specifically, and for a very good reason: The situation facing Whitman's persona here as he looks out on the river is actually a generic one. Like other settings Whitman visited around town, walking on the streets and traveling across the city or crossing its rivers, this favorite setting presents him with the fundamental poetic task of creating order out of disorder. With no inherent or "authorized" system by which to understand and order the "sights and hearings" he typically experienced on his daily outings, Whitman was confronted with the poetic task of contriving verbal and organizational representations.

His response in this section of the poem is simultaneously specific and generic: He sends out his "I" to report on what he now sees and always sees (as "others" before him have also seen and after him will yet see it). In this frame he sets the content of his report, which comes back as a visual catalog of his sightings – ships, waves, people, light, and structures – rendered unified as a formal compositional whole. The primary organizational technique he employs here to present this picture, as he does throughout *Leaves of Grass,* is parallelism, the overriding structural device by which he sets his observations into an ordered sequence and produces the effect of rhythmic balance. On the more local level of the line, however, he also employs a highly active vocabulary made up largely of present participles (as well as of past participles and gerunds) to keep the basic action, the seeing and recording of the scene, flowing and progressing, the various elements of the scene moving toward one another. To imagine this scene without these words would be not only to deprive it of its underlying dynamism but to isolate the individual elements in their own contexts, a situation that would return Whitman to his point of origin and eliminate the fusion of elements, human with human, artistic with natural, to which the poem builds.

An activistic poet like Whitman would naturally often employ a highly verbalized vocabulary to express his vision of the dynamism of life. A fairly typical example of this propensity is the opening stanza from Section 10 of "Song of Myself":

Alone far in the wilds and mountains I hunt,
Wandering amazed at my own lightness and glee,
In the late afternoon choosing a safe spot to pass the night,
Kindling a fire and broiling the fresh-kill'd game,
Falling asleep on the gather'd leaves with my dog and gun by my side.

(37)

Comically absurd as this scene is in picturing its home-centered, Brooklyn poet roaming the woods with dog and gun, linguistically considered it actually has a compelling logic, the logic that Whitman's catalogs, long and short alike, frequently have in riding a generous supply of participles. These catalogs were one of the novel devices of Whitman's poetry, as well as one of its most self-consciously devised and executed practices. They allowed Whitman to incorporate in his poetry the principle of inclusiveness to which he was committed as a political and cultural nationalist. At the same time, they gave free play to an imagination that was remarkably liberated, for its time, from the constraints of specificity and linearity. This particular passage provides a typical case of the way Whitman characteristically made over the prosaic facts of his own life in the energized terms of his poetic replacement, who is flung to far-off places and outfitted for a variety of roles by the ongoing thrust of the poem's participial language. If effective in this passage from Section 10, this device was particularly necessary in his much longer catalogs, where it could be used to sustain their movement and unify their direction. One example of this is the famous "I am afoot with my vision" sequence in Section 33 of this poem, whose accumulating participials, in effect, become the means of transportation of the "I" to distant places and activities. Their effect in that section, however, is not so much to launch the actor or action away from the center vectorially as to loop the movement and return it back to the center, a circling effect that is common in Whitman's poetry and one of its distinguishing characteristics.

A subtle variation on this practice of using participles for geographical or situational mobility occurs in the bathing sequence of the twenty-eight young men in Section 11 of "Song of Myself." With the introduction of the line "Dancing and laughing along the beach came the twenty-ninth bather," Whitman succeeds in intruding a new "female" element into a set situation of twenty-eight male bathers. Similar to this effect is that of Section 41 of "Song of Myself," in which Whitman begins a pan-historic catalog of the various gods of humankind with the line "Magnifying and applying come I," whose effect is to intrude his presence into established quarters to shake up the foundations of the accepted pantheon. These are only two of the instances in his poetry in which Whitman found in such participially introduced phrases a supple verbal conveyance for figuring the fantasy he often played in his mind of sauntering into and out of more or less fixed structures – crowds, buildings, set gatherings, even situations. In such cases, the dynamism that Whitman achieved through his use of participles might as well be situational as physical.

I understand Whitman's systematic use of participles in the first edition of

Leaves of Grass as one of the verbal means he found for conveying his young man's sense of modern life as free, mobile, and changing – that element in Whitman that has generated "open road" readings of his life and poetry. It reminds me of several of Jean-Jacques Rousseau's autobiographical remembrances of his youth, particularly the following: "Jeune, vigoureux, plein de santé, de sécurité, de confiance en moi et aux autres, j'étois dans ce court mais précieux moment de la vie où sa plénitude expansive étend pour ainsi dire notre être par toutes nos sensations, et embellit à nos yeux la nature entiére du charme de notre existence." ["I was young, vigorous, healthy, fearless, and full of confidence in myself and others. I was enjoying that short but precious moment in life when its overflowing fullness expands, so to speak, one's whole being, and lends all nature, in one's eyes, the charm of one's own existence."][6] Especially in 1855, Whitman's poetry often sounded this young man's optimism and egocentrism. At the same time, for Whitman, unlike for Rousseau, the temptation was strong, even irresistible, to identify himself with the national collective, and his creative expression was often an attempt to devise ways to realize that ambition, whether indirectly, as in "Song of Myself," or directly, as in "I Hear America Singing." In the latter case, Whitman imagined the dynamic power of the nation not as a geographical entity spreading westward but as an activity – and one of his favorite ones, at that: singing. The poem consists of a vision of the various units of the country – the mechanic, the carpenter, the mason, the young wife, the boatman – each person separately "singing" his or her individual song. But where in "Pictures" each person acts his or her role separately, this poem blends the individual acts of singing into a harmonious participial ensemble of America singing.

The paradox from which the poem works, the empowerment of each element of the country individually but at the same time their merger in the collective empowerment of the nation as a whole, was one that Whitman saw as forming a fault line across American society. I believe, in fact, that the fear of the failure of the individual parts to conjoin as neatly and harmoniously as the seamless whole orchestrated by this poem was one that Whitman knew profoundly even before his development by the mid-1850s into the poet of *Leaves of Grass*. That anxiety intensified with the growing strains placed on the Union during the late 1850s and with the eventual outbreak of the Civil War. However much he may have wished for societal unity, Whitman was never able to sustain an easy or long-lasting reconciliation between his personal longings and national developments. Perhaps for this reason, Whitman more often than not tended to link the dynamism of his participials, whether used singly or strung together into long chains, to the idea of the individual rather than to that of the collective. That individual is typically the favorite person (in two senses) of his poetry: his "I." Although critics and readers ever since the first publication of *Leaves of Grass* in the mid-nineteenth century have broken their heads against the wall of the biographical fallacy in trying to pierce the plane of the first-person figuration and to read into it personal, psychological, or sexual traits of the author, I will simply say here that, whatever or whoever lay behind it, Whitman found in the figuration of his "I" an extraordinarily congenial vehicle for his vision of freedom and unrestraint. I think, in this regard, of numerous significant passages in Whitman's poetry where Whitman launches his "I" participially as a representative American exploring what he considered a representative situation of American freedom: the opening stanza of "Starting from Paumanok" (with which Whitman was to open the third edition of *Leaves of Grass*); various catalog sections of "Song of Myself"; the nightwalking scene that opens "The Sleepers"; the "sauntering the pavement" scene that opens "Faces"; the dazzling opening strophe of "Out of the Cradle Endlessly Rocking."

One can state the proposition more strongly yet: With his mobility-creating devices, such as the use of the present participle, Whitman found a means for launching his imagination beyond the constraints of time and place into the open dimensions of poetic space. What Whitman could do with the simple grammatical proposition – and, for him, one of the most beloved – "I am" is one of the most revealing phenomena of his poetry. Freed from the limitations of predetermined definition, category, or specification concerning the character of his persona, Whitman's poetic "I" gave a new meaning to the concept of self-determination. It effectively answered the question "Who am I?" with the response: I am anyone, anywhere, anytime. I am the hunter, the trapper, the fisherman, the lover (alternately, male or female), the escaped slave; I am in the hayloft, in the streets of the city, out on the bay, on the margins of the pond; I am back in prehistory, at the site of land and sea battles of earlier generations, on the cutting edge of modern experience (whether it be in 1855, 1955, or 2055). Although Whitman learned various ways to commit this idea to paper, certainly one of the most effective was by way of the present participle, whose inherent dynamism gave his poetic verses the propellent they needed to move beyond the condition of stasis or fixity. One can only imagine how much harder it would have been for Whitman to create this effect in a language that lacked the grammatical element of the present participle (as indeed it is for translators trying to render the dynamic mobility of his poetry in their own tongues but forced to do so without the built-in mechanism available to Whitman in English).

Such usage was most common in but not limited to Whitman's early poems. Even at the end of his long life/career, Whitman was still utilizing the dynamic potentiality of the participle in his poetry. One fine example is in "Unseen Buds," a poem written in extreme old age and poor health and first published in his 1891 *Good-Bye My Fancy:*

> Unseen buds, infinite, hidden well,
> Under the snow and ice, under the darkness, in every square or cubic inch,
> Germinal, exquisite, in delicate lace, microscopic, unborn,
> Like babes in wombs, latent, folded, compact, sleeping;
> Billions of billions, and trillions of trillions of them waiting,
> (On earth and in the sea – the universe – the stars there in the heavens,)
> Urging slowly, surely forward, forming endless,
> And waiting ever more, forever more beyond.

(557)

Back in the 1850s, Whitman had seen "buds" as a suitable trope for the potentiality of life and art that he not only longed to believe in but that he needed to associate with his own existence. But even in old age, with his health and vitality fast waning, his ability – I would say, his compulsion – to figure life as a process of ongoing budding remained staunch. Even beyond the tenacity of his willpower, what I find most remarkable is the way the aged man imagined the buds of life in terms of process (or, to put this proposition grammatically, intransitively), via participial actions whose defined end or direction is never given. Neither in youth nor in old age was it characteristic of Whitman to determine what the end product or specific configuration of the buds would be.

Or, to take another example, one can find a similar phenomenon in – a very different source – Whitman's 1860 "Children of Adam" poem "To the Garden the World," an edenic fantasia of primal life that offers one of the most engaging uses of participles in all of Whitman's oeuvre:

> To the garden the world anew ascending,
> Potent mates, daughters, sons, preluding,
> The love, the life of their bodies, meaning and being,
> Curious here behold my resurrection after slumber,
> The revolving cycles in their wide sweep having brought me again,
> Amorous, mature, all beautiful to me, all wondrous,
> My limbs and the quivering fire that ever plays through them, for reasons, most wondrous,

Existing I peer and penetrate still,
Content with the present, content with the past,
By my side or back of me Eve following,
Or in front, and I following her just the same.

(90)

Others can choose their favorite terms; my personal favorite here is "exist-ing." It seems to me the perfect expression for the poem's situationally conceived concern with life or, to put it more ontologically, with existence. Whitman's speaker does not so much exist as is *existing* – that is, occupying a state in which existence is mobilized. Then, again, the entire poem is an exercise in verbal, physical, and metaphysical mobility. It operates by the circling effect created by the stream of uncompleted participial movements, which leave Whitman's Adam and Eve in a state of ceaseless motion and always incipient preparation. To ask of the poem "motion to where?" or "preparation for what?" is to miss its point; its Adam and Eve exist, as it were, in a state of pure process, whose context is that of the creativity that they in their twin figures symbolize and that the poem in its movement enacts.

What Whitman could do with whole stanzas he could also do with whole poems. A good example of a poem structured entirely by participials is one of Whitman's best late poems, "The Dalliance of the Eagles" (first published in 1880):

Skirting the river road, (my forenoon walk, my rest,)
Skyward in air a sudden muffled sound, the dalliance of the eagles,
The rushing amorous contact high in space together,
The clinching interlocking claws, a living, fierce, gyrating wheel,
Four beating wings, two beaks, a swirling mass tight grappling,
In tumbling turning clustering loops, straight downward falling,
Till o'er the river pois'd, the twain yet one, a moment's lull,
A motionless still balance in the air, then parting, talons loosing,
Upward again on slow-firm pinions slanting, their separate diverse flight,
She hers, he his, pursuing.

(273–4)

From its first to its closing word, the poem is built on present participles. Whitman's fondness for them as conveyors of ongoing action and motion was never clearer. In a poem where an ongoing action, the mating of the eagles, is both the subject and the process of the poem, his availing himself freely of present participles was a natural way of expressing the sight un-folding – as it unfolds – before his eyes. But before I explicate the poem any further, I would like to juxtapose it with a poem of a similar act and, to a certain extent, of a similar manner, a comparison that gives a wider perspective on the issues involved and the possibilities available to a poet writing in a related manner on a related theme. Here is Yeats's "Leda and the Swan":

> A sudden blow: the great wings beating still
> Above the staggering girl, her thighs caressed
> By the great webs, her nape caught in his bill,
> He holds her helpless breast upon his breast.
>
> How can those terrified vague fingers push
> The feathered glory from her loosening thighs?
> And how can body, laid in that white rush,
> But feel the strange heart beating where it lies?
>
> A shudder in the loins engenders there
> The broken wall, the burning roof and tower
> And Agamemnon dead.
>   Being so caught up,
> So mastered by the brute blood of the air,
> Did she put on his knowledge with his power
> Before the indifferent beak could let her drop?[7]

Aside from the resemblance of their treatment of the act of sex on a cosmic scale, what is most obviously similar is the way both poets represent the sex act via present participles. Yeats: the "beating" wings, the "staggering" girl, the "loosening" thighs, the "beating" heart, the "burning" roof; Whitman: the "rushing" contact, the "clinching interlocking" claws, the "living, fierce, gyrating" wheel, the "beating" wings, the "swirling mass tight grappling," the "tumbling turning clustering" loops, the "loosing" talons. The similarity is so close that certain phrases are nearly interchangeable.

This similarity makes the differences between the two poems and the different directions in which the two poets head all the more interesting. Yeats's use of this verbal pattern is crafted onto a tapestry thickly textured in mythical history. Its thicker texturing and powerful outside frame of reference throw into relief the greater self-unity and tighter self-referentiality of Whitman's poem, which seems, by contrast, characteristically ahistorical and atemporal. The action represented by "The Dalliance of the Eagles" is a timeless one, not only unbound by but unrelated to the lines of history or chronology. Although Whitman does mention the time of day and does chart the act through and beyond its climax, he conceives of the mating of the eagles as an act to be repeated endless times and in an endless number of places and circumstances. For this reason, it is an act, unlike that of Yeats, that cannot be contained in the conventionally accepted and formalized terms of a sonnet. Nor, for that matter, does Whitman even commit it to completed grammatical structures; rather than the sentence, his chosen unit is the phrase, a more supple element for conveying the poem's series of interlocking actions.

Moreover, the act of the eagles is linked to the presence of the poet, as deemphasized as it will virtually ever be in Whitman, in the poem. Even if one discounts the slim possibility that the opening participial phrase ("Skirting the river road") refers to the poet rather than to the eagles; the poet, who speaks of "my forenoon walk, my rest," is also caught up in the process of the poem as the observer-describer of the mating of the birds taking place high above his head but still well within his field of vision. That opening line, a virtual signature line for Whitman and perhaps the one marker that would allow an unalerted reader to recognize this as a Romantic rather than an Imagist poem, is essential to Whitman's art, since he was unwilling to allow the poem to fly off, like an unattended kite from its string, out of his on-site control. Rather, Whitman preferred to keep his finger on the string by establishing his presence, if not exactly at the center of the poem, at least in proximity to the act taking place in it. This was crucial for Whitman, since the act described in the poem was analogous to the act of the poet in making the poem. In fact, beyond the narrative of the mating activity of the eagles lies the story of the making of poems generally, an act of self-generation that charts its own movements as freely as the participially propelled eagles do theirs in this poem. For all its concentration on the mating birds, the poem seems, finally, to be itself an act of generation that will continue to generate at other times and venues, allowing for the possibility that there will be more eagles mating, more instances of the poet observing them, and more resultant poems. In this context, it may not be an exaggeration to claim that the grammatical form of the present participle was the closest approximation in the English language to Whitman's conception of the poetry-making process.

I have been speaking of Whitman's heavy reliance on the present participle as though it were exclusively a private matter – a sign and a function of his personal genius. But may it not also be understood more broadly as a cultural response to the conditions of his time and society? Or perhaps to the conditions of modern life generally? Such pieces as the intensely and explicitly ideological preface to the 1855 edition of *Leaves of Grass* would certainly lead one to take seriously Whitman's expressed intentions of writing a self-consciously American poetry addressed to his own people and to their shared condition. In fact, the freedom of the individual (provided, of course, that the individual was a white male Protestant) to be of which

Whitman's poetry "speaks" was so emphatically a characteristic of a segment of his society's white male liberal thinkers that one may reasonably expect to find parallels to Whitman's free verse experimentation in the writing of his greatest contemporaries. Surely, its closest parallel in philosophical literature was in Ralph Waldo Emerson, who once in an early essay spoke of his own endeavor in life as to "essay to be."[8] And, quite likely, Emerson found the form of the essay to be sufficiently open-ended to provide a congenial mode for the expression of his ideas. But, except for occasional works, such as "The Snow-Storm," one will generally be disappointed in trying to find in Emerson's verse a fully worked out and controlled "language experiment" comparable or equivalent to Whitman's.

A closer approximation to Whitman and his freedom with language than Emerson may well be Melville. The comparison is a rich one: exact contemporaries, sea poets, poets pressing language and form beyond their established limits, poets unparalleled in their time for their verbal inventiveness generally and for their flair for the kinaesthetic effect of their writing in particular. Who but Melville could have responded as viscerally as did Whitman to the "gliding wonders" – the phrase is Whitman's but might just as readily have been Melville's – of the physical world? And who but Melville could have matched Whitman in the boldness of his conceptualization of modern individuals confronting the state of human nature in the open air?

In speaking of Melville's style at its most original in *Moby-Dick,* Newton Arvin long ago pointed out the limit-transcending thrust of Melville's language: "One feels . . . that the limits of even the English vocabulary have suddenly begun to seem too strict, too penurious, and that the difficult things Melville has to say can be adequately said only by reaching those limits."[9] Arvin was struck by not only Melville's flair for powerfully expressive words but also his attraction to specific kinds of words, especially verbal nouns, adverbs, and adjectives (the last in both the past and present tenses). His point about the extraordinary use Melville makes of his verbs and verb derivatives is a perceptive one, and one from which a possible bridge can be built to Whitman's practices as an innovative shaper of language and syntax. Particularly in the concluding chapters of *Moby-Dick,* in which the opposed motions of the whale and the *Pequod* finally cross, one can discern the degree to which Melville, like Whitman, achieves his finest kinaesthetic effects through an intensely verbalized vocabulary. No less than Whitman's, Melville's poetic world is a universe pictured as being in a state of generation, throwing off its effects in rapid succession and keeping the gliding wonders of the world passing constantly before the reader's eye: the spectacle of "the gliding whale" passing by in all its majesty, the ocean sound of "small fowls screaming over the yet yawning gulf," the "devious cruising Rachel" perpetually in search of its lost orphan.

But perhaps the closest poetic connection may be made not with a nineteenth-century contemporary but with the quintessentially twentieth-century Wallace Stevens, who for all his strong idiosyncracies and temperamental differences seems to me a true heir of the "participle-loving Whitman" I have been trying to define. In this connection I think, in particular, of his meditation on poetry and the age, "Of Modern Poetry":

> The poem of the mind in the act of finding
> What will suffice. It has not always had
> To find: the scene was set; it repeated what
> Was in the script.
>   Then the theatre was changed
> To something else. Its past was a souvenir.
> It has to be living, to learn the speech of the place.
> It has to face the men of the time and to meet
> The women of the time. It has to think about war
> And it has to find what will suffice. It has
> To construct a new stage. It has to be on that stage
> And, like an insatiable actor, slowly and
> With meditation, speak words that in the ear,
> In the delicatest ear of the mind, repeat,
> Exactly, that which it wants to hear, at the sound
> Of which, an invisible audience listens,
> Not to the play, but to itself, expressed
> In an emotion as of two people, as of two
> Emotions becoming one. The actor is
> A metaphysician in the dark, twanging
> An instrument, twanging a wiry string that gives
> Sounds passing through sudden rightnesses, wholly
> Containing the mind, below which it cannot descend,
> Beyond which it has no will to rise.
>   It must
> Be the finding of a satisfaction, and may
> Be of a man skating, a woman dancing, a woman
> Combing. The poem of the act of the mind.

Whitman was just such an "insatiable actor" whose element was language and whose self-appointed mission was to find the words that would suffice for the men and women of his time. Posted far in advance of the twentieth-century moderns, Whitman self-consciously tossed away the old scripts and turned his back on the old theaters in his search for bold ways of speaking new messages. With his flair for the self-dramatic, Whitman devised his own kind of theater in the round with his one-man troupe positioned at center stage, addressing an audience of both one and many. Never unmindful of that audience, Whitman created for it a script that featured diverse counterparts to Stevens's "man skating" and "woman dancing": armies crossing, eagles mating, lilacs blooming, the globe "swift-swimming in space," individuals walking the open road – and, above all, poets creating. This is, finally, how I see Whitman himself: as the poet creating.

NOTES

1   Randall Jarrell, *Poetry and the Age* (New York: Random House, 1953), p. 105.
2   Although in some cases one might be inclined to read these verbals as gerunds rather than as participles, I would simply point out that, when read as the opening lines of their respective poems, they are used unambiguously as participles. In fact, it is a general rule in Whitman's poetry that they derive from or introduce the grammatical subject, usually pronominal.
3   The quoted passage comes from a 1923 lecture, "The Council of Three"; in *Kino-Eye: The Writings of Dziga Vertov,* ed. Annette Michelson, trans. Kevin O'Brien (Berkeley and Los Angeles: University of California Press, 1984), pp. 15, 17–18.
4   Whitman, Preface to 1855 *Leaves of Grass,* in *Complete Poetry and Collected Prose,* ed. Justin Kaplan (New York: Library of America, 1982), p. 18.
5   *Leaves of Grass: Comprehensive Reader's Edition,* ed. Harold W. Blodgett and Sculley Bradley (New York: New York University Press, 1965). All citations from Whitman's poetry are taken from this edition, and their page numbers are cited in the text.
6   *Les Confessions,* in *Oeuvres Complètes,* ed. Bernard Gagnebin and Marcel Raymond, (Paris: Gallimard, 1959), 1, pp. 57–8. The English version is that of J. M. Cohen, trans., *The Confessions* (New York: Penguin, 1953), p. 63.
7   William Butler Yeats, "Leda and the Swan," in *The Poems/A New Edition,* ed. Richard J. Finneran (New York: Macmillan, 1983), pp. 214–15.
8   The phrase comes from "Literary Ethics," in Ralph Waldo Emerson, *Essays and Lectures,* ed. Joel Porte (New York: Library of America, 1983), p. 98.
9   Newton Arvin, *Herman Melville* (New York: William Sloane, 1950), p. 163.

7

SHERRY CENIZA

"Being a Woman . . . I Wish to Give My Own View": Some Nineteenth-Century Women's Responses to the 1860 *Leaves of Grass*

In Section 49 of "Song of Myself," the Whitman persona marvels at a body that can know the acute sensory experience of giving birth, pain merging into the pleasure of expulsion, the ultimate orgasm, as the persona watches a childbirth. He lies next to the woman, close, in a way like present-day practice in which the male shares in the birthing experience as much as he can. The persona speaks:

> I recline by the sills of the exquisite flexible doors,
> And mark the outlet, and mark the relief and escape.[1]

To a reader familiar with Whitman's images and the valorization of the concepts that these images inscribe, the terms "doors," "sills," and "flexible" signal concepts and characteristics that coalesce into primary motifs in his work – the possibility of beginning anew and the strength gained through an inclusive or expansive point of view. Here, female genitalia image these concepts, the phrase "sills of the exquisite flexible doors" possessing an evocative power that critics have not usually associated with Whitman's images of female sexuality. The word "vulva," if traced back far enough, has as one of its derivations "the leaf of a door" (the leaf-door, i.e., the flexibility of a folding door). The persona marvels at this leaf-door from the vantage point of the sills, which in turn evokes the image of a threshold, a verge, a beginning, and also a level of pain, the threshold of pain. All the while the "l" sounds of the phrase resound in the reader's mind, calling up other images, other poems, other readings.

Marveling at childbirth, at a body that has tensile strength – a ductile anchor?[2] – that dilates to expel new life, the persona addresses death and staves it off. Section 49 begins abruptly:

> And as to you Death, and you bitter hug of mortality,
>   it is idle to try to alarm me.

Almost as if in fear, the persona abruptly shifts focus, ceasing his direct address to death, and begins instead to describe the birthing process.

Through the use of present participles and the effect achieved by the repetition of sound, the poet persona moves from the bravado of his direct address to death to a tone more akin to awe:

> To his work without flinching the accoucheur[3] comes,
> I see the elder-hand pressing receiving supporting,
> I recline by the sills of the exquisite flexible doors,
> And mark the outlet, and mark the relief and escape.

As the persona staves off death, he returns to direct address and negates (nervously scoffs at?) the threat of a corpse:

> And as to you Corpse I think you are good manure, but
>   that does not offend me,

And as before, bravado is followed by images of female fecundity:

> I smell the white roses sweet-scented and growing,
> I reach to the leafy lips, I reach to the polish'd
>   breasts of melons.

The leafy lips (the exquisite flexible doors) and polished breasts become one, then, with roses and melons and counter the threat of stasis.

This passage serves as an entry into a frame of reference for reading and interpreting Whitman's poetry, a frame that sees Whitman's work as empowering his female readers, a view that some of the most progressive-thinking nineteenth-century women supported and defended. However, there is a persistent strand in Whitman criticism that sees Whitman as a less than positive force for his female readers: from D. H. Lawrence's often quoted lines describing Whitman's representation of women – "Muscles and wombs. They needn't have had faces at all" – to Edwin Haviland Miller's extremely negative view of Whitman's mother and on to the most recent negative view of Whitman's representation of women in his poetry and his relationships with women in actual life found in Joyce W. Warren's biography of Fanny Fern (and earlier in *Patrons and Protegees*).[4] Discussion of Whitman and women, however, has been carried on without contextualization of women's history – their lives and writings. There is little if any discussion in Whitman scholarship of the women whose names and addresses appear in Whitman's notebooks, or the women whom Whitman quotes in his notebooks, or the women whom Whitman writes to and who answer back, or the numerous women mentioned in the seven-volume *With Walt Whitman in Camden,* or the women who published articles about Whitman. Many of these women took part in the most significant movement for women's rights up to the late 1960s – the National Woman's

Rights Movement, which took place from 1850 until the outbreak of the Civil War. The decade of the 1850s was also the most creative period in Whitman's life.

In the 1850s, a group of women worked to bring about change in all dimensions of women's lives – political, legal, personal, sexual, educational, and professional. Three of Whitman's friends during this period were women instrumental in these attempts at reform – Abby Hills Price, Paulina Wright Davis, and Ernestine L. Rose. These women were what we would call today radical feminists; they diametrically opposed the status quo. Their arguments, however, in the speeches they made before the National Woman's Rights Conventions and elsewhere did not assume a purist character. They often used cultural conventions subversively. Davis was the most accommodating as she shaped her prose to make her radical calls for change fit into a framework or language acceptable to the culture at large; Price was the most relentless in her calls for change; Rose was the most theoretical. Whitman heard what these women had to say as he carried on conversations with them and read their words. Like theirs, his writing is filled with varying rhetorical strategies and conflicting ideological shifts as he unconsciously worked with his own cultural inconsistencies and consciously with language and form to create *Leaves of Grass*.[5]

Without a full contextualization of the women important in Whitman's life – their history – no reading of Whitman's representations of women in his poetry is finally satisfactory. I mean this criticism to include such otherwise illuminating studies as Harold Aspiz's *Walt Whitman and the Body Beautiful*. Aspiz looks at innumerable nineteenth-century texts, but in the sections of his book dealing with nineteen-century women, he does not study women's texts, except for Eliza Farnham's. Also, though Jimmie Killingsworth's recently well-received *Whitman's Poetry of the Body* uses current theoretical structures to discuss persuasively poems important to a feminist critique such as "Unfolded Out of the Folds," Killingsworth does not quote women's words, does not give an indication that he has spent time reading women's history or listening to their words, their views.

Joyce Warren, however, has, and she interprets Whitman's representations of and attitudes toward women negatively. Warren's exclusivity, however, weakens her argument. Her reading of Fern and Whitman focuses on an either/or dilemma: The reader accepts either Fern or Whitman. This either/or dilemma is unnecessarily restrictive and, I believe, ultimately damaging to our study and understanding of literary history.

Unlike Warren (and two other feminist critics who have recently written about Whitman and women – Sandra Gilbert and Joanne Feit Diehl), Betsy

Erkkila does not see Whitman disempowering women.[6] In her book *Whitman the Political Poet,* Erkkila argues that "[i]f at times Whitman's work seems to reinscribe the conservative sexual ideology of his time, his poems had and still do have a galvanizing effect on women readers."[7] The key phrase in Erkkila's statement is "at times." Even the most radical women's rights activists – women like Elizabeth Cady Stanton and Ernestine L. Rose – would *at times* reinscribe conservative sexual ideology as they worked for change. Domestic fiction writers – such as Susan Warner and Maria Susanna Cummins – were much less outspoken about and critical of the status quo than were women like Stanton and Rose. However, as we speak of nineteenth-century fiction writers' work now, we do not say that their work is or was disabling for women. Rather, we talk about contradictory discourses; we talk about subversive strategies. We give measure. For example, Susan Coultrap-McQuin speaks of the swings in Elizabeth Stuart Phelps's work: "Despite the energy and self-affirmation of these works in the 1870s, other more conservative, somewhat contradictory topics continued to crop up in Phelps's work."[8] Contradictions within nineteenth-century women's fiction, we imply, do not necessarily mean that this fiction disempowered female readers, then or now. Whitman's own contradictions are no different in kind from those of his female contemporaries.

Hearing what some of the most socially involved woman's rights activists of the time said about Whitman's work as they responded to it makes it difficult to read Whitman's sexual politics as reductive for women, problematic though specific passages may be. The main purpose of this essay is to bring to textual life some of these women for whom Whitman's texts had "galvanizing effects," to use Erkkila's term, thereby inscribing into Whitman scholarship what has been omitted – the stories of women important in Whitman's life and their perception of *Leaves.* These stories form a provocative new context for reading *Leaves* and, most specifically, the "Children of Adam" cluster. Put into the context provided by this essay, the "Children of Adam" cluster becomes interesting on its own, rather than simply existing as a pale companion to the "Calamus" cluster, as it is often read.

Here, then, I tell about the women who defended Whitman's 1860 edition of *Leaves of Grass.* This defense took place in June 1860 in the pages of Henry Clapp's *Saturday Press.* The focus of the defense (and the attacks) was the "Children of Adam" cluster, which appeared for the first time in this edition. Henry Clapp, Jr., a figure in Whitman's life who deserves more attention than he has yet received, published the first issue of his paper on October 23, 1858; it ran until December 15, 1860, when Clapp had to cease publication because of lack of money. The paper resumed August 5, 1865, running until it once more folded on June 2, 1866. Clapp's iconoclasm and the writers he attracted to his journal punctuated the cultural dialogue with an acerbity that riled the mainstream press and, through it, mainstream readers. In Clapp's efforts to introduce the 1860 edition of *Leaves* to the public, he put into play his policy of printing negative as well as positive reviews, thus stirring up controversy and, as a consequence, attention. Regarding Clapp, Whitman told his friend Horace Traubel that "Henry was right: better to have people stirred against you if they can't be stirred for you – better that than not to stir them at all."9

The story begins with the June 2 issue of the *Saturday Press*, in which appeared a review of *Leaves* signed "Juliette H. Beach." It's a familiar story now: This article was not Juliette Beach's work but rather her husband's. In this review, Calvin Beach charges Whitman with writing filth, singling out the "Children of Adam" cluster. Whitman's poetry, Calvin Beach says, calls up the feeling of "brute nature [rather] than the sentiments of human love." Beach says that Whitman sees women only as a means to propagate the species and as an outlet for his own desires, that sex to Whitman is a "purely animal affair, and with his ridiculous egotism he vaunts his prowess as a stockbreeder might that of the pick of his herd."

In the next week's issue, Clapp printed a "Correction," explaining the mixup, saying that the confusion was understandable since he had forwarded Juliette Beach a copy of the new *Leaves* and therefore expected a review from her, not from her husband. Implicitly, the "Correction" says that Mr. Beach appropriated the book and wrote his own review of *Leaves*. In this same June 9 issue appeared the first of three reviews written by women. All three allude to Calvin Beach's attack. Only one woman signed her full name: "Mary A. Chilton, Islip, Long Island, June 5th, 1860." Though it is not clear how well Whitman knew Chilton, connections between the two existed, connections in addition to her 1860 defense, that is. Knowing something of her life, then, contextualizes *Leaves* in a new and illuminating way.

Whitman had written down Mary Chilton's name in his notebooks prior to her June 9 defense of him. Her name appears in two of his Brooklyn notebooks, dating sometime between the years 1857 and 1860. In one, Whitman lists next to Chilton's name and Manhattan address the name and different Manhattan address of Theron C. Leland, an active Fourierist and phonographer (who took down the proceedings of the fourth National Woman's Rights Convention, held in Cleveland in 1853). Chilton and Leland eventually married. In another notebook – Whitman's "Dick Hunt" notebook – Chilton's name and address appear on the same page with the addresses of Ernestine L. Rose and Abby Hills Price, Whitman's friends and radical activists for woman's rights, who very likely also knew Chilton.[10] In addition, Whitman knew Chilton through her writing. An issue of the *Social Revolutionist*, a journal supporting free love/free thought, for which Chilton wrote, is among Whitman's papers at Rutgers University. This issue – July 1857, marked by Whitman – contains one of Mary Chilton's articles – "Sexual Purity."[11]

Put in contemporary terms, Mary Chilton was a radical feminist. Moncure Conway – Unitarian clergyman, liberal leader, and writer – once described her as "another Frances Wright."[12] She believed in the rights of the individual and, most significantly for antebellum America, in the rights of the woman as an individual. In a society that censored women's public voice, she sent a radical message: She was an activist for woman's rights, a free-love proponent, and a water-cure physician. Her quest for personal freedom led her to Modern Times, the Long Island community that became known in the early 1850s as a free-love community, though it had many more ideological underpinnings than that, primarily the founder, Josiah Warren's, brand of individualistic socialism.[13] Taylor Stoehr, in *Free Love in America: A Documentary History*, says that it was Mary Chilton who hosted Moncure Conway when he visited Modern Times in 1856. Stoehr, who refers to Chilton as Mary Leland, says that the home where Conway stayed was Theron C. Leland's and that "Mrs. Leland" was Conway's hostess.[14] Conway, who also visited Whitman in 1856, includes his account of the Modern Times visit in his autobiography and in a *Fortnightly Review* article:

> She [Chilton] was a woman I should say, a little over thirty years of age, and had an indefinable grace and fine intellectual powers, united with considerable personal beauty. She was a native of one of the Southern States, – Georgia, I believe, – where she had married. The marriage was unhappy, and on separation she considered herself, as I have heard, most cruelly treated by her husband and the law together, in being deprived of her children. She had studied medicine, and was earning her livelihood by medical practice. Her own experiences led her to sum up the chief evils of society in the one word *marriage*.[15]

During the time of Conway's visit, Chilton was contributing articles to the *Social Revolutionist*, a monthly publication edited by John Patterson, in 1856–7. In these articles, Chilton creates a strong persona who speaks, she says, for the masses, for egalitarianism. She condemns the hypocritical society that pays lip service to a document like the Declaration of Independence yet openly supports and perpetuates enslaving institutions. She holds that freedom is an inherent right for all people. She scorns institutions in general, specifying the church and marriage in particular. She proclaims the natural-ness of sexual feelings and expression and rejects the Calvinist notions of original sin and the depravity of the body. She argues that there is no distinction between the body and the soul. In addition to providing a con-text that invites new readings of passages such as the one that opens this essay, Chilton's *Social Revolutionist* articles inform us of her politics and indicate ways in which her views parallel Whitman's.

Her November 1856 article, "Who Are the Martyrs?", criticizes re-formers who advocate caution because, "they say, the time has not yet come to realize Freedom in social relations." In this article, Chilton makes many of the same points that Whitman's "Song of the Open Road" illustrates, but her language is more direct than Whitman's in naming the objects of her critique. Though she avoids using the term "sexual relations" and instead uses the more conventionally acceptable "social relations" or "most inti-mate relations," she is outspoken in her charges against the institution of marriage as it existed: People form legal bonds out of "selfish, mercenary, bread and clothes considerations" and as a "protection against poverty, combined with a purely selfish fear of the condemnation of the world, should the lovers follow their intuitions and obey the dictates of their hearts by simply remaining lovers." Like many free-lovers, her central goal was to change the laws and assumptions governing the institution of marriage rather than to have multiple sex partners. Chilton ends her article by urging her readers to study the picture she presents and, as a consequence, to work for reform. Using the argument prevalent in diverse reform movements at the time, she says that forced or nonconsensual sexual unions result in unhealthy, diseased children. She sees people locked in marriage with little hope for divorce as the real martyrs:

> Oh! cautious and conservative reformer, look about you and see the careworn faces of your respectable married friends; listen and hear the sighs and groans of heartbroken sufferers! What does all this sickness and misery mean that we see everywhere? Are not these prudent people really the martyrs, and not the brave and fearless, who leave home and friends, and position and luxury, for the love of Freedom and the freedom of love? Not they the martyrs; no, you will find the martyrs among the respectable and those deemed comfortable, and certainly cared-for portion of the community. Could you look behind the scenes, you would find manacles on arms that in secret are raised to Heaven . . . you might see the vinegar-soaked sponge of respectability, tauntingly of-fered in mockery, to the fevered lips.

Interestingly, the last half of Section 13 of "Song of the Open Road" (1856) makes many of the indictments that Chilton does. The parallel between the two texts is significant in considering the reception of Whitman's poetry in his own time; it helps to explain why in 1860 Mary Chilton, and others with similar views, defended *Leaves*. Knowing about Chilton's life, her views, and her defense of *Leaves* also guides us today to contextualize our own readings of Whitman's representations of gender and our politics that influence these readings.

Section 13 of "Song of the Open Road" speaks of living a life of deception, of conforming to popular mores and thereby denying one's authenticity. Though marriage is not named, certainly a reader like Chilton would immediately apply the term to the poem's indictment, as would others who did not subscribe to the culturally encoded valorization of marriage in antebellum America.

Whoever you are, come forth! or man or woman come forth!
You must not stay sleeping and dallying there in the house, though you built it,
   or though it has been built for you.
Out of the dark confinement! out from behind the screen!
It is useless to protest, I know all and expose it.
     . . .
Inside of dresses and ornaments, inside of those wash'd and trimm'd faces,
Behold a secret silent loathing and despair.
     . . .
Home to the houses of men and women, at the table, in the bedroom,
   everywhere,
Smartly attired, countenance smiling, form upright, death under the breast-bones,
   hell under the skull-bones,
Under the broadcloth and gloves, under the ribbons and artificial flowers,
Keeping fair with the customs, speaking not a syllable of itself,
Speaking of any thing else but never of itself.

                                  (CRE, 157–8)

Whitman's picture of couples "smartly attired, countenance smiling, form upright, death under the breast-bones" fits well with the picture that Chilton creates of "the careworn faces of your respectable married friends," both chipping away at the conventional view of the sanctity of marriage (and class), exposing a picture of couples living lives of deception. Both passages speak to people who reject the principle that societal boundaries are inherent, to people who believe that lives can become more fully realized through changes in custom and law – such as divorce laws or the view that heterosexuality is the only acceptable form of sexuality.

Chilton's June 1857 article "Do We Need Marriage?" argues that legal marriages work against living a fully realized life. Marriage, she says, is instituted and regulated by the few to control the many. Marriage, then, must be demystified. Individuals must see the controls placed on their personal lives by the "arrogant few":

> If I took a "leap in the dark," and in the despair of great suffering saw greater light, and found it good and life giving, that does not prove that life and happiness might not have been mine years sooner had I not been blindfolded by those self-righteous interpreters. I would not compel or enforce my code of morals or freedom on any one; but say cut the cords, loose the bonds, break the manacles which now hold the masses forcibly subservient: to a false and infernal system.

Though not with the same amount of righteous indignation, Section 5 of "Song of the Open Road" also calls for the individual to move out of ideology – out of the codes defined as natural but in fact socially constructed:

> From this hour I ordain myself loos'd of limits and imaginary
>   lines,
> Going where I list, my own master total and absolute,
> Listening to others, considering well what they say,
> Pausing, searching, receiving, contemplating,
> Gently, but with undeniable will, divesting myself of the holds that
>   would hold me.
>
>   (CRE, 151)

The cultural resonance between these texts helps us to understand the acceptance – indeed, the galvanizing effect – that *Leaves of Grass* had on readers in 1860 like Mary Chilton. It is also significant that Whitman knew women like Mary Chilton, that the years between 1856 and 1860 – a period of intense creativity for Whitman – were marked by his acquaintance with women active in reform movements.

The July 1857 issue of the *Social Revolutionist* – the marked issue found in Whitman's papers – contains the article "Sexual Purity." This article makes two of the points already enumerated – namely, the debilitating effects of marriage when the relationship is not one of reciprocity and the harmful effects on children of such a relationship. But mainly in this article Chilton argues for the sanity of sexual pleasure. Cleverly, she titles this article "Sexual Purity." Her point is that it is wrong to deny what she calls "the electric spark of energizing health" and "the thrilling power of vital force." It is wrong to deny the sensory pleasure of sexual attraction. Chilton, arguing the politics of sex, says that forced sex in marriage is nothing more than legalized prostitution.

These articles show us Chilton's celebration of sensuality – significantly, for her time, of female sensuality – which explains one of the attractions *Leaves* held for her. Hearing her views of sexuality can sensitize us to passages in Whitman's work with images of the female body (such as "exquisite flexible doors"). The articles serve as preparation for Chilton's 1860 defense; they help to explain why Chilton publicly authorized herself when she wrote that defense; they create for us lines of connection between Whitman and serious, incisive, radical female activists like Mary Chilton.

In Chilton's 1860 defense of *Leaves,* she uses the same rhetorical strategies that she employs in her *Social Revolutionist* articles. She takes culturally loaded terms and shades or skews their meanings to create her own reformist view. In the 1857 article "Sexual Purity," she uses "purity" to mean desire; to act in a "pure" way means to act on that desire. It most explicitly does not mean intercourse submitted to "purely" because of the marriage vow. In the *Leaves* review, she couples purity with religion, calling Whitman the "apostle of purity" and then the "poet of sexual purity." In 1857 she uses the term "vital force" when speaking of sexual attraction; in 1860 she calls Whitman "the teacher of the most vital, and hence the most Divine truth." She uses religious terminology in speaking of sexuality, thus conflating the body and soul and defusing the Calvinist belief in the duality of the psyche, just as Whitman did throughout *Leaves of Grass* and startlingly so early in "Song of Myself," in Section 5. She argues for sexuality on the basis of organicism – that the parts of the body work to create the whole and that therefore no one part can be out of place or vile. Those, however, who assert the doctrine of total depravity (alluding to Calvinism and to Calvin Beach's article) must, she says, "find some part of the person too vile to think of." Her review defends Whitman's poetry, but it also boldly defends sexuality, a defense made by a woman in a society that worked to silence women and to deny them control of their bodies.

On June 10, one day after the *Saturday Press* ran Chilton's defense, an article by Adah Menken titled "Swimming Against the Current" appeared in the New York *Sunday Mercury,* in which Menken defended Whitman. Menken – the actress and writer who in 1860 was married to the prize fighter John Heenan and who Lillian Faderman says in *Surpassing the Love of Men* was "undoubtedly not a stranger to lesbian sex" – knew Whitman and admired his poetry.[16] Menken's June 10 column praises individuals who, she feels, have been courageous in asserting their originality and have gone against the taste and mores of their culture. She singles Whitman out for his courage and his perceptive reading of his culture and says that his contemporaries "cannot comprehend him yet." The editor, R. H. Newell, who eventually married Menken, wrote a disclaimer to her article:

> We are far from endorsing all its sentiments, and are astonished to observe that Mrs. Heenan indulges in a eulogium of that coarse and uncouth creature, Walt Whitman. The lady is entitled to her own opinion, however, though in the present expression of it she is certainly "Swimming Against the Current."[17]

Six days later, on June 16, a long review blasting Whitman appeared in the *Springfield Daily Republican.* The article, titled " 'Leaves of Grass' – Smut in Them," was written in response to Chilton's defense. Like the editorial voice of the *Mercury,* which dissociated itself from Menken's approval of Whitman, the editorial voice of the *Springfield Republican* maintained that it had not intended to "notice" the new edition of Whitman's poetry, but that

> certain of the soft heads, on the shoulders of men and women indiscriminately, have conceived that it is a pure book. In the last number of the New York Saturday Press, Mary A. Chilton gives her ideas of Walt Whitman's poetry generally, and especially of his smut; and to show the public how far into degradation certain new lights are ready to be led, we quote a portion of her letter, simply italicizing such sentences as we wish to call special attention to: –

The editor was especially incensed that the book had "respectable" credentials – a "respectable publisher – the author a writer for the Atlantic Monthly – 'for sale everywhere' on respectable book-shelves – in very respectable type and binding." He goes on to note the attacks on Christianity that he sees *Leaves of Grass* making, principally in its appeal to nature as an authority rather than to "Christianity." He disparages Chilton's term "poet of sexual purity." And he notes what he sees as the book's attack on the institution of marriage: "The very first social institution that falls into contempt after Christianity as a revelation is discarded is Christian marriage, and of all the 'teachings' in the world, we know of none that so inevitably lead to impurity as those attributed to 'Nature.' " And Walt Whitman, he says, is "*par excellence* the 'poet of nature.' " The word "smut" in the title of the review leaves no doubt about the reviewer's scorn of Whitman and *Leaves.* Emily Dickinson, a close friend of the *Springfield Republican* editors (Samuel Bowles and Josiah Holland), would write two years later to her friend Thomas Wentworth Higgingon (April 25, 1862): "You speak of Mr Whitman – I never read his Book – but was told that he was disgraceful –".[18] A regular reader of the *Springfield Republican* as well as a friend of the editors, Dickinson could hardly have missed this review, with its condemnation not only of Whitman, but of Mary Chilton as well.

One week after the *Springfield Republican* review, on June 23, two more defenses of *Leaves* written by women appeared in the *Saturday Press*, responding to the controversy the poems provoked. One article was signed "A Woman" and another "C.C.P." Gay Wilson Allen says that the review signed "A Woman" "seemed designed to counteract Mr. Beach's attack, and this may have been Mrs. Beach's belated review." Justin Kaplan calls the review "Juliette's own article . . . signed 'A Woman.'" Betsy Erkkila also credits Juliette Beach as the author of the review.[19]

The particulars of Juliette Beach's and Whitman's relationship are not clear, but by examining the written evidence we have of their friendship, the following can be ascertained: Beach, a writer for Clapp's *Saturday Press,* had made her admiration of Whitman's work known to Clapp prior to the 1860 *Leaves,* so Clapp told Whitman to send her a copy of the 1860 edition to review. In spite of the furor over the 1860 publication and reviews, Beach and Whitman kept up some sort of friendship, which likely ended around 1871, except for Whitman's mention of her, though not by name, to Traubel in 1889: "There was a woman up there, a marvelous woman, who did some writing for the Press: she wrote about Leaves of Grass: there was quite a stew over it: some day I'll have to unbosom so you may know the ins and outs of the incident."[20] John Burroughs – the naturalist, writer, and Whitman's friend – said of her review (though not mentioning Beach by name): "[T]he most pertinent and suggestive criticism of [*Leaves*] we have ever seen, and one that accepted it as a whole, was by a lady – one whose name stands high on the list of our poets. Some of the poet's warmest personal friends, also, are women of this mould."[21]

Clara Barrus, a physician, and a friend and biographer of John Burroughs, says that Whitman wrote his 1865 poem "Out of the Rolling Ocean the Crowd" for Beach and that Beach had written "many beautiful" letters to Whitman that Burroughs had tried but failed to get her to publish.[22] Ellen O'Connor, Whitman's close friend from the time he moved to Washington, D.C., until his death, mentions Beach to Whitman in three 1864 letters to him. In the original draft of Ellen O'Connor's article on Whitman, which appeared in the 1907 *Atlantic,* O'Connor claims that Whitman felt great sympathy, affection, and admiration for Beach. Like Barrus, O'Connor says that Whitman wrote "Out of the Rolling Ocean the Crowd" for her. O'Connor goes on to say that Calvin Beach had abused Walt in the presence of Juliette and another woman and that in relating the incident, Whitman remarked that he "would marry that woman tonight if she were free." O'Connor claims that "correspondence was kept up between them for some time after that, the only instance I have known where he was strongly attracted toward any woman in this way."[23] It is not surprising that Whitman valued Beach's friendship, for she had what many other women had who figured in Whitman's life – an independent mind and personal courage. O'Connor's romantic interpretation of the nature of Whitman's caring, however, is highly questionable.

Juliette Beach was known to readers of the *Saturday Press* since she contributed poems to the paper and occasionally wrote articles as well. Her work also appeared in other New York papers. Her review calls Whitman the long-awaited American poet; it argues for the acceptance of the body and the soul equally, denying, as Chilton had, the Calvinist rejection of the body. Beach argues for Whitman's (and God's) egalitarianism, again in contradistinction to Calvinism. She embraces Whitman's innovative style, speaking of the blend of prose and verse, and stresses the role of the reader. This last point distinguishes Juliette Beach as a critic and reader and marks her contemporaneity. In essence, she theorizes the role that the reader plays in the formation of textual meaning, anticipating (as did Whitman) our current interest in the reader's role. The parallel between Beach's and Whitman's interest in the reader's empowerment suggests reasons, beyond content, for Beach's interest in Whitman's poetry. It is possible, as well, that her articulation of the reading process helped Whitman to formulate his own articulation of the reader's role ten years later in the closing pages of "Democratic Vistas":

> Books are to be call'd for, and supplied, on the assumption that the process of reading is not a half-sleep, but, in highest sense, an exercise, a gymnast's struggle; that the reader is to do something for himself, must be on the alert, must himself or herself construct indeed the poem, argument, history, metaphysical essay – the text furnishing the hints, the clue, the start or framework.[24]

In 1860, Beach sees Whitman's book doing what Whitman's "Democratic Vistas" advocated. She sees *Leaves* acting as a primer theorizing the role of ideal democratic citizens, "men and women worthy a broad, free country," but in order for the book to be read and comprehended, she calls for educated readers: "If our sons and daughters were educated so that they could appreciate this book, we should in the next generation have men and women worthy a broad, free country." Here is where Beach's and Whitman's stances most directly coincide, with Whitman saying in 1871: "Not the book needs so much to be the complete thing, but the reader of the book does. That were to make a nation of supple and athletic minds, well-train'd, intuitive, used to depend on themselves, and not on a few coteries of writ-ers."[25] Beach says, however, in 1860 that most readers would read *Leaves* "literally only, and blindly, and therefore condemn the whole."

Prior to Beach's review of *Leaves*, she presented her theoretical approach to criticism in a November 26, 1859, article in the *Saturday Press* discussing Augusta Jane Evans's novel *Beulah*. In response to an article written two weeks earlier by the *Press*'s regular columnist, Ada Clare, in which Clare called Evans's book a total failure, Beach argues against this blanket con-demnation of the book, looking at the writer's purposes and analyzing the differences in the reading and writing cognitive processes. She views reading as a holistic process that subverts the sequential nature of language. Writing, however, she sees determined to a great extent by time, by the sequential working out of the language and of the characters, both of which are influenced by the changes in the writer's own circumstances over time. By the time Beach wrote this, Whitman's *Leaves* was already showing the evolving process and circumstantial effects that Beach defends. Beach also sees the role that an individual writer's point of view plays, calling an author's book "his dialect." For Beach, the writer, then, cannot assume the distance from her or from his writing that, ideally, the reader can. Beach's attempts to theorize the cognitive processes that go into reading and writ-ing, and her recognition of the role that ideology plays in language, make her an unusual critic for her time.

Beach's notion of the importance that point of view – the author's "dia-lect" and, by extension, ideology – plays in a writer's work parallels Whit-man's notion of the importance of historical grounding. The final paragraph of Whitman's 1876 Preface spells it out: Whitman tells us that he wrote out of his own distinct times, and his readers must factor in the historicity of the times in reading *Leaves*:

> In estimating my Volumes, the world's current times and deeds, and their spirit, must be first profoundly estimated. Out of the Hundred Years just ending, (1776–1876) . . . my Poems too have found genesis.[26]

Interesting though these parallels are, two letters that Juliette Beach wrote to Clapp, one on June 7 and one on August 13, are even more so.[27] As if to answer Calvin Beach's charge of Whitman's "ridiculous egotism," Juliette Beach tells Clapp in her June letter that she has the greatest faith in the book and that "Its egotism delights me – that defiant ever recurring I, is so irresistibly strong and good." As in her review, she speaks of the role of the reader, or of how to read the book. She realizes that the *way* to read the book would not be recognized as a component of the book itself, but that it should be, that indeed *how* to read the book *should* be taken into consideration. She talks about the book's spirit, the need to take the book as a whole, and the influence one's frame of reference has on one's reception of the book. "It is useless," she writes Clapp, "in judging this book to draw dividing lines and say this is good, and this bad. It is to be accepted and examined and pronounced upon en masse." The book, she says, "is unfit to be read if read superficially, and not to be tolerated for an instant if *viewed from the commonest social standpoints*" (emphasis added). She likes Whitman's rejection of what she calls "the vagueness of creeds" and says that Whitman is the poet that the age has waited for, an American original with a "fierce wild freedom from anything conventional."

Beach's June 7 letter to Clapp also speaks of her silencing: "I regret extremely that I have been obliged to deny myself the pleasure of writing at length and for publication, my view of "Leaves of Grass." I feel sure that I could have reviewed the book in a manner worthy of it, and yet have been not misunderstood myself." She speaks of her inability to follow her own inclination to write to Whitman because she had promised not to. In her August 13 letter, she speaks of her bitter regret that because she is a woman, she is denied the "happiness" of Whitman's friendship:

> Believe me there is nothing which I so passionately and bitterly regret, (and all the more passionately and bitterly, because the regret is useless,) as the fact that I am a woman and therefore obliged to deny myself the happiness of Walt Whitman's friendship. But to return to my notice of "Leaves of Grass": you know yourself that the book has a strong, real personality; it is not like any book that was ever written before.

"Outwardly," she writes to Clapp, "[*Leaves of Grass*] has caused me more pain and trouble than I have ever known before. – I do not deny that inwardly it has given me happiness and peace" (June 7 letter).

"Being a woman, and having read the uncharitable and bitter attacks upon the book," the author of the other June 23 article, signed "C.C.P.," says, "I wish to give my own view of it." Because we know Whitman's record of self-reviewing and Clapp's practice of assuming personae, the question of this review's authorship arises. However, numerous women who were Whitman's friends could have authored this piece. Whitman's friend Abby Hills Price was one. Price had connections with Henry Clapp dating back to the 1840s, and in 1859 the *Press* printed one of her poems. The *Press*'s columnist Ada Clare, also a friend of Whitman's, was another, as well as Adah Isaacs Menken.[28] Women such as Ernestine L. Rose and

Paulina Wright Davis – activists and also Whitman's friends – could have written the defense. And then, again, C.C.P. may not have been involved in any movement and may not have been a writer or public figure at all. She may have been what is claimed in the review – a woman writing because she wished her voice, her view, to be heard.

C.C.P.'s review echoes points that Chilton and Juliette Beach made: the democratic or leveling effect Whitman achieves by not making distinctions, the recognition of sex as a principle of life equal with birth and death, the organic form of *Leaves of Grass,* and the force it holds in the creation of an American literature. C.C.P.'s review criticizes the current literature, calling it sentimental and hypocritical, as it assumes a "semblance of virtue." The review also indirectly comments on Calvin Beach's article, his singling out for censure the "Children of Adam" cluster and what he sees as the poetry's complete degradation of women. C.C.P., however, speaks of Whitman's regard for women: "a reverence . . . which holds the 'woman just as great as the man' and a mother 'The melodious character of the earth, the finish beyond which philosophy cannot go and does not wish to go.'"

The controversy stirred by the publication of the 1860 *Leaves of Grass,* and specifically the "Children of Adam" cluster, has not ceased. In Whitman's time, he was damned because he did not protect women by veiling their sexuality; in our time, some say that he protects women too much – makes too much of women as mothers, cannot see beyond timeworn gender stereotypes, does not see women as individuals. The "Children of Adam" cluster, which by the Boston district attorney's estimation contained the largest number of offensive passages in *Leaves,* passages that thereby had to be excised because of their excessive sexual openness, now is seen by some as conservative.

The Boston district attorney's attempt to ban the sale of *Leaves* unless specific passages and poems were expurgated occurred in the spring of 1882. That June, Whitman's article "A Memorandum at a Venture," addressing the treatment of sexuality in literature and the issue of censorship, appeared in the *North American Review.* The opening sentences stage the question as if in debate:

> Shall the mention of such topics as I have briefly but plainly and resolutely broach'd in the "Children of Adam" section of "Leaves of Grass" be admitted in poetry and literature? Ought not the innovation to be put down by opinion and criticism? and, if those fail, by the District Attorney?[29]

Sexual passion, Whitman says, is part of life and thus must be treated in his poetry: "as the assumption of the sanity of birth, Nature and humanity, is the key to any true theory of life and the universe – at any rate, the only theory out of which I wrote – it is, and must inevitably be, the only key to 'Leaves of Grass,' and every part of it."[30] As if circling back to the 1860 controversy, Whitman mentions the *Springfield Republican* and its attack on him. He also directly addresses the connection between women's rights and female sexuality:

> To the movement for the eligibility and entrance of women amid new spheres of business, politics, and the suffrage, the current prurient, conventional treatment of sex is the main formidable obstacle. The rising tide of "woman's rights," swelling and every year advancing farther and farther, recoils from it with dismay. There will in my opinion be no general progress in such eligibility till a sensible, philosophic, democratic method is substituted.[31]

In contrast to the 1850s, when Price, Rose, Davis, and Stanton had argued for liberalized divorce laws, property rights for married women, women's entry into the professions, and equal educational opportunities, by 1882 the woman's rights movement had become more conservative, more of a one-issue movement. A woman like Mary Chilton would have no voice in a movement that had as one of its primary spokespersons Frances Willard, whose 1889 autobiography, *Glimpses of Fifty Years,* Whitman read in 1890.[32] Frances Willard was not a "Frances Wright woman," a phrase Whitman used to speak of women he admired, such as Anne Gilchrist or Mary Whitall Smith Berenson, and which in the 1850s the press used (disparagingly) in reference to Ernestine L. Rose. To some extent, there is a correlation between the changes the women's rights movement experienced and the changes Whitman made in his representations of women as *Leaves of Grass* evolved. However, structurally, the cluster Whitman called his "sex odes" – "Children of Adam" – changed little.

Of the original fifteen poems in the "Children of Adam" cluster, Whitman removed only one: "In the New Garden" appeared only in the 1860 edition. In terms of Whitman's sexual politics, the omission is significant. The editors of the *Comprehensive Reader's Edition* say that "In the New Garden" "in part resembles" the poem that opens the cluster, "To the Garden the World" (*CRE,* 594). However, the endings of these two poems differ dramatically in terms of gender politics. "In the New Garden" ends with the lines "For the future, with determined will, I seek – the woman of the future, / You, born years, centuries after me, I seek" (*CRE,* 594). The ending of "To the Garden the World" reads: "By my side or back of me Eve following, / Or in front, and I following her just the same" (*CRE,* 90). The coordinating conjunctions linking Eve and the poet-persona in "To the Garden the World" carefully play off the interchange of leadership positions. In the other poem, "In the New Garden," Eve is nonexistent, not yet evolved. The omission of "In the New Garden" is significant.

Eleven of the poems in this cluster were new to the 1860 edition. One, "I Sing the Body Electric," appeared in the 1855 edition. Two poems – "A Woman Waits for Me" and "Spontaneous Me" – appeared in the 1856 edition. Two poems were added after 1860: "Out of the Rolling Ocean the Crowd," which first appeared in *Drum-Taps* in 1865, and "I Heard You Solemn-Sweet Pipes of the Organ," which first appeared in the 1865–6 *Sequel to Drum-Taps*.

A trope running through much of the cluster is expressed in the first poem, "To the Garden the World": "Curious here behold my resurrection after slumber" (*CRE,* 90). The cluster, as a whole, turns on the idea of awakening, of seeing the world anew (and sexually) once the individual strips off societal frames of reference. The law that the persona sees, then, is the law of unity, the conflation of body and soul, rather than the Calvinist (and transcendentalist) elevation of the soul over the body – a hierarchical relationship – and rejection of the body's essential goodness, thus fragmenting the psyche.

"We Two, How Long We Were Fool'd," the ninth poem in the "Children of Adam" cluster of sixteen (in the 1891 edition), holds a central position in both the 1891 and 1860 editions of *Leaves*. Like "To the Garden the World," "We Two" plays on the idea of awakening, though in this poem the awakening involves recognizing false consciousness and shedding it. The entire poem focuses on the trope of transmutation. The change or transmutation is seen positively in that the "we" of the poem awaken to desire, but there is also a tonally bitter reading as the two recognize the deceit that existed in their lives prior to their awakening. Here are the first eleven lines of the 1860 version of the poem:

> You and I – what the earth is, we are,
> We two – how long we were fooled!
> Now delicious, transmuted, swiftly we escape, as Nature escapes,
> We are Nature – long have we been absent, but now we return,
> We become plants, leaves, foliage, roots, bark,
> We are bedded in the ground – we are rocks,
> We are oaks, – we grow in the openings side by side,
> We browse – we are two among the wild herds, spontaneous as any,
> We are two fishes swimming in the sea together,

> We are what the locust blossoms are – we drop scent around the lanes,
>   mornings and evenings,
> We are also the coarse smut of beasts, vegetables, minerals,[33]

The acts of shedding false consciousness and awakening to one's essence are societal and personal acts that have for a model in the natural world a popularized notion of the Lamarckian concept of evolution. This pre-Darwinian reading of evolution takes into account the role that the environment plays in bringing about an organism's change, but it also posits an Enlightenment twist when it views the organism's role in its change. The popularized view of Lamarck took what Lamarck called "sentiment intérieur" and saw in this concept an organism's "right" (or will) to develop unfettered. Women's rights activists like Paulina Wright Davis and Abby Hills Price substituted "right" society for environment and the inherent rights of women (and men) for Lamarck's notion of "sentiment intérieur" to argue by analogy that a society that obeyed "natural" laws would allow individuals to develop unthwarted.[34] In such a society, women would have equal rights with men. The two in "We Two," then, are to cast off society's (false) projections and become what their ("natural") selves desire. Once society's restrictions are removed, the "two" unfold to their desired essences.

> We are Nature, long have we been absent, but now we return,
>   . . .
> We have circled and circled till we have arrived again, we two,
>   (*CRE*, 107–8)

When read by free-love advocates, this poem confirms the principles the movement supported: Love must grow out of attraction, and love must be allowed conditions for growth and change, like nature. Marriages, then, should not be irrevocable. When read by women working within the woman's rights movement, the poem creates an image of perfect equality – the two of "we two" are equal two's; thus, read this way, the poem argues for the active participation by women that the more radical women in the movement promoted. When read by gay men and lesbians (terms that did not exist in 1860), the poem confirms the authenticity of their desires as it rejects models imposed by society. Throughout the poem, the scientific basis of change or transmutation or evolution undergirds its argument.

Since this poem appears in the "Children of Adam" cluster, most readers expect the "we" persona to be male and female – male and female plants, fish, hawks, suns. If it is read this way, then by 1860 Whitman had made the move Harold Aspiz claims he had made: that Whitman's notion of sexuality became more a matter of reciprocity as his own ideas evolved. Aspiz says that Whitman "sometimes employs the premise (particularly in the early editions of *Leaves of Grass*) that the male is the sole transmitter of the electric spark of life and that the female is the source chiefly of the life-giving sustenance."[35] Aspiz cites Dr. Edward Dixon and Dr. Russell Trall as authorities for Whitman. He then cites lines from the 1856 "Poem of Procreation" (later titled "A Woman Waits for Me"), lines that Whitman deleted in the 1860 *Leaves*:

O! I will fetch bully breeds of children yet!
They cannot be fetched, I say, on less terms than mine,
Electric growth from the male, and rich ripe fibre from the female are the terms[36]

Aspiz feels that through the deletion of these lines, "the principle of electric maleness which animates the Adamic persona in *Leaves of Grass*" has been blurred.[37] Thus, if the "we" in "we two" is read as male and female, the poem is a model of egalitarianism.

Likewise, blurring takes place in the following line from "We Two": "We are two resplendent suns, we it is who balance ourselves orbic and stellar, we are as two comets" (*CRE*, 108). If indeed "we" in this poem was read by Whitman's contemporaries as male and female "we," then the two equal suns cut away any notion of polarized heavenly bodies, one more energized than the other. The blurring of the polarized male/female essences creates conditions of equality between male and female in Whitman's poem, but the blurring also creates the possibility of same-sex unions. "We," cleverly on Whitman's part, is never named a "he" and a "she." Thus, depending on the reader, "we" could be two "he's," two "she's," androgenous "he's" or "she's," or, more conventionally, a heterosexual coupling. Gender typing conventional for the times is blurred throughout the poem: "We are what locust blossoms are . . . We are also the coarse smut of beasts . . . We prowl fang'd and four-footed . . . We are two clouds . . . We are what the atmosphere is, transparent, receptive, pervious, impervious." These two "we's" slide in and out of gender-marked associations gleefully. They are not naive, however, for they know the issue in the gender debate – whether one is gendered primarily by society or by biology: "we are each product and influence of the globe." They know balance: "we it is who balance ourselves orbic and stellar, we are as two comets." Finally, the use of "you" in the first line, a line that appeared only in the 1860 edition, directly addresses the reader, ensuring that the reader becomes intimately part of the "we," sharing in the possibilities it suggests.[38]

The whole premise of this poem – how long we were fooled – claims, then, that arbitrary social and legal structures have denied the we-personae their desired essence, whether that essence is a radically different heterosexual relationship from what society endorsed and enforced or a homosexual one – female–female or male–male. The actual lives of Mary Chilton, Adah Menken, and Ada Clare rejected the arbitrary structures this poem challenges, and the more radical woman's rights activists challenged their antebellum societal structures in public words, written and spoken. These women spent time with Whitman; he considered them his friends.

Once we are aware of the numerous women who were Whitman's friends and of their highly politicized lives, we realize that the assessment of Whitman made by one of his friends, Charles Eldridge, fails to to make its case. Eldridge, one of the publishers of the 1860 *Leaves of Grass* and a longtime friend of Whitman's, wrote a letter in 1902 to be read at the ninth annual convention of the Walt Whitman Fellowship. Eldridge's point was to establish Whitman as a conservative. In the letter, Eldridge said that "[Whitman] delighted in the company of old fashioned women; mothers of large families preferred, who did not talk about literature and reforms."[39] Whitman's mother doesn't neatly fit that description; much less do Chilton, Beach, Clare, Menken, Price, Rose, and Davis, not to mention Whitman's extreme admiration of Frances Wright and of numerous other women not mentioned in this essay. The facts of Whitman's life cancel out Eldridge's interpretation, an interpretation that can be used to establish an argument for the representation of women in Whitman's poetry and prose as reductive.

Eldridge, however, wasn't the only friend to misinterpret Whitman's view of gender. On the evening of July 4, 1889, Horace Traubel walked over to Whitman's Mickle Street house to pick up the revisions Whitman had made in Traubel's manuscript, which was to become *Camden's Compliment*. Traubel mentions some of Whitman's changes:

> [Whitman] proposed speaking of "army hospitals" instead of simply "hospitals," and "secession war" instead of "war," and "the *person* Walt Whitman" instead of "the *man* Walt Whitman" – certainly this last, a radical improvement in musicalness; suggested also "His love for the *aggregate race*" instead of "for the whole race of *man*."[40] (emphasis added)

Whitman was seventy years old at the time, Traubel thirty-one, but Whitman's awareness of the political power of language far exceeded his young, progressive friend's. Whitman's concept of American democracy demanded gender equality, and so "musicalness" was not in Whitman's mind when he changed "man" to "person" and "race of man" to "the aggregate race." Rather, Whitman's awareness of his audience prescribed the change, his awareness of the role language played both in terms of his own poetic program – to address *all* of America – and his belief in the role poetry played in creating the kind of democracy he felt the future held for the United States. Women took part in that democracy.

NOTES

1   Walt Whitman, *Leaves of Grass: Comprehensive Reader's Edition,* ed. Harold W. Blodgett and Sculley Bradley (New York: New York University Press, 1965), p. 87. Hereafter, quotations of poems will be parenthetically noted and will refer to this edition as *CRE,* unless otherwise indicated. All of the Whitman citations come from *The Collected Writings of Walt Whitman,* general editors Gay Wilson Allen and Sculley Bradley (New York: New York University Press, 1961–), 22 volumes, unless otherwise cited.

2   "Ductile anchor" comes from Whitman's "A Noiseless Patient Spider," *CRE,* p. 450.

3   In the years preceding the 1855 *Leaves,* the *Water-Cure Journal* was one of the many periodicals Whitman read. This journal was dedicated to health reform, especially hydropathy, a methodology that influenced Whitman's own health practices throughout his life. Evidence of the journal's influence on Whitman surfaces on a linguistic level in his use of the word "accouchment," a term regularly used in the journal. Whitman used variations of the term in "Song of Myself," "A Song of the Rolling-Earth," and "To Think of Time."

Dr. Joel Shew, in speaking about the book he had recently written, *The Water Cure in Pregnancy and Childbirth,* in the *Journal* said that he had written it to work against the "almost universal custom of employing man-midwives in this country at the present day" 7 (1849):122.

4   See my review of Warren's biography, *Fanny Fern,* in the Fall 1993 issue of the *Walt Whitman Quarterly Review* and my comments on Edwin Haviland Miller in my unpublished dissertation "Walt Whitman and 'Woman Under the New Dispensation': The Influence of Louisa Van Velsor Whitman, Abby Hills Price, Paulina Wright Davis, and Ernestine L. Rose on Whitman's Poetry and Prose" (University of Iowa, 1990, note 68, pp. 217–219); for criticism of Whitman and women, see D. H. Lawrence, "Whitman," *Selected Literary Criticism,* ed. Anthony Beal (New York: Viking, 1966), p. 397; Joyce W. Warren, "Subversion versus Celebration: The Aborted Friendship of Fanny Fern and Walt Whitman," in *Patrons and Protegees,* ed. Shirley Marchalonis (New Brunswick, N.J.: Rutgers University Press, 1988), pp. 59–93; and Warren, "Walt Whitman," *Fanny Fern: An Independent Woman* (New Brunswick, N.J.: Rutgers University Press, 1992), pp. 160–78.

5   I discuss these strategies and inconsistencies in my dissertation; in "Walt Whitman and Abby Price," *Walt Whitman Quarterly Review* 7 (Fall 1989):49–67; and in "Whitman and Democratic Women," *Approaches to Teaching Whitman's Leaves of Grass* (New York: Modern Language Association, 1990), pp. 153–8.

6   Sandra Gilbert, "The American Sexual Poetics of Walt Whitman and Emily

Dickinson," *Reconstructing American Literary History,* ed. Sacvan Bercovitch (Cambridge, Mass.: Harvard University Press), 1986; Joanne Feit Diehl, "From Emerson to Whitman," *Women Poets and the American Sublime* (Bloomington: Indiana University Press, 1990).

7   Betsy Erkkila, *Whitman the Political Poet* (New York: Oxford University Press, 1989), p. 314.

8   Susan Coultrap-McQuin, *Doing Literary Business: American Women Writers in the Nineteenth Century* (Chapel Hill: University of North Carolina Press, 1990), p. 174.

9   Horace Traubel, *With Walt Whitman in Camden* (New York: Rowman and Littlefield, 1961), 1, p. 237. For background information on Clapp and the *Saturday Press,* see M. Jimmie Killingsworth's article "The *Saturday Press*" in *American Literary Magazines: The Eighteenth and Nineteenth Centuries,* ed. Edward E. Chielens (Westport, Conn.: Greenwood Press, 1986), pp. 357–64.

10   Walt Whitman, *Daybooks and Notebooks,* ed. William White (New York: New York University Press, 1978), 1, p. 100; 3, p. 788; 3, p. 834; Walt Whitman, *Notebooks and Unpublished Prose Manuscripts,* ed. Edward Grier (New York: New York University Press, 1984), 1, p. 248 and 248n. Neither Grier nor White correctly identifies Chilton.

11   See Kenneth Price's "Whitman, Free Love, and the *Social Revolutionist,*" *American Periodicals,* 1 (Fall 1991):70–82.

12   George E. MacDonald, *Fifty Years of Freethought* (New York: The Truth Seeker Company, 1929), 1, p. 450.

13   John C. Spurlock's *Free Love, Marriage and Middle-Class Radicalism in America, 1825–1860* (New York: New York University Press, 1988) provides a helpful discussion of Josiah Warren (1798–1873), whose principles Spurlock summarizes: "The happiness of society could be insured by giving each person sovereignty over his or her own person and property, an equal share of natural wealth, and an equivalent whenever property was exchanged" (p. 108).

14   Taylor Stoehr, *Free Love in America: A Documentary History* (New York: AMS Press, 1979), p. 432.

15   *The Fortnightly Review* 6 (July 1, 1865):427. The account of Conway's visit also appeared in his *Autobiography: Memories and Experiences* (Boston: Houghton Mifflin, 1904), 1, pp. 264–8.

16   Lillian Faderman, *Surpassing the Love of Men: Romantic Friendship and Love between Women from the Renaissance to the Present* (New York: William Morrow, 1981), p. 275.

17   In addition, in the January 14, 1860, issue of the *Saturday Press,* Ada Clare, a regular weekly columnist for the *Press,* criticized her friend William Winter's poem "Song of the Ruined Man" and praised Whitman's "Child's Reminiscence."

18   Emily Dickinson, *Selected Letters,* ed. Thomas H. Johnson (Cambridge, Mass.: Harvard University Press, 1986), p. 173. Ezra Greenspan pointed out this connection to me.

19   Gay Wilson Allen, *The Solitary Singer* (Chicago: University of Chicago Press, 1985), p. 261; Justin Kaplan, *Walt Whitman: A Life* (New York: Bantam,

1980), p. 242; Betsy Erkkila, *Whitman the Political Poet* (New York: Oxford University Press, 1989), pp. 311–12.

20 Horace Traubel, *With Walt Whitman in Camden,* ed. Sculley Bradley (Philadelphia: University of Pennsylvania Press, 1953), 4, p. 196.

21 John Burroughs, "Walt Whitman and His 'Drum Taps,'" *Galaxy* 2 (Fall 1866):608.

22 Clara Barrus, *The Life and Letters of John Burroughs* (New York: Houghton Mifflin, 1925), 1, p. 120.

23 Gay Wilson Allen lent me Clifton Furness's Ledger, in which Furness had copied Ellen O'Connor Calder's original draft of the article that appeared in the 1907 *Atlantic.* The section on Beach did not appear in the published article.

24 Walt Whitman, "Democratic Vistas," *Prose Works 1892,* ed. Floyd Stovall (New York: New York University Press, 1964), 2, pp. 424–5. Whitman reiterated this point eighteen years later: "I round and finish little, if anything; and could not, consistently with my scheme. The reader will always have his or her part to do, just as much as I have had mine. I seek less to state or display any theme or thought, and more to bring you, reader, into the atmosphere of the theme or thought – there to pursue your own flight." "A Backward Glance O'er Travel'd Roads," *CRE,* p. 570.

25 Whitman, "Democratic Vistas," *Prose Works 1892,* 2, p. 425.

26 Walt Whitman, "Preface 1876," *CRE,* p. 754. See also Whitman, "Backward Glance," *CRE,* p. 565, 135–41.

27 Juliette Beach's letters are part of the Feinberg Collection, Library of Congress.

28 The most revealing comment Whitman made of Ada Clare came right after her death in a letter to Ellen O'Connor: "Poor, poor, Ada Clare – I have been inexpressibly shocked by the horrible & sudden close of her gay, easy, sunny free, loose, but *not ungood* life – I suppose you have seen about it, but I cut the enclosed from the *Herald* in case you have not –": Walt Whitman, *The Correspondence,* ed. Edwin Haviland Miller (New York: New York University Press, 1961–77), 2, p. 285.
     Clare died from rabies on March 4, 1874, as a result of a dog bite five weeks earlier. Clare, Whitman, and Adah Isaacs Menken frequented the same circle of "Bohemians" at Pfaff's beer cellar. Whitman mentions Mencken's article in the *Sunday Mercury* in a June 12 letter to Henry Clapp (*Correspondence,* 1, p. 55).

29 Whitman, "A Memorandum at a Venture," *Prose Works 1892,* 2, p. 491.

30 Ibid., 2, pp. 493–4.

31 Ibid., 2, p. 494.

32 Horace Traubel, *With Walt Whitman in Camden,* ed. Gertrude Traubel and William White (Carbondale: Southern Illinois University Press, 1982), 6, p. 335. Frances Willard led the WCTU for twenty years, including suffrage as one of the organization's reform efforts. Whitman met her at the home of the Smith family: Mary, Alys, Logan – the children – and Robert Pearsall and Hannah Smith, the parents. Whitman refers to Mary Whitall Smith and Anne Gilchrist frequently in Traubel's account of his and Whitman's conversations. For example, see vol. 4, p. 188, and vol. 3, pp. 512–13.

33 *Leaves of Grass [1860],* Intro. Roy Harvey Pearce (Ithaca, N.Y.: Cornell University Press, 1961), p. 309. Needless to say, the "smut" in line 11 was not what

the writer of the *Springfield Republican* had in mind when he titled his article "Leaves of Grass: – Smut in Them."

34 For a discussion of "sentiment intérieur," see Leslie J. Burlingame, "Lamarck," in *Dictionary of Scientific Biography,* general ed. Charles Coulston Gillispie (New York: Scribner's, 1973), 7, p. 591.

35 Harold Aspiz, *Walt Whitman and the Body Beautiful* (Urbana: University of Illinois Press, 1980), p. 147.

36 Walt Whitman, *Leaves of Grass: A Textual Variorum of the Printed Poems,* ed. Sculley Bradley et al. (New York: New York University Press, 1980), 1, p. 239.

37 Aspiz, *Body Beautiful,* p. 148.

38 C. Carroll Hollis, in *Language and Style in Leaves of Grass* (Baton Rouge: Louisiana State University Press, 1983), discusses Whitman's use of the personal pronoun "you," pp. 94–5, 97–100, 101–2, 107–11, 116–23. Also see Ezra Greenspan's *Walt Whitman and the American Reader* (Cambridge: Cambridge University Press, 1990), especially the last chapter.

39 "Walt Whitman as a Conservative," *New York Times,* June 7, 1902. Eldridge's letter makes up most of this article.

40 Horace Traubel, *With Walt Whitman in Camden,* ed. Gertrude Traubel (Carbondale: Southern Illinois University Press, 1964), 5, p. 347.

8

ED FOLSOM

Appearing in Print: Illustrations of the Self in *Leaves of Grass*

I

When *Leaves of Grass* appeared in 1855, one of the most remarkable aspects of Whitman's idiosyncratic volume was the engraving of a daguerreotype of the poet that appeared opposite the title page (see Figure 8.1). Since the title page did not contain the author's name, the visual image stood as a kind of surrogate identification, as if the authorizing presence of the volume was more effectively represented by an illustration than by the more conventional linguistic sign. The reader was greeted with a body in print unaccompanied by a name in print.

That engraving has come to be one of the most familiar icons in American literature. Much has been written about the image – how it represented Whitman as a "common man," a worker instead of an intellectual, a poet whose poems emerged from his body and not just his head, a person who lived outdoors (or at least who was so contemptuous of social conventions that he wore his hat indoors and would not, as he indicated in the preface to his book, take it off to signal subservience to anyone, even – and especially – the president). It was an emblem of the poet of the body more than of the poet of the soul. The image centered on the torso instead of the face, and the portrait indicated that the poetry that would emerge from such a poet would be different from what had come before – earthier and more direct and more sensual. Over the next century, the image would prove to be highly influential: It gradually worked to transform the way most American poets portrayed themselves on their book jackets and frontispieces. A growing number of poets traded their coats and ties and face portraits for al fresco body poses in informal clothes – poses that echoed, again and again, Whitman's originating image of the poet as literal outsider. Today, any poetry section of any bookstore in the United States bears testimony to the fecundity of Whitman's portrayal of a distinctly American poetry.

In Whitman's own time, though, his friends were often uneasy about the

Figure 8.1 Steel engraving by Samuel Hollyer of an 1854 daguerreotype by Gabriel Harrison. Frontispiece portrait for the 1855 edition of *Leaves of Grass*.

messages the portrait seemed to convey. Although William Douglas O'Connor liked "its portrayal of the proletarian – the carpenter, builder, mason, mechanic" (*WWC* 3: 13) – William Sloane Kennedy hoped "that this repulsive, loaferish portrait, with its sensual mouth, can be dropped from future editions." For Kennedy, the image was of a "defiant young revolter of thirty-seven, with a very large chip on his shoulder, no suspenders to his trousers, and his hat very much on one side."[1] Whitman himself, always a careful critic of his own image, worried that in this portrait he looked "so damned flamboyant – as if I was hurling bolts at somebody – full of mad oaths – saying defiantly, to hell with you!" (*WWC* 4: 151). But he nonetheless liked the image "because it is natural, honest, easy: as spontaneous as you are, as I am, this instant, as we talk together" (*WWC* 3: 13). The image, in other words, set the tone for the poetry: natural, easy, spontaneous, inviting, yet also defiant and even a bit outrageous.

Virtually all the early reviews of *Leaves of Grass* commented on the portrait and on the fact that the reader *saw* the author before knowing the author's name: "Here is a quarto volume without an author's name on the title page; but to atone for which we have a portrait engraved on steel of the notorious individual who is the poet presumptive." This London *Critic* reviewer goes on to describe the man in the portrait as "the impersonation of his book – rough, uncouth, vulgar."[2] Whitman's own anonymously published self-review also emphasized the way the portrait substituted for the name and suggested that the portrayed body of the poet was somehow analogous to the body of the book: "His name is not on the frontispiece but his portrait, half length, is. The contents of the book form a daguerreotype of his inner being, and the title page bears a representation of its physical tabernacle" (*Imprints* 50). Whitman's association here of the words of his poem with the visual image of his body is telling. The reader opens the book to confront an engraving of a daguerreotype of the poet's physical self and then turns to the poems to encounter a daguerreotype of his soul. The ink and paper have created visual and linguistic signs that reify the poet, construct an identity we can grasp with the eyes and hands as well as with the intellect. Whitman thus begins what C. Carroll Hollis has called "the most successful metonymic trick in poetic history"[3] – his insistence on the book as a man ("Camerado, this is no book, / Who touches this touches a man" [*LG* 505]) – by conflating two bodies, his own and that of his book. As Roger Asselineau has observed, Whitman's intent was to insist on a direct and unsettling encounter with his readers, to avoid an easy and orthodox introduction: "Whitman had not wanted to be a name, but a presence; he wished to be a man rather than an author, and had therefore placed his portrait at the beginning of the book facing the title page. . . . He has not dressed up to meet his reader."[4]

Whitman had always been concerned that the transference of life into words, of presence into book, involved a depletion of vitality, and he set out to find a way to prevent, and perhaps reverse, that slippage. In the original version of "A Song for Occupations," Whitman had mourned the loss of life when living poems were embodied in a book: "I was chilled with the cold types and cylinder and wet paper between us. / I pass so poorly with paper and types. . . . I must pass with the contact of bodies and souls" (*LGV* 84). Similarly, he had warned about the danger of loving images more than the life they represented: "The well-taken photographs – but your wife or friend close and solid in your arms?" (*LG* 78). The danger of art, Whitman argued, was that it could make us worship the images of reality rather than point us back to the reality that the art only signaled.

As *Leaves* grew, however, Whitman gained more faith in the ability of the cold types to carry life, to embody an identity, to become a man. Whitman thereby developed a complex strategy for forcing the reader into an athletic struggle with his poems, challenging the reader to be active, not passive; to enter into the creative act; to bring the poem to life; not to sit back and wait for the *author*ity to pour meaning into the vessel-reader. The portraits of himself that he included in his books were part of this strategy – printed faces that fixed the reader with a gaze, fragments of ink casting out a look that the reader would have to answer, energize, bring to life. It was all part of Whitman's radical democratic aesthetics, what Alan Trachtenberg (paraphrasing Karl Mannheim) has called "the ecstasy of identifying with the physical point of view of another, seeing through the other's eyes into one's own, as the psychological basis of a truly democratic culture."[5] Photographs of himself allowed Whitman to see into his own eyes (a necessary act of democratic self-regard), and they encouraged readers to see through his eyes into their own, to imagine what thoughts lay behind the face mask (a necessary act of democratic identification).

Throughout his poetic career, Whitman would carefully coordinate illustrations of himself with the song of himself: Every portrait, he once noted, "has its place: has some relation to the text"; he wanted "all the pictures [to] have a significance which gives them their own justification . . . whether the fortunate (or unfortunate) reader sees it or fails to see it" (*WWC* 2: 536). The inclusion of portraits, then, was a challenge to the reader to work, to struggle for meaning, to respond. The portraits were as essential a part of the book as the poetry was, and they demanded the same athletic involvement from the reader, who was required to interpret actively not only the words but the visual images as well.

Whitman's challenging practice of illustrating the self is what I want to investigate in this essay. I will look at the ways that Whitman characteristically adapted and utilized the various emerging technologies of printing illustrations in books in order to enhance his self-representation. During most of Whitman's life, the technology to print photographs in books did not exist. Instead, photos had to be engraved, and the results – although often impressively photolike – would never be mistaken for a photograph. Engravings had their own set of conventions, their own history of techniques, that distinguished them in essential ways from photographic representations. As he did with so many developing technologies of his time, Whitman appropriated the technology of engraving and the tradition of frontispiece portraits and made them uniquely his own. As a reviewer for *Life Illustrated* in 1855 noted, *Leaves* "is like no other book that ever was written," and equally it was like no other book ever *printed:* "The discerning reader will find in this singular book much that will please him, and we advise all who are fond of new and peculiar things to procure it."[6] One of the new and peculiar things in Whitman's book was his use of an unnamed frontispiece portrait, an engraving that becomes more surprising the more we examine it. Let's look at it once again.

This 1855 frontispiece portrait has become the most familiar of all the images of Whitman – hat on, shirt open, head cocked, arm akimbo. Early reviewers could not get over the engraving and would describe it again and again in a variety of tones: "a gentleman in his shirtsleeves, with one hand in a pocket of his pantaloons, and his wide-awake cocked with a damne-sir over his forehead" (*Imprints* 45–6); "the damaged hat, the rough beard, the naked throat, the shirt exposed to the waist, are each and all presented to show that the man to whom these articles belong scorns the delicate art of civilization" (*Imprints* 42); "he stands in a careless attitude, without coat or vest, with a rough felt hat on his head, one hand thurst [sic] lazily into his pocket and the other resting on his hip . . . the picture of a *perfect loafer;* yet a thoughtful loafer, an amiable loafer, an able loafer" (Wallace 137). Clearly Whitman had hit on a culturally resonant and ideologically charged representation of himself, and his decision to continue to reprint the engraving in edition after edition of *Leaves* (it appeared in the 1856, 1867, 1876, 1881–2, 1884, 1888, 1889, and 1892 printings of *Leaves,* as well as in his 1875 *Memoranda during the War*) suggests just how vital he believed the image was to the overall effect of his poetic project. The repeated printings – often appearing opposite the opening lines of "Song of Myself" – insisted on this engraving as something more than a simple picture of the author. "The portrait," Whitman said, "in fact is involved as part of the poem" (Kennedy 248).

The figure stands against the most democratic of backgrounds – a blank page. But although there is no visible background, the pose (and the fact that the portrait remains anonymous, unnamed) invites us to read this figure symbolically, to place it in a social context that makes sense of the figure, and in so doing to question traditional assumptions about what a poet can be, where a poet can come from, and how a poet can be portrayed. The portrait is Whitman's announcement of his first poetic pose – the worker-poet, his physicality signaled by the costume, by the suggestion of outdoors. Whitman referred to the photo as "the street figure" (*WWC* 2: 412), thus suggesting an urban background, but that background has to be gradually filled in by the reader, catalog by catalog, as the poems unfold, just as the reader is allowed access to the name of Walt Whitman only about halfway through the first long poem (which he would eventually name "Song of Myself") when he announces "Walt Whitman, an American, one of the roughs, a kosmos" (*LG* 52) – a line that names Whitman, only to dissolve him again into the universe. As Byrne Fone has recently observed, "certainly the author of this book was not left unnamed for anonymity's sake merely, but instead to unsettle text, reader, and poet": . . . . "The text at that moment surely creates him, and how much more unsettling it is that when he is named at last, the name is almost immediately lost in a cosmos of definition – of renaming."[7] The portrait, the acts of naming and unnaming, all foreground the question of identity, the central concern of *Leaves*. How does anyone become a self in a democracy, where the central tenet is that everyone is equal? If all selves are potentially the same, if everyone contains (at least in embryo) everyone else, then what is identity? These are questions that would occupy Whitman throughout his life, and the visual portraits appearing in his books are part of his attempt at an answer.

The 1855 portrait, marking perhaps the first time an engraving of a daguerreotype was used as a frontispiece for a book of poems, makes its point in a number of ways: It is in sharp contrast to the expected iconography of poets' portraits, portraits that conventionally emphasized formality and the face instead of this rough informality, where we see arms, legs, and body all serving to diminish the centrality of the head, or at least to put the head in its place. Poets' portraits in the nineteenth century indicated that poetry was a function of the intellect, was a formal business conducted in book-lined rooms where ideas fed the head through words.[8] Whitman, of course, was out to undermine this conception, to move poetry to the streets, to deformalize it, to yank it away from the authority of tradition, and to insist that poetry emerged from the heart, lungs, genitals, and hands, as much as from the head. He wanted the representative democratic poet to speak in his poems, and the absence of his own name from the title page allowed the representative portrait to speak to authorship: These were poems written by a representative democratic person, living in the world, experiencing life through the five senses, a self that found authority in experience, that doffed its hat to no one, that refused to follow the decorum of removing one's hat indoors or even in books.

In 1850, Mathew Brady had published his *Gallery of Illustrious Americans,* containing a dozen portraits of what he called "representative" Americans – presidents, senators, generals, even a poet (William Ellery Channing). Alan Trachtenberg has shown how Whitman offered his own 1855 image as a different kind of "illustrious American," redefining Brady's notions and rejecting his "emphasis on established leaders and dignitaries," proposing a new conception of "illustrious" that was more democratically representative (Trachtenberg 69), allowing access to parts of the body and to parts of society that had up to that point been considered anything but illustrious. Since there were as yet no methods for reproducing photographic images, Brady's "illustrious American" daguerreotypes were distributed as lithographs (by Francis D'Avignon), and part of their effect, as Trachtenberg has noted, results from the necessary transformation of the photographic image to a lithograph engraving, a process that produced "a general likeness in place of the original vibrancy and presence": "the daguerrean image is drained of its vitality in the processed picture, product of the engraver's interpretation." Such compromises were inevitable, given the limitations of the available technologies; daguerreotypes offered a new vitality and accuracy to portraiture, but when mass duplication was needed, that vitality and accuracy gave way to "a formal look preserved and popularized by lithography" (Trachtenberg 46).

Whitman, however, worked against this effect; instead of seeking an engraving that pretended to be a copy of a daguerreotype, he had Samuel Hollyer – a young British engraver visiting the United States, who would after the Civil War settle in New Jersey and become one of the finest portrait engravers in the country – engrave Gabriel Harrison's daguerreotype in a way that did not attempt to *disguise* but rather *emphasized* the artificial and constructed nature of the steel-cut image. Although Hollyer's engraving renders Whitman's face and upper torso in photographic detail, its intensity of realistic detail fades toward the bottom of the image; Whitman's legs are rendered with less and less detail until they diminish to simple sketch lines, then fade into the blankness of the paper itself. The image advertises its constructedness. The lower part of the image insists on the fact that the embodied self in the portrait is composed of *lines*.

We do not know how much or in what ways Whitman was involved in supervising Hollyer's engraving, but we do know that he often requested alterations and revisions of engravings and photographs of himself. Late in life, Hollyer recalled how, soon after he had engraved the portrait, he met Whitman at a restaurant and asked him how he liked the engraving: "he [Whitman] said it was all right but he would like one or two trifling alterations if they could be made." Whitman then brought the plate to Hollyer's studio, where the artist "made them to his entire satisfaction."[9] We can only imagine what alterations Whitman insisted on, but clearly they had to do with enhancing his first attempt to create the organizing metonymy of *Leaves of Grass* – the book as man, the pages and the ink as identical to (the embodiment of) the poet himself. We might imagine that if he had had the means, he might have made his portrait in the 1855 *Leaves* a pop-up figure, literally springing from the page ("I spring from the pages into your arms" [*LG* 505], he announced in 1860). The effect of Hollyer's engraving in fact suggests this, for the background of the unframed portrait is nothing but the page itself: This author literally lives in his book. Hollyer intensifies this effect by adding the odd bent-oval shading around the barely sketched-in legs, suggesting a dent in the page, a hole out of which the poet literally emerges into ink, springing out of the page into the reader's eyes. The legs are not truncated in this portrait; rather, they simply disappear into (or appear out of) the dark dent in the paper, and we witness the poet rise on the page, through the ink lines into an illusion of presence, a presence captured by Hollyer's careful rendering of the detailed, half-shadowed face of the daguerreotype. The image allows Whitman to play on the relationship between engraving and photograph, suggesting an analogous relationship between poem and poet, each a reflection of the other, artifice creating reality while emphasizing the fabricated nature of that reality.

If we look even more closely at the shading around Whitman's half-erased (or barely sketched-in) legs, we can see that Hollyer has etched a series of wavy sketch lines around the shading, creating the illusion that he has finished off the shading roughly with a pencil. The whole portrait emerges from an intriguing tension between the rough, half-sketched quality that emphasizes the artificial, constructed nature of the image and the finished, highly detailed quality that imitates the verisimilitude of the original daguerreotype. It is as if Hollyer (and Whitman) want to underscore the *process,* the labor involved in making ink turn into identity, of making lines turn into humanity, of making a book turn into a man. As we read the image from bottom to top, we read that process: sketch lines, a dent of ink, four bare lines suggesting the continuation of legs that have faded into the blankness of the page, out of which arises a laboriously constructed impression of ink on paper that finally strikes our eyes as a man, an unmistakably individualized person made entirely out of ink and paper and art.

This emphasis on process, on the artifice of constructing a detailed identity out of initial bare sketches, is part of the tradition of portrait engraving. Most portrait engravings in the early nineteenth century emphasize to some extent the artifice of the engraving by leaving part of the image unfinished or barely sketched in. We can see this trait clearly in a famous frontispiece portrait appearing some eight years before Whitman's, a portrait Whitman would have known: the representation of Frederick Douglass in his *Narrative of the Life of Frederick Douglass, An American Slave. Written by Himself.* This portrait (see Figure 8.2) exaggerates the convention of empha-

Figure 8.2 Frontispiece engraving for Frederick Douglass, *Narrative of the Life of Frederick Douglass, An American Slave* (Boston: Antislavery Office, 1847).

sizing the rough sketch out of which the detailed portrait emerges; from the shoulders down, Douglass is represented only by a bare, primitive line drawing, whereas from the shoulders up, he emerges into a fully realized presence. It is easy to see how such a portrait enhances the pattern of his narrative, where Douglass the successful author and orator emerges from a slave who is prevented from having any access to his personal history, whose ability to learn and form an identity is stunted by the restrictions on movement and education imposed by slavery. Douglass's book traces his rise from a generic "American slave" with an empty identity to "Frederick

Douglass," a newly named and fully realized individual who has taken control of his life and now is the agent of his own narrative instead of a faceless product of the slavery system. His ability to gain access to writing and reading, to learn to "write by himself," brings his past under his own guidance and control, and his signature under his half-sketched, half-realized portrait is as significant to his iconography as the *lack* of Whitman's name is to the iconography of *Leaves*. Douglass's signature is ink affirming a literacy that creates and verifies identity; for much of Douglass's life, that signature was impossible, for the name and the ability to sign it were absent. His page was blank; his narrative is the story of learning to sign his name, at first literally and later figuratively, and to fill the blank pages with his identity. His book is his signature, and it ends literally with the act of signing his name, a full circle back to the title page. The visual emblem of himself imitates his emergence from blankness and sketchy beginnings into a distinguished selfhood.

Engraved portraits, then, served as particularly appropriate openings to slave narratives, which were confirmations of identity and celebrations of free individuals emerging out of an institution that strove to keep such individuality invisible, blank, and unformed. Engravings – with their emphasis on the process of creating verisimilitude, their habit of incorporating in the same image various stages of composition (from rough sketch to finished portrait) – thus were more effective vehicles than photographs for representing identity as an act of labor. There was artistry involved in making lines cohere into a recognizable and distinctive self, whether they were lines of words created by a writer or incisive lines on wood or metal cut by an engraver.

Like Douglass, Whitman was fascinated with the ways that lines could construct the self. His experiments with the long lines of *Leaves* created a radical new sense of self in relation to the world – absorptive, expansive, unfettered by conventional line length and meter. The poems of the 1855 *Leaves* were in some ways based on what Whitman learned from slave narratives like Douglass's. Whitman's 1855 poems in fact incorporate a slave narrative, from the "runaway slave [who] came to my house and stopped outside" and "staid with me a week, before he was recuperated and passed north, / I had him sit next me at the table" (*LG* 37–8) to the moments when Whitman speaks *as* the slave: "I am the hounded slave. . . . I wince at the bite of the dogs" (*LG* 66) and "I hate him that oppresses me, / . . . How he informs against my brother and sister and takes pay for their blood, / How he laughs when I look down the bend after the steamboat that carries away my woman" (*LG* 627–8). Whitman appropriated aspects of slave narratives in order to concretize the expression of desire for freedom and equality in his poetry. Like a slave narrative, *Leaves* was the record of a human seeking a new name, an unfettered identity, an open road that would lead away from all forms of enslavement – whether social conventions, literary traditions, or the actual institution of slavery.

It is fitting, then, that Whitman's frontispiece portrait would echo certain aspects of Douglass's even as it contrasted other elements: For Douglass, the escape was from work clothes to formal clothing, a change that signaled success and the acquisition of education and manners; for Whitman, the escape was in the opposite direction (though his later portraits would portray him in more formal attire, as if he gradually felt the need to have his radicalism garbed in respectability). The same social conventions that marked an achievement of identity for Douglass threatened identity for Whitman; an African-American posing as a distinguished writer was every bit as singular in the culture of mid-nineteenth-century America as a white poet posing as a day laborer. Just as Douglass's portrait undermines the generally expected image of a slave, Whitman's portrait undermines the expectations that his readers would bring to an engraving in this context; his is anything but the conventional image of the poet on the frontispiece of a book. He offers us an image of informality, physicality, and rough manners and dress unbefitting the anticipated environment of poetic pages. This image of the poet is just as much out of place in the tradition of poetry books as the poetry itself is. Thus the portrait effectively announces Whitman's new American poetic project, with all its ironies and its dissolving tensions between "poetry" and "work," between "poet" and "working man."[10]

II

Over the years, Whitman would continue to illustrate himself in his books with a variety of photoengraving and photoduplication technologies. The technologies of photoreproduction were developing with dizzying speed during the years when Whitman was publishing his various editions and issues of *Leaves of Grass*. Ezra Greenspan has convincingly demonstrated how Whitman's conception of poetry was thoroughly intertwined with the advancing technologies of printing, and how his early years in print shops and on newspapers led to "the peculiar literalness with which he saw print and paper."[11] The same is true of his relationship to the technologies of photoduplication. He knew engravers and photographers and confidently oversaw their work. By the end of his life, half-screen processes had been developed to the point where wood engravings and stereotypes of photographs were quickly becoming anachronistic, if not obsolete. By the 1890s, halftone photographs could be printed on the same machines and on the same pages as print, and could thus be integrated more fully into mass-produced books than Whitman could have imagined in 1855. Although photoengraving techniques were available in the 1870s and 1880s, it was only in the decade following Whitman's death that advances in half-screen processes and photoengraving techniques led to the virtual displacement of woodcut and steel engravings by photographs, which in a short time became the common mode of illustration in mass-printed journals and books.[12]

In the second half of the nineteenth century, the creation of a cheap, reliable process for producing halftones was the key problem for publishers wanting to reproduce photographs. Until such processes were perfected (they had been attempted as early as 1852 [see Taft 436]), all techniques of photographic reproduction reduced the rich tones of a photograph to stark contrasts of black and white. This chiaroscuroization of photographs, instead of creating the illusion of presence, emphasized the page and the ink as the light and dark ingredients out of which illustrations were composed. We have seen how Whitman used this self-referential nature of engraving to his advantage in the 1855 frontispiece engraving.

He would return to the same effect and even intensify it by including a woodcut portrait by William J. Linton in his 1875 *Memoranda During the War* and again in his 1876 issue of *Leaves* (see Figure 8.3). In chronological terms, the woodcut represented a retreat from the advancing technologies, for it was, of course, an older form of portrait reproduction than the steel engraving technique that Hollyer used. But we can see why Whitman was attracted to the Linton engraving, which was based on a photograph by George Potter. Just as Hollyer did with Harrison's photo, Linton turned Potter's photographic likeness of Whitman into an image that insisted on its constructedness. Although Whitman would note in the 1876 *Leaves* that this image was "Photograph'd from life," he liked the woodcut precisely because it was different from the photo; it was based on the photograph "from life," but it turned the "real" photographic image into a printed artifact every bit as suggestive as a poem.

Linton's engraving technique creates a powerful image, especially the riveting eyes – eyes that Whitman immediately realized were certainly no true reflection of his own: "My eyes are by no means bright, liquid, startling – no, not a bit that sort of eyes: they are rather dull – rather sluggish" (*WWC* 2:144). So when Whitman wrote a poem ("Out from Behind This Mask") about this engraving and published the engraving on the page oppo-

Figure 8.3 Engraving by William J. Linton, based on a photograph by George C. Potter, 1871?.

site the poem (he subtitled the poem "To Confront a Portrait"), he emphasized how the woodcut differed from the photograph on which it was based: It is "this bending rough-cut mask" with "burin'd eyes, flashing to you to pass to future time, / . . . To you whoe'er you are – a look" (*LG* 382). The woodcut forms a mask instead of a mirror, emphasizes its roughness (Whitman's assessment was that it was "rather rough as a woodcut, but if rough then like me" [*WWC* 2: 144]), and underscores its labored, cut quality (Whitman called the engraving "the cut, my head" [*WWC* 2: 208]). Its highly artificial eyes contain etched concentric circles around the irises, creating the riveting, targetlike effect that grips the reader. These eyes are made with a burin, cut with a blade, proclaiming that they are the product of an artist familiar with paper and ink and the engraver's trade. These eyes are eternalized in ink, and their ability to hold the reader (long after the historical Whitman has died) is a sign of the power of art to defeat time and space, to continue to flash to unspecified future times, to pass on a look to "whoe'er you are" reading this poem in whatever time.

By emphasizing the devices used to construct such a riveting stare, Whitman and Linton were able to accomplish more than a photograph could in terms of imitating the charged reader–author relationship Whitman was striving to achieve. This engraving becomes a visual exercise in creating the intense one-on-one relationship that Whitman always insisted must occur between his book and his readers: Only by such active union, by our giving the inked words voice and breath again in our time and place, can the poet enter our present as we enter the poet's past. It is the active conspiracy that Whitman is always trying to beguile his reader into: "What is more subtle than this which ties me to the woman or man that looks in my face? / Which fuses me into you now, and pours my meaning into you?" (*LG* 164). Whitman's retrogression from steel engraving to woodcut, then, serves to intensify the sense of artifice and to indicate ways that inked words and inked portraits could mutually support each other as they advertised themselves as artists' constructions of identity. It is fitting that Whitman intervened in the manufacturing of Linton's image (just as he had done with Hollyer), insisting that the engraver have it printed particularly dark in order to intensify the stipple of the engraved lines (see *WWC* 2: 208). There is a way that woodcut portraits, in their very artificiality, exist outside of time in a perpetual present, whereas photographs exist, by definition, in a past time. Whitman, trying to create the perpetual present of reader encountering poem (and poet), worked hard to erase the built-in sense of past in his original photographic portraits by transforming the photographic momentariness into engraved permanence.

Whitman's development of illustrations of himself in his books did not, however, continue to be retrogressive in terms of technology. As the technologies of pictoral reproduction advanced, Whitman carried on his experimentation with ways to illustrate the self, and in his 1876 *Two Rivulets* volume he included an actual photograph in one of his books (an 1872 photo by G. Frank Pearsall). This was a photographic print that had to be glued into each volume: "My work is extremely personal," he said at this time, "and on the fly-leaf of each volume I have put my photograph with my own hand" (quoted in Greenspan 221). He signed many of these photos, adding his autograph to his pictograph, and in this way further personalized the volume, literally touching the book to the life of the author, who, as he would testify on the title page of his 1888 *Complete Poems & Prose,* "handled" each volume. He wanted readers to know that the book they held in their hands had once been held literally in the author's hands. The illusion of physical touch – the act of holding the book in hand as akin to the act of holding hands – was essential to the metonymy of book as man, and the pasted-in, signed photographs grounded the illusion, just as his actual signature on the title page of his 1876 and 1889 volumes confirmed that the author had indeed "handled" (hand-held) each book.

By looking at the way some of Whitman's self-images refer to each other, we can see how he experimented with the illustration duplication technologies available to him. In his 1856 edition of *Leaves,* Whitman had again used the Hollyer engraving, but in his much-expanded 1860 edition, he switched to an engraving of a painting by his friend Charles Hine. This image appeared opposite another anonymous title page, serving again as a pictorial signature. Gay Wilson Allen has called this "the most artificial and uncharacteristic portrait that Whitman was ever to use in any of his books" (Allen, 244); and although that is true, it is also important to note that, of all his book portraits, this one least emphasizes the artificiality of its construction. Since it began as a painting, the engraving (signed by an engraver named S. A. Schoff) – unlike Hollyer's engraving of a daguerreotype – could not illustrate the transformation of an unmediated photographic image into the work of an artist's hand. Although the bottom of Schoff's engraving, representing Whitman's chest, does fade into single lines, echoing the tradition of leaving the engraving unfinished, the overall effect falls far short of Hollyer's more suggestive use of figural incompletion. Whitman would never again reprint the 1860 portrait, a clear sign that he too saw it as a mistake.

Another, more suggestive illustration of the self appears in the 1860 edition, however, though it seldom gets noticed – a decoration repeated three times: once at the beginning of the book, once a little more than halfway through, and again at the end. It is a rough engraving of a disembodied hand, with index finger pointing; on the index finger is a perched butterfly (see Figure 8.4). One of Whitman's favorite marks in his manuscripts and marginalia is the roughly drawn pointing hand, which he often used to highlight important passages. In the 1860 *Leaves,* the engraved finger works the same way, initially pointing the reader into the book. The first engraving comes at the end of the table of contents, opposite "Proto-Leaf," the open-

Figure 8.4 Engraving of
a hand with a butterfly;
margin decoration in
the 1860 edition of
Leaves of Grass.

ing poem; Whitman has here printed the finger tilting up toward the title of
the poem on the opposite page, as if to direct the reader personally to the
opening of the text. Halfway through, the pointing hand appears again, this
time on the right-hand page, pointing straight to the next page, a visual
encouragement to the reader to continue. On the last page, after the end of
the final poem, "So Long!," the hand points one last time, now indicating
the way straight out of the book and into the world. Whitman would often
seek ways in his poetry to hook his readers around the waist and take them
into the poems, only to tell them finally that they must depart on their own,
freeing themselves not only *with* the poems but *from* the poems as well. The
disembodied hand is a visual representation of that very process. The butterfly on the finger seems to lift, as much as to rest on, the disembodied
hand; the emblem suggests a joining of humans and nature, as well as a
marriage of body and soul, each supporting and guiding the other.

Over twenty years would pass before readers would discover that this
engraving of a hand also represented Whitman himself. In the early 1880s,
Whitman had a photographic portrait taken by Phillips and Taylor in Philadelphia, which he would use as the frontispiece for his 1889 issue of *Leaves*
(see Figure 8.5). This portrait serves to flesh out the 1860 decorative engraving by attaching the rest of Whitman's body to the pointing hand with the
butterfly perched on it. In the photo Whitman sits, hand raised, with what
appears to be a real butterfly on his index finger. This portrait became
infamous, since Whitman claimed on a couple of occasions that "it was a

Figure 8.5 Walt Whitman. Photograph by Phillips & Taylor.

real butterfly on my finger"; when a scholar many years later found a cardboard butterfly among Whitman's papers in the Library of Congress, Whitman's reputation for exaggeration and self-promotion was fixed.[13] But the later expanded photographic representation of the 1860 engraving can be seen as part of Whitman's attempt to weave himself fully into his text;

just as his 1855 engraving moves from sketched ink lines to photograph-ically complete image, the sketched ink lines of the 1860 pointing-hand emblem move to the fleshed-out tones of the 1880s photographic image. The represented Whitman lives in his books, and the illustrations of himself from book to book comment on each other as much as his new and revised poems comment on his earlier ones. In reprinting and using the "butterfly" photograph during the last decade of his life, Whitman casually reversed the image, so that his hand was pointing whichever way he needed it to point for his particular purpose at any given time. He did not view these images as honest or accurate representations of a self that lived outside the pages of his book but rather saw them as visual representations of the constructed self that lived only *in* the pages of his book. The interplay between rough engraving and finished photograph that we find in this pair of images sepa-rated by twenty years is characteristic of Whitman's handling of his self-visualizations; he would mix the media of visual representation within sin-gle images, and he would mix them across time.

The "butterfly" photograph was not the first actual photograph Whit-man had used in his books. In his 1882–3 *Specimen Days,* he included another photograph (an 1880 portrait by Frederick Gutekunst), and then in 1888 he used for the first time one of the new halftone processes of photo reproduction that allowed the mass printing of photographs on specially treated paper, so that the photo could be bound directly into the book (instead of being tipped in or glued in, as the 1876 photo was). When Whitman finally gained access to this technology that would allow him to mass-produce his photographic image easily as a bound page in his book, he chose what has seemed to critics over the years an inexplicably idiosyncratic image. In anticipation of his seventieth birthday, he had gone to Frederick Gutekunst's photographic studio in Philadelphia. He labeled the resultant photograph "THE 70th YEAR . . . taken from life," and he decided to have it touched up and engraved so that he could use it as the frontispiece for his *November Boughs* volume of poetry and prose (see Figure 8.6). He found it to be "a satisfying picture, all in all" (*WWC* 2: 99). To Whitman's dismay, his friends and associates vehemently disagreed: "no one likes the fron-tispiece," he reported; "All the boys turn up their noses – smell something wrong – think it won't do" (*WWC* 2: 411). Whitman's friend Horace Traubel, who was helping to get Whitman's last books into print, com-plained to the photoengraver that he had done a poor job, and according to Traubel, the engraver admitted "It is bum – I wouldn't have been surprised if you had turned it down" (*WWC* 2: 189). But Whitman was unfazed by all the criticism; something in the weird result appealed to him deeply, and he

Figure 8.6 Frontispiece portrait for *November Boughs* (1888).
Photograph by Frederick Gutekunst, Philadelphia, 1888.

claimed that it "serves our purpose – is appropriate" (*WWC* 2: 411). When
his friend Thomas Harned complained about it, Whitman allowed that the
image was not "high art" but went on to insist that he was "not looking for
high art": "sometimes a picture which is elementally very simple, crude, has
something to say, says something, in fact, which no amount of added finesse
would strengthen or improve" (*WWC* 2: 428). But just what did Whitman
think this odd image was saying?

In some surprising ways, the image calls us back to his originating 1855
engraving. The poet is again (and for the first time since 1855) portrayed in

a full-body pose. His hat is on and cocked, his arm is akimbo, his hand is in his pocket, and his collar is wide open, all echoing the 1855 pose. If we put the two images side by side, we get a warped mirror-image effect, with the 1855 portrait leaning right, the 1888 one leaning left, as if we are seeing the same self in the same pose through a lens of thirty-plus years. Whitman would in fact include both the 1855 and the 1888 portraits in his 1889 issue of *Leaves*, thereby offering the attentive reader a study in the process of a life, the echoing of youth and old age, leaves of grass and November boughs. The poet who appeared arrogant and erect in 1855 now appears softened and bent; he sits instead of stands, and one weakened arm is supported by a cane.

There are other kinds of echoes between the two portraits, a resonance of technique. Although the 1888 image is clearly a photograph and thus does not have the qualities we saw in the 1855 image – the foregrounding of artifice by portraying the self emerging out of ink and lines on a blank page – it creates a very similar effect through different means. The 1888 image is a true full-length shot; unlike the early image, this Whitman is not cut off at the knees – we apprehend him right down to his very real and fully detailed shoes. But those shoes are planted on a very *un*real ground, a ground that is only roughly etched onto the photographic plate. The photographically real image of Whitman sits on a one-dimensional chair that is barely suggested by the engraver, a chair that is half scratched out, as if the engraver had second thoughts about including it. Unlike the blank background of the 1855 image, which allowed us to imagine an outdoor setting but which ultimately indicated that the poet's true context was the page itself, this later image places the poet outside, but the nature in which he sits flaunts its artificiality. The effect is of a real person in an artificial world, akin to recent cinematic efforts to incorporate real people into cartoon settings: The poet sits on a fading, etched chair in a make-believe woods.

The setting in this photoengraving is not a photographer's studio (although Whitman did have several photos taken in studios with props that created the illusion that he was outside, he never used these images in his books), but rather is once again a self-consciously inked, constructed page. The scene the poet resides in is one-dimensional; he seems to sit *on* or *against* the engraved drawing of nature rather than *in* it. The background, in other words, is as much the page of a book as was the blank page of the 1855 engraving. It's as if Whitman has adapted the more recent technology of photoengraving so that he could create an updated study of how his identity is situated in and on the pages of his book. Here the illusion of a real self emerging out of the artifice of ink and paper is even more striking than in 1855. Again, viewing the two images side by side, we discover the early engraving of a daguerreotype reflected in the later photoengraving of a photograph, different technologies producing the same metonymy of book as man. In the first, a photographically real Whitman arises gradually out of a smudge of ink on paper; in the second, he rests on an engraved cartoon drawing.

Satisfied with such resonance, Whitman was undeterred by his friends' disdain for the portrait; he admitted he didn't care for the "technicalities" of the photoengraving, but "damn the technicalities if the rest is all right!" (*WWC* 2: 189). And what for him was all right was that the portrait had "the same ruggedness, unstudiedness, unconventionality" (*WWC* 2: 198) that his book had. It was a fitting emblem precisely because it did not hide its half-finished nature, its halfway state between art and reality. He liked the portrait for its failure to be a perfect illusion, for its botched technicalities, for its lack of "finish": Whitman would always be an artist who lacked finish, whose very poems did not "end" in any usual sense. He believed his poetry, like his identity, was always in process, and so it is fitting that he sought out visual emblems of himself that represented the process, not the product.

III

Whitman's love of process – his sense that the self was always in formation, always changing – is what drew him so eagerly to the new technology of photography.[14] He was of the first generation to experience the world photographically. The first daguerreotypes appeared in the United States in 1839, and by the early 1840s Whitman had already been photographed; he would continue throughout his life; "No man has been photographed more than I have" (*WWC* 2: 45), he once said; "I have been photographed, photographed, photographed, until the cameras themselves are tired of me" (*WWC* 1: 367). Many contemporary observers agreed with his assessment: Horace Traubel in 1889 raised the question to William Douglas O'Connor and Richard Maurice Bucke: " 'I wonder if Walt is not the most photographed man that ever lived?' William said, 'It looks to me as if he was.' Bucke said: 'There's no doubt of it' " (*WWC* 4: 260). Over 125 photographs of Whitman still exist today; the fact that he used only 8 of the photographic images to illustrate himself in his books suggests the careful culling that he undertook to construct a visual, textually bound Walt Whitman that would correspond to the linguistic Whitman that lived in the poems. The proliferating set of self-images handed to him by photography was at once exhilarating and terrifying, and as he looked at his many photographs, he was like the persona of "Song of Myself," expanding out into a risky and contradictory set of images before the threatening diffusion forced him to contract back into a unified self. Faced with a hundred versions of himself, he finally chose only a handful as representative.

As an old man, Whitman was part of the first generation of humans who could observe themselves as young people, who could examine traces of themselves along a visual continuum leading directly up to the image of themselves in the present. This revelation was immediately seen at the advent of photography as one of its most revolutionary aspects; photography yielded a series of permanent and accurate images of a self as it grew up and grew old. It is probably something of a cruel irony that Whitman was the first person to illustrate, fully and dramatically, such a process of aging through photographs. As he tried to puzzle out the meaning of the process that the photos revealed, his concerns ran deeper than just determining the effects of age on his features; his photos seemed to him to track an identity, to capture in the changing contours of his face the sweeping changes in his life. He was not always satisfied with what he found, and so he often rejected photos of himself because they revealed a glumness or a misanthropy or a despondency that he believed would be dangerous to associate with his poetry: "No man has any excuse for looking morose or cruel: he should do better," Whitman said while looking at one photograph; "That is so important to me: to not look downcast – cloud up things" (WWC 3:378). Whitman used his abundance of photographs to perform a penetrating and often depressing self-examination.

The sheer number of images bothered him; in his final years, he seemed to lose touch with many of the selves they represented, almost as if some of the self-images were of strangers: "Can a man by searching find God?" he asked one day; "can a man by searching find the origin of a picture of himself?" (WWC 4: 393). Stumbling upon photos of himself he had forgotten had been taken, he joked, "I meet new Walt Whitmans every day. There are a dozen of me afloat. I don't know which Walt Whitman I am" (WWC 1: 108). Different photographers brought out different angles, shadowed different features and highlighted others, until the number of paper mirrors began to add up at times to a bewildering fragmentation of self: "What a study it all is – this of portraits: no two of them identical: every interpreter getting another view. What amazing differences develop in the attempt of a dozen observers to tell the same story . . . there are as many views as there are people who take them" (WWC 2: 45). This confusion of Whitmans created something of an identity crisis as he thought about what all these images over the years suggested about the wholeness of his life: "It is hard to extract a man's real self – any man – from such a chaotic mass – from such historic debris" (*WWC* 1: 108). Although he knew that "the man is greater than his portrait" (*WWC* 1: 108), he also believed that his photographs over a lifetime were adding up to something, were capturing a persisting quality that had never before been revealed in human experience: "The human expression is so fleeting – so quick – coming and going – all aids are welcome" (*WWC* 5: 478). When Horace Traubel suggested that "A photograph is a fragment [but] a painted portrait may be a whole man," Whitman rejected the implied slight to photography; he saw that photography affirmed his belief that identity was not some transcendent quality but rather was an embodied process: "I am getting more and more in spirit with the best photographs, which are in fact works of art" (*WWC* 4: 434).

At times, though, Whitman seemed to wish that his multiple photographs would collapse into a composite form, like the English scientist Francis Galton's experiments in the 1870s and 1880s; Galton built on the growing realization that photography was transforming identity into a process, and he sought ways to make the fragmented nature of individuated portraits yield a transcendent identity. His composites, as Miles Orvell has noted, were formed "by combining individual portraits into a single homogenized facial image": "By photographing an individual as many as twenty times and printing a single composite print at the end, Galton argued that he would avoid the hazard of the single image and would arrive at an averaged expression that was the sitter's true self."[15] The variety of discrete and partial images could be melded into one true and whole image. In a similar way, Whitman in the 1880s carefully read and interpreted his photos, looking for clues to their individual and momentary significance and also looking for ways the single images added up to a totality, ways the "elements" formed a "compound": "I guess they all hint at the man" (*WWC* 6: 395; 2: 156). Most of the photos, he believed, were "one of many, only – not many in one," each picture an image that was "useful in totaling a man but not a total in itself" (*WWC* 3: 72). Each photo was like a word in a giant lexicon, one small, fragmented representation of a giant self: The poet kept working to lift the diffusion into wholeness, to prevent it from slipping into dispersion.

There was no doubt for Whitman that his portraits tracked a life *in* time and demonstrated that life was a process of continuity and change. And he even began to wonder whether the photos finally demonstrated that life was "evolutional or episodical," a unified sweep of a single identity or a jarring series of new identities: "Taking them in their periods is there a visible bridge from one to the other is there a break?" (*WWC* 4: 424). Whitman tried to maintain the faith that his photos finally were like the catalogs in his poems, an infinite and contradictory variety that piled up a wild randomness that created a unity, a form and a plan, a happiness. *Leaves of Grass* was modeled on the procession of a life from the starting through the parting, and it set out to embrace the shifting moments of change into an overarching identity: "It is not chaos or death – it is form, union, plan – it is eternal life – it is Happiness" (*LG* 88). Whitman looked at his photos and said, "We judge things too much by side-lights: we must have a care lest we pause with the single features, the exaggerated figures, individuals, facts – losing thereby the ensemble" (*WWC* 1: 283).

Whitman's adult lifetime of photographs thus forms at once the most intimate and most public record of any nineteenth-century writer. To look at this impressive series of images is to wonder whether we are seeing one of the great narcissistic acts of the century – an obsessive turning in, a fascination with his own uniqueness – or one of the most public acts, an exfoliation of the self through filmic images out into the world, a replication of the self analogous to the publication of his poems, an attempt to become the representative American. As with his best poetry (a poetry that defined the self as infinitely absorptive as it turned out to the world to embrace the vast contradictions of experience, then pulled that variety firmly into the self to hold it, contain it, caress it, and unify it), his photographic project seems an attempt to define the self by sharing it with the world, but also by casting it into a represented image so that he could contemplate it, dwell on it, look outward into his own eyes. Most of the images – including all the photos of himself with his young male friends – remained unpublished in Whitman's lifetime. The fact that so many photos remain (although he destroyed some, he retained most of them, even the ones he intensely disliked and did not want to make public) seems to indicate a very public dimension to Whitman's project of fully illustrating the self, but the fact that so few were published suggests the furtiveness that always undercuts Whitman's apparent candor.

Toward the end of his life, Whitman and his friends began thinking about publishing a book or an album containing a selection of his photographs. The idea was to have a visual song of the poet's self, a carefully selected set of images without poetry that would indicate the passage of a life as effectively as the poems did. "If I could get a book to suit me," Whitman mused, "into which I could put the pictures to suit me, I would be happy" (*WWC* 5: 86). Such a controlled series of images would ease the panicked sense of self-fragmentation that he felt when he rummaged through the welter of photographs. The project also offered Whitman's friends an opportunity to control and correct the poet's image; several of his disciples, for example, much preferred a second daguerreotype of Whitman taken by Gabriel Harrison in 1854; Whitman's friend Richard Maurice Bucke called the preferred image the "Christ likeness" and claimed it showed signs of Whitman's illumination, unlike the arrogant and rough pose Whitman had chosen for his 1855 frontispiece (and had continued to reprint). But the book of portraits was never completed; Whitman and his associates could not agree on which images would form the sanctioned sequence tracking the particular identity that would best serve posterity.

As Whitman came to realize the futility of this project, he turned his attention to a related project that brought together his lifelong attempt to meld illustrations of himself with his songs. For his 1888 *Complete Poems & Prose,* he selected four photographs to accompany his text, and for his 1889 issue of *Leaves,* he selected five. On the title page of this volume, he described it as "a special, complete, final utterance, in one handy volume, . . . stamp[ed] and sprinkl[ed] all with portraits and facial photos, such as they actually were, taken from life, different stages." In a grand final flourish, he mixed all the technologies of self-representation, combining steel engravings with woodcuts with photoengravings with actual photographs. These volumes stand not only as Whitman's summary statement of his textually visualized self, but also as a gallery of nineteenth-century portrait reproduction techniques: The methods of "stamping" the various "facial photos" is as important as the original photos themselves. In Whitman's hands, each phase of image making emphasized how the portraits were as much a product of ink and paper as the poems were; they were constructs pointing the way to productive engagements with the reader. He did not set out to publish a full record – in words or in pictures – of Walt Whitman, the man who lived from 1819 to 1892; rather, he set out to incorporate an identity in print. "Doubtless, anyhow," he said on the 1889 title page, "the volume is more A PERSON than a book." So his selection of images (and his selection of techniques of imaging) was crucial for the self that the text embodied (a self that continues to live on long after the self that existed outside the text died).

For his 1888 *Complete Poems & Prose* volume, Whitman added a new frontispiece portrait, a profile photograph (see Figure 8.7). Once again, he chose a portrait that his friends did not care for, one that he himself saw problems with, but one that finally served his specific purpose of weaving himself fully into his book. Like the Gutekunst portrait that we have already discussed, this portrait echoes the 1855 engraving: Both are open-collar

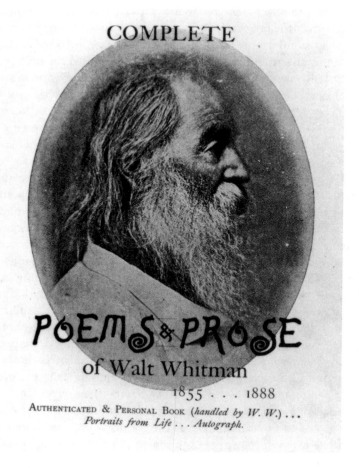

Figure 8.7 Frontispiece for *Complete Poems & Prose of Walt Whitman 1855 ... 1888*. Photograph by Charles H. Spieler, Philadelphia, early 1880s.

photos, both are unorthodox poses, and both demand a redefinition of the image of "poet."

Whitman's choice of a profile shot is telling, for one thing a profile does is to make the face unfamiliar to the person being photographed. Most of our portraits tend to imitate the angles on ourselves that we normally observe in the mirror. Since we seldom see ourselves from the side, putting a face in profile turns it slightly alien, even as it heightens the features. The resultant image is less personal and less familiar (the eyes of a face in profile, of course, are never looking at the viewer), more distant. For Whitman it was crucial that the profile portrait of himself was looking *out,* away from the spine of the book, away from the book itself, inviting the reader to follow his gaze out into the world, not to rest within either the book or the self: "It is appropriate: the looking *out:* the face *away* from the book," he said; "Had it looked *in* how different would have been its significance." And that gaze out into the world, with unfamiliar eyes, from the poems to what is around us, became for Whitman as good an emblem as any for the distinctive quality of American poetry, a poetry that would look to nature and experience for its authority, not to the past and to tradition: "I am after nature first of all: the out look of the face in the book is no chance" (*WWC* 2: 460). This portrait thus functions in much the same way as the disembodied pointing-hand engraving in the 1860 edition – a visual guide for the reader as the poet takes us into and then out of the textual experience.

The profile of American poetry, Whitman suggests with this portrait, is a face looking out into the world, seeking words out of experience instead of out of books, attaching the filaments of language to *things* more than to ideas, discerning and describing the unfamiliar – or the familiar in an unfamiliar way. This photo and another (one that he came to call the "Lear" photo) taken at the same session were the first pictures he had had taken since the Civil War in which he did not wear a coat; the shirtsleeves informality hearkened back to his 1854 daguerreotypes and to the photos Alexander Gardner had taken in the mid-1860s. The profile portrait thus echoes Whitman's self-image from his more robust earlier days, and he sees it as "so thoroughly characteristic of me – of the book – falls in line with the purposes we had in view at the start" (*WWC* 3: 254). He stood firm on the use of the image despite the objection, even ridicule, of his friends. The photo was even more generally unpopular than the 1854 daguerreotype: "I think I am the only one who likes it," Whitman said, but went on to justify its use in a number of ways:

> What does it express? . . . it says nothing in particular – suggests, what? Not inattention, not intentness, not devil-may-care, not intellectuality: then what is it? . . . It is truth – that is enough to say: it is strong – it preserves the features: yet it is also indefinite with an indefiniteness that has a fascination of its own. I know this head is not favored, but I approve it – have liked it from the first.
>
> (*WWC* 2: 513)

Whitman even altered the title of his book so as to avoid a possible joke. Originally he had wanted to call this retrospective volume *Walt Whitman Complete,* but as Horace Traubel prepared to take the portrait to the printer, he looked uneasily at it, and Whitman asked, "What's the matter?"

Traubel explained, "I was thinking that if we put above this portrait 'Walt Whitman Complete' they'll laugh at us" (*WWC* 2: 412). Traubel reports that Whitman laughed, too, said he had already thought of that, and went on to change the title. The portrait, in significant ways, does contrast to the 1855 image: Where the 1855 pose emphasized "Walt Whitman Complete" by including the torso and limbs, the 1880s pose clearly signals a diminishing sense of physicality; and where the 1855 pose is literally confrontational, challenging in its direct stare at the onlooker, the 1880s shot looks away, as if the poet's interests have shifted from direct encounter with the reader to a search for something beyond the book, and perhaps – in keeping with the theme of the later poetry – beyond this life. Still, Whitman insisted on containing both images within the book; the 1880s pose never displaced the 1850s one – it only complicated the image by contradicting it while joining it, clashing with it while echoing it in its informality. As such, the two images work with the other images in this same book to suggest the changes that a lifetime of photos record in a life full of contradictions but still strung on a single identity: If a lifetime of photos teaches anything, it is that life is a series of contradictions and echoes.

It is important to note one more aspect of this 1888 frontispiece portrait. When Whitman designed the title page, he chose to deemphasize the verisimilitude of the image by allowing print to invade the oval of the portrait. The photo is graffitoed over by the words of the title, which form a linguistic incursion into the space of the portrait, the first time Whitman experimented with language literally overlaying a photographic surface. So although he worked against the artificiality of the representation itself – he had complained vociferously when the photoengraver had touched up the photo by adding what Whitman called a "top-knot and Romeo Italian curls" (*WWC* 2: 479), embellishments that he insisted be removed – he nonetheless continued to emphasize the artifice of visual representation itself. Part of his reason for choosing this particular photo was its resemblance to "beautiful medallions we sometimes see" (*WWC* 2: 475). The photo was an "accurate" representation of the poet, but a representation made out of ink, medallioned and written over, a man made out of the materials of art, a self become a book.

Whitman's photos, by the time they made it into print, could not be mistaken for mirrors of reality ("miraculous mirrors," as photos were sometimes called in the nineteenth century) or windows to the world. Instead of presenting his photos as direct impressions of sunlight on photographic plates, Whitman had them worked over in various ways – mediated by engravers and designers – until they became visual pathways into *textual* identity. Whitman's face looked out from his book to the world, but the face itself was firmly embedded in that book, absorbed into the leaves like ink. He pulls his readers into his text with a significant look, a glance: eye/I contact. Then he sends us on our way: "Now I will you to be a bold swimmer," he says near the end of "Song of Myself," as he prepares to release us from his liberating text. Meanwhile, he stops somewhere and waits, always literally undercover.

NOTES

1   William Sloane Kennedy, *The Fight of a Book for the World* (West Yarmouth, Mass.: Stonecroft Press, 1926), p. 248.

2   *Leaves of Grass Imprints* (Boston: Thayer & Eldridge, 1860), p. 42. References to this volume will hereafter be given as *Imprints* and cited marginally in the text.

3   C. Carroll Hollis, *Language and Style in Leaves of Grass* (Baton Rouge: Louisiana State University Press, 1983), p. 252.

4   Roger Asselineau, *The Evolution of Walt Whitman: The Creation of a Personality* (Cambridge, Mass.: Harvard University Press, 1960), p. 48.

5   Alan Trachtenberg, *Reading American Photographs: Images as History, Mathew Brady to Walker Evans* (New York: Hill and Wang, 1989), p. 68.

6   James K. Wallace, "Whitman and *Life Illustrated*: A Forgotten 1855 Review of *Leaves*," *Walt Whitman Review* 17 (December 1971):137.

7   Byrne F. S. Fone, *Masculine Landscapes: Walt Whitman and the Homoerotic Text* (Carbondale: Southern Illinois University Press, 1992), p. 7.

8   See Constance Harris, *Portraiture in Prints* (Jefferson, N.C.: McFarland & Co., 1987), p. 211.

9   Quoted in Gay Wilson Allen, *The Solitary Singer: A Critical Biography of Walt Whitman* (New York: New York University Press, 1955), p. 150.

10 For an illuminating discussion of the relationship between poetry and labor in Whitman, see Alan Trachtenberg, "The Politics of Labor and the Poet's Work: A Reading of 'A Song for Occupations,'" in Ed Folsom, ed., *Walt Whitman: The Centennial Essays* (Iowa City: University of Iowa Press, 1994), pp. 120–32.

11 Ezra Greenspan, *Walt Whitman and the American Reader* (Cambridge: Cambridge University Press, 1990), p. 42.

12 See Robert Taft, *Photography and the American Scene: A Social History, 1839–1889* (1938; rpt. New York: Dover, 1964), pp. 419–50; and William Welling, *Photography in America: The Formative Years, 1839–1900* (Albuquerque: University of New Mexico Press, 1978), p. 364.

13 Mary G. Woodhull, "Walt Whitman – A Memory Picture," *Literary Era* 8 (March 1901):160; see also William Roscoe Thayer, "Personal Recollections of Walt Whitman" (1919), in Joel Myerson, ed., *Whitman in His Own Time* (Detroit: Omnigraphics, 1991), p. 304. The cardboard butterfly is revealed in Esther Shepherd, *Walt Whitman's Pose* (New York: Harcourt, Brace, 1938), pp. 251–2.

14 In *Walt Whitman's Native Representations* (Cambridge: Cambridge University Press, 1994), I discuss at length Whitman's relationship to photography and photographers, and I discuss his photographic portraits. In the opening paragraphs of this section, I offer an overview of my argument in chapters 4 and 5 of that book.

15 Miles Orvell, *The Real Thing: Imitation and Authenticity in American Culture, 1880–1940* (Chapel Hill: University of North Carolina Press, 1989), p. 92.

GUIDE TO FURTHER READING

Allen, Gay Wilson. *The Solitary Singer: A Critical Biography of Walt Whitman.* New York: Macmillan, 1955.

"The Iconography of Walt Whitman." In Edwin Haviland Miller, ed., *The Artistic Legacy of Walt Whitman.* New York: New York University Press, 1970, pp. 103–52.

Clarke, Graham. *Walt Whitman: The Poem as Private History.* New York: St. Martin's, 1991.

Folsom, Ed, ed. " 'This Heart's Geography's Map': The Photographs of Walt Whitman." *Walt Whitman Quarterly Review* 4 (Fall/Winter 1986–7):1–76. [Special double issue containing all known Whitman photographs.]

"Whitman and the Visual Democracy of Photography." *Mickle Street Review* 10 (1988):51–65.

Greenspan, Ezra. *Walt Whitman and the American Reader.* Cambridge: Cambridge University Press, 1990.

Harris, Constance. *Portraiture in Prints.* Jefferson, N.C.: McFarland & Co., 1987.

Orvell, Miles. *The Real Thing: Imitation and Authenticity in American Culture, 1880–1940.* Chapel Hill: University of North Carolina Press, 1989.

Reisch, Marc S. "Poetry and Portraiture in Whitman's *Leaves of Grass.*" *Walt Whitman Review* 27 (September 1981):113–25.

Saunders, Henry S. *Whitman Portraits.* Toronto: Privately published, 1922.

Taft, Robert. *Photography and the American Scene: A Social History, 1839–1889.* 1938; rpt. New York: Dover, 1964.

Trachtenberg, Alan. *Reading American Photographs: Images as History, Mathew Brady to Walker Evans.* New York: Hill and Wang, 1989.

Welling, William. *Photography in America: The Formative Years, 1839–1900.* Albuquerque: University of New Mexico Press, 1978.

ABBREVIATIONS

LG: Sculley Bradley and Harold W. Blodgett, eds., *Leaves of Grass.* Norton Critical Edition (New York: Norton, 1973).

LGV: Sculley Bradley, Harold W. Blodgett, Arthur Golden, and William White, eds., *Leaves of Grass: A Textual Variorum of the Printed Poems,* 3 vols. (New York: New York UP, 1980).

WWC: Horace Traubel, *With Walt Whitman in Camden,* 6 vols. Vols. 1–3 (1906–14; rpt. New York: Rowman and Littlefield, 1961); Vol. 4, ed. Sculley Bradley (Philadelphia: University of Pennsylvania Press, 1953); vol. 5, ed. Gertrude Traubel (Carbondale: University of Southern Illinois Press, 1964); vol. 6, ed. Gertrude Traubel and William White (Carbondale: University of Southern Illinois Press, 1982); vol. 7, ed. Jeanne Chapman and Robert MacIsaac (Carbondale: University of Southern Illinois Press, 1992).

9

RUTH L. BOHAN

"I Sing the Body Electric": Isadora Duncan, Whitman, and the Dance

Only months before she died in a freak automobile accident in Nice, France, in 1927, strangled by the same scarf with which she danced the impassioned *Marseillaise,* Isadora Duncan completed her autobiography, *My Life.* Twenty-five years after catapulting to international acclaim as the "barefoot dancer" from California, Duncan proclaimed the poet Walt Whitman one of her three "dance masters."[1] With the bravado typical of her after-concert lectures, she hailed Whitman as the "supreme poet of our country" and credited his poetry with having instilled in her "my great spiritual realization of life" (Duncan, *My Life,* 31, 341). To many of those who had followed the progress of her dance across three continents and nearly as many decades, Duncan's disclosure only confirmed what they had long since determined for themselves. Writer and editor Max Eastman was among those who perceived in Duncan's dance a strong Whitmanic presence. In his memoirs, Eastman extolled "that warm witty magnetism" with which she danced, terming her "not only a supreme artist . . . [but] also a creative and a moral force." For him as for others of his generation, "[s]he really became, as she thought to, a winged apostle to the whole world of Walt Whitman's vision of a poised and free-bodied and free-souled humanity, carrying his thought to hearts that never heard of him."[2]

As the self-appointed national poet, Whitman had repeatedly reminded his readers that it was to the future that he directed his verse. "Poets to come!" he exclaimed in one of the opening poems in *Leaves of Grass,* ". . . Not to-day is to justify me and answer what I am for, / But you [of the future], a new brood, native, athletic, continental, greater than before known, / Arouse! for you must justify me." The poem's closing lines confirmed the urgency of his appeal. He was, he stressed, "Leaving it to you to

Research for this project was begun with a generous fellowship from the J. Paul Getty Trust and a residency at the Smithsonian Institution's National Museum of American Art. I would also like to thank Barbara Kachur and Barbara Day for their helpful suggestions and editorial assistance.

prove and define it, / Expecting the main things from you."[3] The poet's refusal to be bound by the time-honored traditions of his craft, his blurring of the distinctions between elite and popular modes of representation, and his ringing endorsement of the invigorating, self-realizing authority of the individual seemed creatively reborn in Duncan's willful subversion of traditional dance practices. Through the expressive vehicle of her body, Duncan negotiated and re-presented Whitman's potent claim to be "the caresser of life wherever moving" (Whitman, "Song of Myself," 40). Both the construction and the reception of Duncan's dance are best understood in light of the high esteem in which Whitman was held by modernist artists and social reformers in the early decades of the twentieth century. During a period in which the established norms of artistic discourse were constantly being renegotiated and reevaluated, Whitman served as an important energizer and guide. How the poet's presence resonated through Duncan's dance is the focus of this essay.

Duncan's early upbringing laid the foundation for her later engagement with Whitman. Born in San Francisco in 1877, Duncan grew to maturity in genteel poverty in a household that placed a premium on individual creativity and the arts.[4] In the evenings, her mother, Dora Duncan, a piano teacher and follower of the radical free thinker Robert Ingersoll,[5] performed selections from Beethoven, Schumann, Schubert, and Chopin or read aloud from the works of Shelley, Keats, and Burns, instilling in each of her children a lasting appreciation of music and poetry. Isadora and her sister Elizabeth, who would later serve as the administrator and principal instructor at her schools, began to dance while still very young. By their teenage years they were instructing other children in the neighborhood. "We called it a new system of dancing," Duncan recalled, "but in reality there was no system. I followed my fantasy and improvised" (Duncan, *My Life,* 21). In 1896 Isadora and her mother moved to Chicago, where the young dancer launched her professional career. For two years she toured with Augustin Daly's well-known theatrical company, dancing such roles as a fairy in *A Midsummer Night's Dream* and a spirit in *The Tempest.*

Once freed from the regimen of Daly's company, Duncan enjoyed a modest initial success dancing privately for wealthy socialites in New York and New England. Her earliest solo dances were often accompanied by poetry or a combination of music and poetry. She danced to works by Milton and Joachim du Bellay and choreographed an entire dance around Omar Khayyam's *Rubaiyat.*[6] The narrative line of the poetry guided her gestures, but from the beginning Duncan strove to represent something more than the simple unfolding of the narration. In an interview in 1898, the year before her remove to London, Duncan declared it her intention "to blend together – a poem, a melody and a dance – so that you will not listen to the music, see the dance or hear the poem, but will live in the scene and thought that all are expressing." She insisted, furthermore, that for her "the greatest worth of dancing" stemmed from its contribution to the development of character and self-knowledge.[7] This dual emphasis on the organic expressiveness of the dance and its existence as a moral and ethical force would color her entire career and form the basis for her later engagement with Whitman.

As Duncan immersed herself in the work necessary to reconstitute the art of dancing, she consistently sought out the company of poets and writers. During her year-long stay in London, she enjoyed an active association with such well-known writers and poets as William Butler Yeats, Sir Edwin Arnold, Austin Dobson, and the Pre-Raphaelites.[8] In addition, she spent long hours reading from the poetry of Keats, Browning, Rossetti, and Oscar Wilde with the Oxford-educated poet Charles Ainslie. On her move to Paris in 1900, her interests shifted to the French realists and symbolists – Flaubert, Gautier, Maeterlinck, and "all the modern French books of the day" (Duncan, *My Life*, 72) – which she studied with the writer André Beaunier. Duncan also read widely in more historical literature, and in Germany read Dante with the German writer and teacher Heinrich Thode.[9]

When and in what context Duncan first encountered Whitman is unknown. Toward the end of her life Duncan traced her fascination with his work to the very beginning of her dancing career. In *My Life* she claimed to have presented herself to Augustin Daly as "the spiritual daughter of Walt Whitman" (Duncan, *My Life*, 31) a full two years before setting out on her own. However, like much in Duncan's autobiography, this story is inconsistent with the known facts of her life. It was probably not until several years after her removal to Europe and her phenomenally successful debut as a solo performer in Budapest in 1902 that Duncan began to give serious attention to Whitman's poetry.

When Duncan settled permanently in Europe in 1899, Whitman's reputation was already well established among a small but growing group of artists and intellectuals. A contemporary critic observed "a veritable tidal wave of Whitman enthusiasm" sweeping the Continent. Interest had been building "with increasing intensity" since the appearance of the first translations of Whitman's poetry in the 1870s and 1880s.[10] Interest was particularly keen in Germany, where it rode the coattails of the phenomenal popularity accorded the writings of Friedrich Nietzsche, the country's recently deceased native son. "Nietzschemania was the beginning of Whitmania in Germany," declared the critic O. E. Lessing. To German audiences eager for a more egalitarian and democratic order, *Leaves of Grass* and *Thus Spoke Zarathustra* struck a responsive chord, with each offering to replace the "old, traditional institutions" with "new ethical standards" and a heightened sense of self.[11] Between 1899 and 1909 no fewer than three German editions of *Leaves of Grass,* three editions of Whitman's prose writings, and more than two dozen essays on Whitman appeared in both the popular and scholarly presses.[12]

Duncan enjoyed direct access to both the Whitman and Nietzsche cults through her association with the Austrian scholar Dr. Karl Federn (1868–1925), whom she met while dancing in Berlin in 1903. With Federn, Duncan read *Thus Spoke Zarathustra* in German, pondering at length its assessment of the overman, the eternal recurrence, its innovative narrative structure, and its inspiring oracular tone.[13] Years later Duncan acknowledged that the "seduction of Nietzsche's philosophy ravished my being." So involved did she become that it was only with "the greatest reluctance" that she agreed to separate herself from Federn and her readings long enough to fulfill her performing obligations in other German cities (Duncan, *My Life,* 141). During the days and weeks that Federn and Duncan read Nietzsche, the Austrian scholar was also busily completing a major translation of eighty poems from *Leaves of Grass.* The translation appeared the following year, prefaced by a lengthy essay in which Federn praised Whitman for, among other things, "the shaggy roughness, the playful joy, and [the] brutal power" of his verse, a power whose appeal was all the more profound because it seemed "tamed by an all-illuminating love of man" and "elevated by the highest ethical and prophetic enthusiasm."[14] Federn and Duncan surely discussed Whitman, but for each, it was Nietzsche, not Whitman, who exerted the stronger appeal and whose ideas seemed more fully illuminated in her dance. "What Nietzsche suspected and perceived in his artistic and poetic awareness, Isadora has brought to reality," Federn exalted in his foreword to Duncan's treatise on the dance, *Der Tanz der Zukunft (The Dance of the Future),* published in Leipzig the year they met.[15]

If Federn opened the door to Duncan's interest in Whitman, it was the brilliant British theatrical innovator and Whitman enthusiast Edward Gordon Craig (1872–1966) who led her across the threshold. Duncan met Craig, as she had Federn, in the bustling international city of Berlin (Figure 9.1). From the moment they met in December 1904, these "Two Villains," as Craig dubbed the pair in an early photograph, recognized in each other a kindred spirit. As Craig put it: "We both spoke the same language – hers the American brand, mine the English."[16] Craig, too, rebelled against the mimetic and aesthetic traditions of his craft and devoted his life to creatively

Figure 9.1 *Edward Gordon Craig and Isadora Duncan,* Berlin, 1904.
Dance Collection, The New York Public Library for the Performing Arts,
Astor, Lenox, and Tilden Foundations.

reinventing the art of the theater. Like Duncan, he favored a complete break with the realistic mise-en-scene of his predecessors. He constructed instead a nonlocalized, spatial environment in which movement, not words, predominated.[17] Within days of their introduction the two became lovers, and in 1906 a child, Diedre, was born. The intensity of their affair diminished rapidly thereafter, but its impact endured for years to come.

As the son of the acclaimed British actress Ellen Terry, Craig grew up among England's literary and theatrical elite, where an interest in Whitman had been building since the 1868 publication of William Michael Rossetti's first English edition of Whitman's verse, the controversial *Poems of Walt Whitman.*[18] In 1884 Terry's leading man, Britain's great Shakespearean actor-manager, Sir Henry Irving (1838–1905), whom Craig held in the greatest esteem and whose biography he would later write, visited Whitman at his home in Camden, New Jersey.[19] With him was his secretary, Bram Stoker (1847–1912), who, twelve years previously, had written Whitman a youthful letter of admiration and who would return to Camden twice more before the decade was out.[20] Stoker probably helped Terry secure for Craig a first-edition copy of *Leaves of Grass* and some original manuscript poems, one of which Craig later gave Duncan.[21] Shortly after receipt of the volume,

Figure 9.2 Edward Gordon Craig, *Portrait of Walt Whitman, The Mask* 4 (July 1911).

and perhaps in response to Whitman's death the preceding year, Craig produced a handsome woodcut of the poet based on Samuel Murray's compelling photograph (Figure 9.2). Craig's enthusiasm for Whitman infused much of his life's endeavor but manifested itself most openly during and just prior to his meeting with Duncan.

In the May 1898 issue of his journal, *The Page* (1898–1901), Craig extolled the American poet as "The greatest man of the century; the greatest and most splendid of all poets" and expressed special fondness for "Song of Myself," "A Song of Joys," and "A Song of the Rolling Earth."[22] As one raised in the theater, Craig was particularly attracted by the gestural presence and spatial dimension with which Whitman transformed the art of poetry. It was in many ways as if Whitman's own early interest in the theater had finally come full circle. The young scenographer expressed particular delight in Whitman's "audacious and native use of his own body and soul," his acceptance of women equally with men ("I am the poet of the woman the same as the man"), and his radical rejection of the outmoded traditions of his craft, themes that would attract Duncan's attention as well. "Every word that falls from his mouth shows silent disdain and defiance of the old theories and forms," Craig noted with delight.[23] The poet's insistence, as he wrote in "A Song of the Rolling Earth," that "Human bodies are words . . . / Every part able, active, receptive, without shame or the need of shame" (Whitman, "A Song of the Rolling Earth," 219), encouraged Craig in his commitment to reorient the theater toward a language of gesture rather than words. Above all, it was the open-air quality of Whitman's verse, its undulating rhythms, its evocation of the qualities and textures of nature, and its sense of the largeness and freedom of the outdoors that most fired Craig's imagination. In perhaps the most telling acknowledgment of Whitman's appeal, Craig paired a passage from *Specimen Days,* which extolled the "silent beauteous miracles that envelope and fuse me – trees, water, grass, sunlight, and early frost –," with another of his meticulous woodblock prints showing the poet in his signature broad-brimmed hat, a giant presence surveying a spreading landscape (Figure 9.3).[24] Like the poet, the landscape seemed not to be contained by the defining boundaries of the frame, but to extend indefinitely outward from its center.

By late 1906 Craig was corresponding with Whitman's literary executor, Horace Traubel, whose cluttered Philadelphia office served as an important clearing house for the dissemination of information on Whitman worldwide. Traubel presented Craig with additional Whitman manuscripts, and in 1911 Craig ran an announcement of Traubel's proposed reprint edition of Whitman's Blue Book in his new journal, *The Mask* (1908–15, 1918). Craig accompanied the half-page announcement with his own earlier profile portrait of Whitman and two Whitman poems, the four items forming a kind of Whitman cluster in the opening pages of the July 1911 issue. The two poems, "To a Foil'd Revolutionaire" and "When I Heard the Learned As-

FIGURE 7   1898

Figure 9.3 Edward Gordon Craig, *The Good Grey Poet, The Page* II, no. 1 (1899).

tronomer," gave added voice to the rebellious self-confidence that fueled Craig's theatrical endeavors.[25]

When Craig first saw Duncan dance in Berlin shortly after they met, he was immediately struck by the freedom, boldness, and invigorating humanity of her dance. The unobstructed openness with which she moved, the unorthodoxy of her gestures, and the daring frankness with which she presented her loosely clad body on a stage stripped bare of the mimetic trappings of the ballet greatly appealed to both his reformist instincts and his aesthetic sensibilities. Above all, Duncan's dance resonated for Craig with an absorbing Whitmanic presence. This young American dancer seemed to Craig, as she would to others similarly steeped in Whitman's poetry, the moving expression and living embodiment of the American poet's call for a "new brood, native, athletic, contintental, greater than before known" (Whitman, "Poets to Come," 14). Shortly after first observing Duncan dance, Craig joyously wrote to his friend and collaborator, the composer Martin Shaw, that he had "seldom been so moved by anything." "Now for the first time do I *see* (& I watch with breathless interest) [what] the young American Walt sang for and loved to see growing to a god. The Daring !!!" (Craig, quoted in Steegmuller, *"Your Isadora,"* 63). In another letter he exclaimed: "I am drinking in 'American *push*' – Walt in a book is alive – but Walt walking, dancing is LIFE" (Craig, quoted in Steegmuller, *"Your Isad-*

ora," 72). Many years after Duncan's death, in a statement for the BBC, Craig recalled that "one had but to see her dance for one's thoughts to wing their way, as it were, with the fresh air, . . . she said everything that was worth hearing; and everything that anyone else but the poets had forgotten to say" (Craig, quoted in Steegmuller, *"Your Isadora,"* 362).

Duncan always considered Craig one of the most astute observers of her dance and within days of their first meeting began in earnest to probe for herself the depths of Whitman's poetry. Duncan soon came to regard Whitman as her spiritual father and *Leaves of Grass* as her *"livre de chevet"* (Duncan, *My Life,* 233). When Craig gave her one of his treasured Whitman manuscripts, she responded with a hushed sense of awe. "I often take it out – alone – and look at it, & think how wonderful it is – the paper left, & his vanished hands –" (Duncan, quoted in Steegmuller, *"Your Isadora,"* 242). Two weeks after meeting Craig, Duncan took a copy of *Leaves of Grass* with her on her first Russian tour and thereafter traveled with it regularly. The long train ride across the snow-covered terrain between Berlin and St. Petersburg reverberated with the sights and sounds of Whitman's "To a Locomotive in Winter." In a letter to Craig, written just after her arrival in the Russian capital, Duncan described with pleasure the steady "pim de pim" of the train as it crossed "over Great fields of snow – vast plains of snow – Great bare Countries covered with snow" – a terrain that reminded her of the expansive vistas of Whitman's verse. "Walt could have written 'em up fine," she exclaimed (Duncan, quoted in Steegmuller, *"Your Isadora,"* 34).

As with many of her contemporaries, Duncan's favorite poem was the spirited "Song of the Open Road" (Duncan, *My Life,* 233). With its rousing call to "go where winds blow, waves dash, and the Yankee clipper speeds by under full sail," the poem gave voice to artistic rebels like herself whose art boldly challenged established social, artistic, and professional norms. "Allons! from all formules!" Whitman urged. "My call is the call of battle, I nourish active rebellion." The poem's rejection of the ordinary rules of rhythm and rhyme ("The music falling in where it is wanted, and stopping where it is not wanted"), its glorification of the freedom and expansiveness of nature ("I think heroic deeds were all conceiv'd in the open air, and all free poems also"), its praise of "sweet and determin'd bodies," and, above all, its tribute to the "efflux of the soul [which] comes from within through embower'd gates, ever provoking questions" (Whitman, "Song of the Open Road," 154, 155, 158, 150, 151, 155, 153) would find creative rebirth in the absorbing physical expression of Duncan's dance. For one who would later choose as her motto *"sans limites,"*[26] Whitman's rejection of "the old smooth prizes" in favor of "rough new prizes" echoed her own dogged determination to chart a daring course independent of established dance practices. Duncan, too, would ordain herself "loos'd of limits and imaginary lines, / Going where I list, my own master total and absolute, / . . . / Gently, but with undeniable will, divesting myself of the holds that would hold me" (Whitman, "Song of the Open Road," 155, 151).

When Duncan began her dancing career, the most powerful "hold" on theatrical dance practices in both Europe and America was the ballet. With its long-standing ties to the aristocratic court dances of Western Europe, the ballet stressed formal correctness, technical proficiency, and an ethereal, antiphysical approach to the body. The lexicon of the ballet comprised a well-defined, rigorously codified catalog of movements designed to transcend gravity and matter. Movement was limited principally to the legs and arms, which moved independently of an upright torso. Virtuosic passages alternated with simpler, less demanding sequences to create a dazzling but discontinuous pattern of movement. The introduction of toe shoes early in the nineteenth century facilitated a more aerial dance with higher elevations, more soaring leaps, and longer balances. Shorter costumes, composed of layers of airy tulle, reinforced the gravity-defying focus of the movements. Elaborate trompe l'oeil settings completed this spectacle of idealized beauty.

Duncan rejected both the ideological foundations and the formal characteristics of the ballet, which she had studied briefly in London and New York.[27] Her repudiation of the ballet stemmed in large measure from her belief that the actions and intentions of the ballet were "not worthy of the soul" (Duncan, My Life, 75). She often insisted that the only "truly creative dancer[s]" were "those who convert the body into a luminous fluidity, surrendering it to the inspiration of the soul."[28] To better achieve this end, Duncan replaced the formal classicism of the ballet with an expressive individualism. Her movements were more earthbound than ethereal and involved the entire body, not just the arms and legs. In lieu of the fanciful narratives common to the ballet, Duncan revived the ritualistic and religious focus of ancient dances. In her earliest treatise on dance, published during her association with Federn, Duncan forthrightly declared: "the dance of the future will have to become again a high religious art as it was with the Greeks" (Duncan, Dance of the Future, 24).

Duncan's understanding of the function of the dance in Greek drama followed closely Nietzsche's discussion of the dance in The Birth of Tragedy (1872). In that youthful examination of the Apollonian–Dionysian split in Greek culture, Nietzsche extolled the life-affirming function of the dancing, chanting satyrs of the Greek chorus. The satyrs, he explained, represented "the archetype of man[,] . . . the true human being," whose nature was not yet corrupted by "the lie of culture" and whose frenzied movements, in opposition to the highly rationalized Apollonian side of human nature, connected tragedy with the fullness of life.[29] Against the invariably false world of appearances, the chorus exposed the layers of life that had been covered up or obscured by civilization. Duncan forcefully identified with the chorus and throughout her career continually invoked the image of the chorus when discussing the intentions of her dance. "To unite the arts around the Chorus," she explained, "to give back to the dance its place as the Chorus, that is the ideal. When I have danced I have tried always to be the Chorus" (Duncan, *Art of the Dance*, 96).

The first step toward dancing the chorus was to reaffirm the essential goodness of the undraped human form, to acknowledge, that is, what Duncan believed the arts of painting, sculpture, and poetry had never forgotten: that the "noblest in art is the nude" (Duncan, *Dance of the Future*, 18). To this end Duncan discarded the tight bodice, gathered skirt, salmon-colored leggings, and padded toe shoes of the ballet to drape her body in a loose-fitting, lightweight, Grecian-style tunic worn over bare legs and feet. The garment revealed rather than concealed the natural contours and physical dimensions of her body even as it complemented the more fluid and relaxed movements of her dance.

As the self-proclaimed "poet of the Body" (Whitman, "Song of Myself," 48), Whitman conferred poetic authority on Duncan's pioneering resolve to represent her body openly and without shame. Throughout his oeuvre, but especially in poems like "I Sing the Body Electric," Whitman extolled the physical delights of both male and female bodies with unparalleled frankness and indulgence. At a time when women's bodies were still largely shielded from public scrutiny under yards of ruffles and ankle-length fabric, Duncan danced the "discorrupted" body of Whitman's poems. As her garment shifted with each movement of her dance, even covered parts of her body, especially her breasts, were frequently exposed to public view. "With Whitman, Isadora sang the body electric," forthrightly declared Rosamond Gilder in her 1928 review of the dancer's autobiography,[30] and indeed, like Whitman's poetic tribute to the body, Duncan's dance celebrated the beauty, physicality, and mystery of the human form while forcefully rejecting prurient Victorian attitudes toward morality and sexuality.

"If any thing is sacred," Whitman exclaimed in one of his poem's most memorable passages, "the human body is sacred, / . . . / And in man or woman a clean, strong, firm-fibred body is more beautiful than the most beautiful face" (Whitman, "I Sing the Body Electric," 99). The poet's fear less naming of even the most intimate body parts, including "the womb, the teats, nipples, [and] breast-milk" (Whitman, "I Sing the Body Electric," 101), assumed a new immediacy in the throbbing reality of Duncan's dance. By underscoring what novelist Floyd Dell termed "the goodness of the whole body,"[31] Duncan and Whitman challenged audiences to an important new awareness of the self. "Have you seen the fool that corrupted his own live body? or the fool that corrupted her own live body?" the poet asked in his assessment of "a woman's body at auction." "For they do not conceal themselves, and cannot conceal themselves" (Whitman, "I Sing the Body Electric," 99).

In this new democracy of the body, concealment denied the sacred authority invested in the self. Most important, in this new emphasis on the body was inscribed the foundation for a revitalized society, one based not on the traditional determinants of class, race, and power, but on an expanded sense of self. Duncan was adamant in her commitment to the life-sustaining potential of the dance. "For me," she explained, "the dance is not only the art that gives expression to the human soul through movement, but also the foundation of a complete conception of life, more free, more harmonious, more natural" (Duncan, *Art of the Dance*, 101). As Duncan matured and her body lost its youthful slimness, the added girth only confirmed the initial impetus of her dance. Writing in 1912, critics Caroline and Charles Caffin advised their readers to regard the dancer's increasingly chunky proportions as integral to her dance. "[I]t is no drawback," they declared, "that she herself has not the absolute perfection of proportion demanded by the Broadway show-girl. Rather it is a confirmation of her ideal, that the body naturally and simply used as a means of expression is a thing to be revered."[32] In his 1921 novel *The Briary-Bush*, Floyd Dell paid tribute to both Whitman and Duncan when he had his protagonist decide to become a dancer after pondering "a woman's body at auction." "Uncouth, wonderful lines," she exclaimed, "– not so much poetry to me as a revelation." For this clergyman's daughter, as for Duncan, Whitman's poem offered empowering evidence "that her body was a poem."[33] "O I say these are not the parts and poems of the body only," Whitman chanted in the concluding lines of his poem, "but of the soul, / O I say now these are the soul!" (Whitman, "I Sing the Body Electric," 101).

Particularly in her later years, Duncan took pleasure in associating her dances publicly with Whitman's poetic daring. When audiences vigorously objected to the dancer's bared breast, as they did in Boston in 1922, the same city that forty years earlier had banned *Leaves of Grass* as obscene, Duncan countered her critics with her own calculatedly Whitmanesque retort. "Why should I care what part of my body I reveal?" she cried. "Why is one part more evil than another? Is not all body and soul an instrument through which the artist expresses his inner message of beauty?" (Duncan, *Isadora Speaks*, 48). Later that same year, Duncan acknowledged Whitman directly following a concert witnessed by Hart Crane in Cleveland. Crane wrote a friend that at the conclusion of the performance, Duncan returned to the forestage, "her right breast and nipple quite exposed," and instructed those present "to go home and take from the bookshelf the works of Walt Whitman, and turn to the section called 'Calamus.'" Crane surmised that "[n]inety-nine percent" of the audience "had never heard of Whitman" but judged that "part of the beauty of her gesture."[34] For Crane as for Duncan, Whitman's unexampled audacity served as a potent reminder of the country's glaring need to throw off the constraining shackles of the past in order to move forward into a more vital and sustaining future.

If Whitman's rebel spirit infused Duncan's rebellious presentation of her body, his uncompromising rejection of the norms of poetic discourse was creatively reborn in the unorthodox movements of her dance. As Whitman willfully abandoned conventional linguistic structures, so Duncan rejected the codified structures of the ballet. Like the lines and stanzas in Whitman's poetry, Duncan's movements followed no externally mandated pattern and intentionally blurred the boundaries that had traditionally distinguished dance from other forms of movement.[35] Her gestures alternated between an astounding lyricism and an animallike vitality. Gordon Craig once remarked that Duncan "spoke of & read [Whitman] because she liked his 'barbaric yawp,'" whereas he "loved Whitman for his music & hated his 'yawp'" (Craig, quoted in Steegmuller, "*Your Isadora*," 63). But it was not just Whitman's barbarisms that attracted Duncan's attention. "Had she danced . . . rantingly, or ravingly," explained Max Eastman, "or even with the romantic extremism with which she talked about dancing, the revolution would have been a dud." Instead, "[s]he danced with a sense for the contained rapture, the never too completed deed, the dignity of the inner spirit" (Eastman, *Heroes I Have Known*, 72). Most important, she brought to the dance a mystical involvement that elevated even the simplest gesture to a level of captivating intensity such that, as Craig observed, she seemed to reinvent movement, "to move as no one had ever seen anyone move before" (Craig, quoted in Steegmuller, "*Your Isadora*," 360).

The anthropomorphized representation of the locomotive in "To a Locomotive in Winter," that "Type of the modern – emblem of motion and power – pulse of the continent" that had attracted Duncan's attention from the moment of her first serious encounter with the poetry no doubt struck her as a prescient trope for her dance. Like the California native, the willful locomotive surged ahead, "rumbling like an earthquake, rousing all, / Law of thyself complete, thine own track firmly holding." The locomotive's "ponderous side-bars," like arms, gyrated, "shuttling at thy sides," while "long, pale, floating vapor-pennants, tinged with delicate purple" enveloped the train's "cylindric body" in a manner suggestive of Duncan's diaphanous garment. Like the speeding locomotive, with its "great protruding head-light fix'd in front," Duncan, too, was lighting the way, not for a "train of cars behind, obedient, merrily following," but for a new generation of dancers and, more important, a new concept of the self. Her dance exhibited a similar lawless abandon, and it, too, reverberated with the expansiveness of nature. "For once come serve the Muse and merge in verse, even as here I see thee," Whitman urged the locomotive in his poem. For Duncan it was Whitman, not the locomotive, whom she would call on as her Muse and whose presence would resonate in the throbbing, swaying motion of her dancing form, "unpent and glad and strong" (Whitman, "To a Locomotive in Winter," 471–2).

In contrast to the ballet, where movement emanated from the base of the spine, Duncan centered her movement in the solar plexus in the upper torso, the area of the body traditionally associated with feeling and emotion.[36] It was here, in the body's midsection, that Duncan located the body's mystical center, the source of all movement and power. The dancer's discussion in *My Life* of her awakening to the spiritual authority of the solar plexus vividly recalls Whitman's mystical awakening to the soul in Section 5 of "Song of Myself." "For hours," she recalled, "I would stand quite still, my two hands folded between my breasts, covering the solar plexus." She remained in this position "as if in a trance" (Duncan, *My Life,* 75), until overcome by the discovery that here was the "temporal home of the soul" (Duncan, *My Life,* 341); here resided "the central spring of all movement, the crater of motor power, the unity from which all diversities of movements are born" (Duncan, *My Life,* 75). For both Duncan and Whitman the soul expressed itself through the physicality of the body, and for both its center radiated from the region of the heart. And although Whitman's was a decidedly genitalized heart, for both the awakening of the soul brought with it "the peace and knowledge that pass all the argument of the earth" (Whitman, "Song of Myself," 33). Duncan described how, after months of learning to "concentrate all my force to this one Centre," she found that "when I listened to music the rays and vibrations of the music streamed to this one fount of light within me." There they revealed themselves "in Spiritual Vision . . . and from this vision I could express them in Dance" (Duncan, *My Life,* 75). Elsewhere Duncan likened the centrally located solar plexus to the Chorus, "center of the drama, . . . center of a harmonious ensemble." Toward each "everything converged; from them everything went out like rays from a light" (Duncan, *Art of the Dance*, 94).

Both the centralizing authority and the mystical intensity of the solar plexus are inscribed in this dramatic and characteristic pose from her dance

Figure 9.4 Arnold Genthe, *Isadora Duncan.* Dance Collection, The New York Public Library for the Performing Arts, Astor, Lenox, and Tilden Foundations.

caught by the photographic lens of Arnold Genthe (Figure 9.4). With her feet firmly anchored to the bare earth and her arms extended up toward the sky, that is, with her extremities radiating outward from the soul, Duncan's body seems joined in a mystical union with the opposing forces of the universe. As dance historian Susan Leigh Foster has observed, Duncan's outstretched extremities made of her body "a conduit from earth to sky" (Foster, *Reading Dancing,* 79), a link between the mundane and the spiritual, between the present and the future. The backward thrust of her head, what Duncan termed "the universal Dionysiac movement" (Duncan, *Art of the Dance,* 91), similarly invokes the surrender of the intellect to the impulses of the soul.

As Duncan stripped away the artifices of the ballet, she removed as well the layers of civilized veneer that had distanced humans from their more vital human instincts. Like Whitman's call to cultivate one's unadulterated self, the lexicon of her dance signaled a return to more essential human movements. Her gestures were both more universal and more accessible than the highly conventionalized movements of the ballet. Included in her repertoire were such common, everyday movements as walking, skipping, hopping and light running steps. She even prostrated herself on the floor of the stage when the mood of the dance called for it. There were "no [stock] steps, no pirouettes, no elevation on to the toes, no display of trained agility," noted the Caffins, "nothing but natural poses, changing and melting into each other harmoniously and insensibly." They judged her movements "even somewhat limited in variety, because her aim is not to multiply poses but to discover in her own body a free and natural expression of what her intelligence and spirit prompt" (Caffin and Caffin, *Dancing and Dancers of Today,* 59). Reviewers continually commented on the seeming artlessness of her dance, often making distinctions between the movements they considered "dance" and those they did not. "Of late years Isadora has danced (in the conventional meaning of the word) less and less," observed dance critic, Carl Van Vechten following her third American tour.[37]

Similar observations were often leveled against Whitman, whose verse was criticized for its lack of conformity with the norms of poetic discourse. Its absence of standard rhythm, meter, and rhyme, together with its informal, conversational style, its diversionary asides to the reader, and its many colloquialisms, allied it more with the everyday language of the street than with the elevated diction of the academy. In the Preface to the 1855 *Leaves of Grass,* Whitman dismissed the commonly held notion that "the genius of the United States" resided "best or most" in its individuals and institutions of elevated stature and authority (Whitman, 1855 Preface, 712). For the poet who would dare to utter the "word of the modern, the word En-Masse" (Whitman, "Song of Myself," 51), the country's greatest prize lay "always most in the common people." "[T]hese too," he exclaimed, "are unrhymed poetry" (Whitman, 1855 Preface, 712), and it was these, the "divine average" (Whitman, "Starting From Paumanok," 21), whom Duncan elevated to new visibility in her dance. By stripping away the stilted language of the ballet, Duncan danced the vernacular Whitman sang. Her everyday movements resonated with the simplicity, directness, and infectious spontaneity of Whitman's earthbound, conversational rhetoric. "It used to be said," wrote the reviewer for the Boston *Transcript* in 1917, "that her whole stock in trade consisted of the movements which every normal man and woman can do; now it consists of the things which every normal man and woman habitually do."[38]

Inscribed in the gently evolving rhythms of Duncan's dance, and crucial to her understanding of the innate beauty and largeness of the human spirit, was a sense of the organic wholeness and fluid expressiveness of the great outdoors. As one who grew up a short distance from the ocean and often danced outdoors, Duncan shared Whitman's commitment to the freedom and spontaneity of nature. For both, nature represented an invigorating alternative to the limits and conventions associated with indoor life and a model of the organic wholeness essential to a sustained revitalization of the self. In her earliest treatise on the dance, Duncan explained the relationship between nature and her dance in the religious terms familiar to Whitman. She judged it her "holy mission" to "mirror" in her body "the waves, the winds, the movements of growing things, the flight of birds, the passing of clouds and finally the thought of man in relation to the universe" (Duncan, *Dance of the Future*, 26). Elsewhere she noted: "I always put into my movements a little of that divine continuity which gives to all of Nature its beauty and life" (Duncan, *Art of the Dance*, 102–3). In contrast to the discontinuous movements of the ballet, where passages of exquisite beauty alternated with moments of virtual inaction and where a rigid torso contravened the flowing movements of the body's arms and legs, Duncan's entire body moved as one flowing and continuous whole. Like the lapping motion of waves or the forward thrust of Whitman's wavelike lines, each movement of her dance seemed to grow out of the movement that preceded it and to anticipate that which followed. Crane acknowledged the powerful organicism of her efforts when he likened her dance to a "wave of life, a flaming gale" (Crane, *Letters of Hart Crane*, 109).

Among those early-twentieth-century observers who mediated their perception of Duncan's dance through the lens of Whitman's poetry, the Russian-born American painter Abraham Walkowitz left a legacy of drawings of Duncan's dance that resonate with the fluidity, organicism, and lyrical beauty of the dances themselves. "She was a Muse," Walkowitz enthused. "She had no laws. She didn't dance according to rules. She created. Her body was music. It was a body electric, like Walt Whitman."[39] In his drawings, Walkowitz employed the same economy of means, formal simplicity, and linear expressiveness that distinguished Duncan's work from that of other dancers. In this cluster of six drawings from the Hirshhorn Museum and Sculpture Garden (Figure 9.5), each movement seems organically linked to every other movement, and the whole seems larger than the sum of its parts. These drawings reveal as well that even when drawn to nature's melodic beauty, Duncan eschewed the refined artificialities of the ballet as resolutely as Whitman rejected the rhetorical flourishes of conventional poetry. Her leg, when raised, was always bent at the knee, never extended fully as in the ballet, and her bare feet, "instead of being a point of escape from reality as in the ballet, became the essential contact with the life-charged earth."[40] But it was not just nature's lyricism that attracted Duncan to the vibrancy of the outdoors. Like Whitman, she responded as well to nature's power, its roughness, and, above all, its magnitude. "Those who like to see pretty dancing, pretty girls, pretty things in general," cautioned Van Vechten, "will not find much pleasure in contemplating the art of Isadora." Her dancing was more "titanic" than pretty, characterized more by the challenges offered by nature's jagged mountains than by the beauty contained in its luscious and fertile valleys (Van Vechten, "The New Isadora," 31). Others discovered in her dance "occasional flashes of something animal" (quoted in Steegmuller, "Your Isadora," 44), qualities that resonate across the page of John Sloan's rugged drawing for *The Masses* (Figure 9.6).

Nature's largeness, its vast, uncharted vistas, and the freedom it offered the lone individual informed not only the lexicon of Duncan's dance, but its spatial, temporal, and aural dimensions as well. In contrast to the ballet, where elaborately appointed backdrops provided a realistic frame for the dance, Duncan danced alone on a bare stage covered only with green carpeting and surrounded by blue-gray curtains. The appointments suggested but did not literally describe the green grass and blue sky of nature. Initially the curtains were strung between classical columns, which reflected the Greek origins of her dance and were only slightly taller than she. After meeting Craig, Duncan eliminated the columns and stretched the curtains to the ceiling. Without the Greek filter, her dance achieved a more timeless and universal dimension, which approximated more nearly the unbounded largeness that Craig and Duncan both admired in Whitman's verse and that

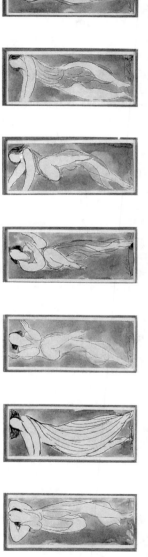

Figure 9.5 Abraham Walkowitz, *Isadora Duncan: Seven Studies*, pen & ink & watercolor on paper, 6 3/4 × 2 5/8 in. Hirshhorn Museum and Sculpture Garden, Smithsonian Institution, Gift of Joseph H. Hirshhorn, 1966. Photographer: Lee Stalsworth.

ISADORA DUNCAN IN THE "MARCHE MILITAIRE"

Figure 9.6 John Sloan, *Isadora Duncan in the "Marche Militaire," The Masses* VI, no. 9 (June 1915).

had informed Craig's earlier woodcut for *The Page.*[41] The boundlessness of nature, the timeless universality of the cosmos, and the panoramic vista of Whitman's verse resonated with compelling intensity in this expansive zone of personal, physical, and spiritual extension.

Shortly after they met Craig produced a portfolio of six drawings of

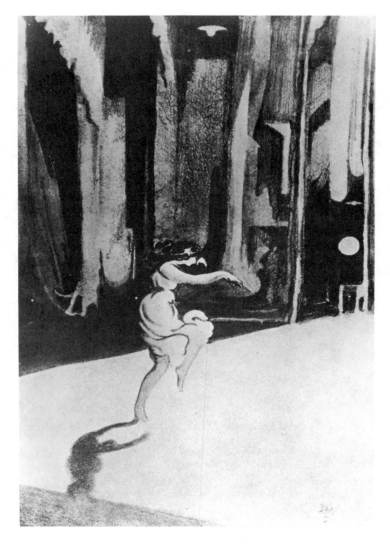

Figure 9.7 Edward Gordon Craig, *Isadora Duncan, Sechs bewegungstudien, 1906* (Leipzig: Inselverlag, 1906). Dance Collection, The New York Public Library for the Performing Arts, Astor, Lenox, and Tilden Foundations.

Duncan dancing, the most striking of which represented Duncan in a lively prancing gesture, alone on the stage of the Thalia Theater in Breslau, Germany (Figure 9.7).[42] Drawn from the wings, the image recalls Degas's informal, behind-the-scenes representations of French ballet dancers, but without the complicating angles and harsh lighting that Degas so loved. The smallness of Duncan's figure, contrasted against the undifferentiated largeness of the empty stage on which she performed, finds its most striking counterpart in Whitman's enchanting short poem "A Noiseless Patient Spider." Like the small, vulnerable spider, who "on a little promontory . . . stood isolated," Duncan confronted the "vacant vast surrounding" with nothing more than her own slight body. As her body noiselessly traversed the uncharted vista around her, she, too, seemed "Surrounded, detached, in measureless oceans of space." By her movements she not only defined the space but created an elaborate network of connectors between herself and her audience, a network that, although invisible, was every bit as significant as the richly patterned, life-sustaining web created by the spider. As she moved, she, too, "launch'd forth filament, filament, filament" out of herself, not the physical filament of the spider but the spiritual filament of her solar plexus. The "bridge" she established between herself and her audience, the "ductile anchor" (Whitman, "A Noiseless Patient Spider," 450) that penetrated to the core of all who experienced her dance, seemed to connect her as well with the universal brotherhood of humanity. In this arena of unhampered freedom, Duncan danced the "amplitude of time" (Whitman, "Song of Myself," 48), the link between present, past, and future, between the material and the immaterial, between the lone individual and the challenges of the unknown. Above all, she danced Whitman's claim that "the unseen is proven by the seen" (Whitman, "Song of Myself," 31).

A musical largeness complemented the spatial and temporal magnitude of Duncan's work, as it did Whitman's verse. In place of the standard and often banal music of contemporary ballet, Duncan danced sections of Beethoven's stirring *Seventh Symphony,* Tchaikovsky's *Marche Slave,* Gluck's *Iphigenia in Aulis,* and Schubert's *Unfinished Symphony.* The music amplified the humanity, emotional expressiveness, and animallike vitality of her movements even as it underscored the organic wholeness of her dance. As she moved, Duncan's body evoked the beauty, largeness, and emotional intensity of the music, much as Whitman's free-verse line evoked the tonal richness and operatic range of the human voice.[43] "[I]n surrendering my body unresistingly to [the] rhythms [of the world's great composers]," Duncan observed, "I have hoped to recover the natural cadences of human movements which have been lost for centuries" (Duncan, *Art of the Dance,* 90).

Like *Leaves of Grass,* Duncan's dance was firmly anchored in the present yet compellingly suggestive of a more fulfilling, humane, and harmonious future. She, too, sought to "launch all men and women forward with [her] into the Unknown" (Whitman, "Song of Myself," 80). Dancing on a bare stage devoid of props and distracting scenery, yet accompanied by the rich, full music of the great romantic composers, Duncan exuded the dignity, daring, and untrammeled potential of the individual. "[I]n watching her we had a sense of satisfied longing," observed her sister-in-law, Margherita Duncan. It was not that she was "supremely right in every movement she made," but rather that she "translated into visibility" the "latent aspirations" of her audience.[44] For those like the American painter Robert Henri, who were themselves steeped in Whitman's verse, Duncan's dance brought to mind "the great voice" of the American poet. In the program of one of her New York concerts, Henri explained: "Back of her gesture I see a deep philosophy of freedom, and of dignity, of simplicity and of order. She is one of the prophets who open to our vision the possibility of a life where full natural growth and full natural expression will be the aim of all people. When I see her dance it is not only the beauty of her expression that fills me with emotion, but it is this promise she gives of a full and beautiful life for those who are to come."[45] In similar fashion, in the socialist journal *The Masses,* Floyd Dell hailed Duncan's dance as projecting "a future more radiant than any I had ever seen in my Socialist and Nietzschean visions." It was not enough, he argued, "to throw God from his pedestal, and dream of superman and the co-operative commonwealth: one must have *seen* Isadora Duncan to die happy."[46]

Duncan danced an intoxicating voyage of self-discovery and continually reminded her audiences that "[t]o see in the dance only a frivolous or pleasant diversion [was] to degrade it" (Duncan, *Art of the Dance,* 103). More important, she linked the discovery of the self with the procreative function of the female body. In *The Dance of the Future,* in a statement worth quoting at length, Duncan termed it the role of the dancer to "help womankind to a new knowledge of the possible strength and beauty of their bodies and the relation of their bodies to the earth nature and to the children of the future." The dancer of the future

> will dance not in the form of nymph, nor fairy, nor coquette but in the form of woman in its greatest and purest expression. . . . She shall dance the freedom of woman. . . . She will dance the body emerging again from centuries of civilized forgetfulness, emerging not in the nudity of primitive man, but in a new nakedness, no longer at war with spirituality and intelligence, but joining itself forever with this intelligence in a glorious harmony.

"It is not only a question of true art," Duncan stressed, ". . . [i]t is a question of the development of perfect mothers and the birth of healthy and beautiful children. The dancing school of the future is to develop and to show the ideal form of woman" (Duncan, *Dance of the Future*, 23–5). Strong, assertive, earthbound, and fully in control of her body and her future, Duncan danced the "new woman." By denying what she termed the "inane coquetry" of the ballet (Duncan, *My Life*, 342), she gave new respect to the female body, treating it not as an object of sexual desire, but as a formidable locus of power and authority. She even danced pregnant. At a time when pregnant women were virtually banished from public view, Duncan danced until the sixth month of both of her pregnancies, her swelling body fully revealed under the loose folds of her garment. "Everything rustling, promising New Life. That is what my Dance means –" Duncan exclaimed (Duncan, *My Life*, 242).

Whitman, too, discovered in the female body a striking model of creative power, and he, too, considered a "sane athletic maternity" to be woman's "crowning attribute." "I have sometimes thought," he wrote in *Democratic Vistas*, ". . . that the sole avenue and means of a reconstructed sociology depended, primarily, on a new birth, elevation, expansion, invigoration of woman." His parameters for a reconstituted literature underscored on every level and with uncanny precision Duncan's demands for a new dance. A "new founded literature," he explained, was "not merely to copy and reflect existing surfaces, . . . not only to amuse, pass away time, celebrate the beautiful, the refined, the past, or exhibit technical rhythmic, or grammatical dexterity." Rather, such a literature was to probe "underlying life, [to be] religious, consistent with science, . . . teaching and training men – and, as perhaps the most precious of its results, [to achieve] the entire redemption of woman."[47] The poet reiterated these beliefs shortly before his death when, in conversation with Horace Traubel, he termed *Leaves of Grass* "essentially a woman's book."[48] Whitman's outspoken support for "the woman as well as the man" (Whitman, *Prose Works* II, 373) earned him a place of honor among early-twentieth-century feminists and prompted Floyd Dell to declare that "[w]hen the true history of this movement is written it will contain more about Herbert Spencer and Walt Whitman, perhaps, than about Victoria Woodhull and Tennessee Claflin. In any case, it is to the body that one looks for the Magna Charta of feminism" (Dell, *Women as World Builders*, 44–5). Duncan fully agreed. For her and for those eager to reinvent both themselves and their society, her dance seemed the cornerstone of such a charter with Whitman as its poetic foundation.

NOTES

1 The other two were Nietzsche and Jean Jacques Rousseau. Isadora Duncan, *My Life* (1927; rpt. New York: Liveright, 1955), p. 80. Subsequent quotations from this text will be cited parenthetically as *My Life*.

2 Max Eastman, *Heroes I Have Known* (New York: Simon and Schuster, 1942), pp. 70, 71, 86. Subsequent quotations from this work will be cited parenthetically as *Heroes I Have Known*.

3 Walt Whitman, "Poets to Come," *Leaves of Grass, Comprehensive Reader's Edition*, ed. Harold W. Blodgett and Sculley Bradley (New York: New York University Press, 1965), p. 14. Subsequent quotations from Whitman's poetry will be taken from this edition and cited parenthetically in the text.

4 Duncan's parents divorced when she was less than a year old, and she rarely saw her father, a banker.

5 Ingersoll was a friend of Whitman's in his later years and spoke at his funeral. It is not known whether Dora Duncan knew of this connection.

6 See Fredrika Blair, *Isadora Duncan* (New York: McGraw-Hill, 1986), p. 26; Duncan, *My Life,* p. 43; "Emotional Expression," *The Director* 1 (March 1898):109–10.

7 Duncan, quoted in "Emotional Expression," pp. 110–11.

8 Sir Edwin Arnold visited Whitman in Camden in September 1889 while returning to England from Japan, but there is no evidence that Duncan knew of this visit or ever discussed Whitman with Arnold. Gay Wilson Allen, *Solitary Singer* (1955; rpt. Chicago and London: University of Chicago Press, 1985), p. 534.

9 Duncan took pride in the fact that her father, whom she rarely saw, was an amateur poet and claimed that one of his poems "was in a way a prophecy of my entire career." Unfortunately the poem is not known. See Duncan, *My Life,* p. 16. In 1922, when she was forty-five, Duncan married a Russian poet, the youthful Sergei Essenin.

10 Edward Thorstenberg, "The Walt Whitman Cult in Germany," *The Sewanee Review* 19 (January 1911):71.

11 O. E. Lessing, "Whitman and German Critics," *Journal of English and German Philology* 9 (Winter 1910):89.

12 Thorstenberg, "Walt Whitman Cult," pp. 76–7; see also Monika Schaper, *Walt Whitmans "Leaves of Grass" in deutschen Übersetzungen – Eine rezeptionsgeschichtliche Untersuchung* (Frankfurt: Peter Lang; Bern: Herbert Lang, 1976), pp. 171–4.

13 For the remainder of her life, Duncan kept a translation of *Zarathustra* by her bed. See Ross McDougall, *Isadora: A Revolutionary in Art and Love* (New York: Thomas Nelson and Sons, 1960), p. 17; Victor Seroff, *The Real Isadora* (New York: Dial, 1971), p. 53.

14 Karl Federn, *Walt Whitman, Grashalme, Eine Auswahl* (Minden: 1904). This passage appears in translation in A. Von Ende, "Walt Whitman in Germany," *Town & Country* (June 20, 1901):12; Von Ende's article was reprinted in Horace Traubel's journal, *The Conservator* 14 (January 1904):167–9 and (February 1904):183–5. Federn's essay was originally published in *Die Zeit* in 1897 and was reprinted in *Essays zur amerikanischen Literatur* (Halle: 1899).

15 Karl Federn, "Einleitung," in Isadora Duncan, *Der Tanz der Zukunft (The Dance of the Future)* (Leipzig: Eugen Diederichs, 1903), p. 7 (translation by Steven Rowan and the author). Duncan's essay was first published in English in *The Dance* (New York: Forest Press, 1909). Subsequent quotations from this work will be cited parenthetically as *Dance of the Future.*

16 Craig, quoted in Francis Steegmuller, *"Your Isadora": The Love Story of Isadora Duncan and Gordon Craig* (New York: Random House and the New York Public Library, 1974), p. 63. Subsequent quotations from this work will be cited parenthetically as *"Your Isadora."*

17 For Craig's contributions to the theater, see his *Index to the Story of My Days* (New York: Viking Press, 1957), *On the Art of the Theatre* (Edinburgh and London: T. N. Foulis, 1905), and *Towards a New Theatre* (London and Toronto: J. M. Dent and Sons, Ltd., 1913); see also Christopher Innes, *Edward Gordon Craig* (Cambridge: Cambridge University Press, 1983); and Irene Eynat-Confino, *Beyond the Mask* (Carbondale and Edwardsville: Southern Illinois University Press, 1987).

18 William Michael Rossetti, ed., *Poems of Walt Whitman* (London: John Camden Hotton, 1868). For Whitman's reception in England, see Harold W. Blodgett, *Walt Whitman in England* (Ithaca, N.Y.: Cornell University Press, 1934).

19 Irving described the visit in "Mr. Irving's Second Tour in America," *The Theatre* 5 (April 1885):178–9. Strangely, Craig makes no mention of the visit in his biography, *Henry Irving* (London: J. M. Dent and Sons, 1930).

20 For Stoker's account of the visit with Whitman and of his own interest generally in the poet, see Bram Stoker, *Personal Reminiscences of Henry Irving* (1906; rpt. Westport, Conn.: Greenwood Press, 1970), II, pp. 92–111. See also Horace Traubel, ed., *With Walt Whitman in Camden* (Philadelphia: University of Pennsylvania Press, 1953), IV, pp. 179–86.

21 Craig, *Index to the Story of My Days,* p. 141; Edward Craig, *Gordon Craig: The Story of His Life* (London: Victor Gollancz, 1968), pp. 80–1; for Duncan's response to the manuscript, see the following discussion.

22 In the same issue Craig praised Queen Victoria, born within a week of Whitman in 1819, as "the greatest lady of the century." "Walt Whitman," *The Page* I, no. 5 (May 1898):n.p. Craig was undoubtedly aware of Whitman's earlier tribute to Queen Victoria, "For Queen Victoria's Birthday."

23 "Quotations. Walt Whitman, 1855," *The Page* I, no. 12 (December 1898):n.p.

24 "Walt Whitman, October 20th, 1876," *The Page* II, no. 1 (1899):n.p. *The Page* also reviewed Richard Maurice Bucke's *Notes and Fragments* (II, no. 4 [1899]) and reproduced in facsimile one of Craig's Whitman manuscripts, a partial draft of "After the Sea-Ship" (II, no. 2 [1899]).

25 *The Mask* 4, no. 1 (July 1911):1–3. For more on Craig's relationship with Traubel, see the Craig–Traubel Correspondence, Horace Traubel Papers, Box 60, Library of Congress, Washington, D.C.

26 Duncan, *Isadora Speaks,* ed. Franklin Rosemont (San Francisco: City Lights Books, 1981), p. 123. Subsequent quotations from this work will be cited parenthetically as *Isadora Speaks.*

27 In London Duncan studied with Ketti Lanner and in New York with Marie Bonfanti. Blair, *Isadora Duncan,* pp. 28–9.

28 Duncan, "The Philosopher's Stone of Dancing," in Sheldon Cheney, ed., *The Art of the Dance* (1928; rpt. New York: Theater Arts Books, 1977), pp. 51–2. Subsequent quotations from this work will be cited parenthetically as Duncan, in *Art of the Dance*.

29 Friedrich Nietzsche, *The Birth of Tragedy and the Case of Wagner*, trans. Walter Kaufmann (New York: Vintage Books, 1967), p. 61. In Brooklyn in the 1850s Whitman had engravings of Dionysus and his teacher, the satyr Silenus, on the wall of his room. Moncure Daniel Conway, *Autobiography: Memories and Experiences* (1904; rpt. New York: Negro Universities Press, 1969), p. 218.

30 Rosamond Gilder, "'I Sing the Body Electric,'" *Theatre Arts Monthly* 12 (March 1928):224.

31 Floyd Dell, *Women as World Builders: Studies in Modern Feminism* (Chicago: Forbes and Co., 1913), pp. 48–9. Subsequent quotations from this work will be cited parenthetically as *Women as World Builders*.

32 Caroline Caffin and Charles F. Caffin, *Dancing and Dancers of Today* (New York: Dodd, Mead and Co., 1912), p. 53. Subsequent quotations from this work will be cited parenthetically as *Dancing and Dancers of Today*.

33 Floyd Dell, *The Briary-Bush* (New York: The Macaulay Co., 1921), pp. 192–3.

34 Hart Crane, *The Letters of Hart Crane, 1916–1932*, ed. Brom Weber (Berkeley and Los Angeles: University of California Press, 1965), p. 109. In contrast to the majority of those present, Crane found Duncan's dance "glorious beyond words" and claimed that it left him "stimulated almost beyond the power to walk straight" (p. 109). Subsequent quotations from this work will be cited parenthetically as *Letters of Hart Crane*.

35 Outside established balletic traditions, Duncan found much that attracted her in the popular movement theories of François Delsarte (1811–71), whose mystically inspired exercise manuals claimed a link between body poses and emotional states. For Delsarte's contribution to the dance, see Nancy Lee Chalba Ruyter, *Reformers and Visionaries: The Americanization of the Art of the Dance* (New York: Dance Horizons, 1979), pp. 17–30.

36 Susan Leigh Foster, *Reading Dancing: Bodies and Subjects in Contemporary American Dance* (Berkeley: University of California Press, 1986), p. 79. Subsequent quotations from this work will be cited parenthetically as *Reading Dancing*.

37 Carl Van Vechten, "The New Isadora," in Paul Magriel, ed., *Nijinsky, Pavlova, Duncan: Three Lives in Dance* (New York: Da Capo Press, 1977), p. 31. Subsequent quotations from this work will be cited parenthetically as "The New Isadora."

38 Quoted in "Isadora Duncan Dances the Marseillaise," *Current Opinion* 62 (January 1917):31.

39 Abraham Walkowitz, "A Tape Recorded Interview with Abraham Walkowitz," *Journal of the Archives of American Art* 9 (January 1969):15.

40 Louis Horst and Carroll Russell, *Modern Dance Forms in Relation to the Other Modern Arts* (San Francisco: Impulse Publications, 1961), n.p.

41 In his copy of *My Life*, Craig sketched the stage with the curtains strung between classical columns, terming the whole "all very modest & useful." His sketch is reproduced in Steegmuller, "*Your Isadora*," p. 24. What, if any, contri-

bution Craig made to Duncan's revised setting is unknown. In later years heforcefully denied any involvement whatsoever, but Craig's notebooks and letters from 1905 record a variety of staging instructions, including the comment, in a letter to his mother, that he was "sending designs for new scene for Miss D to the scene painters." During this same period, he designed the monogram for Duncan's stationery, program covers, and kiosk posters for her 1905 tour. See Cynthia Splatt, *Isadora Duncan & Gordon Craig* (San Francisco: Book Club of California, 1988), pp. 32–49.

42   Each drawing was accompanied by a few bars of Duncan's dance music. A free-verse poem, which stressed the mood of joyous harmony Craig admired in her dance, served as the prologue. Edward Gordon Craig, *Isadora Duncan, Sechs bewegungstudien, 1906* (Leipzig: Inselverlag, 1906), n.p. The poem and the drawings are reproduced in Magriel, *Nijinsky, Pavlova, Duncan,* pp. 64–9.

43   On the musical character of Whitman's verse, see especially Robert D. Faner, *Walt Whitman and Opera* (Carbondale and Edwardsville: Southern Illinois University Press, 1951).

44   Margherita Duncan, "Isadora," in Cheney, *Art of the Dance,* p. 17.

45   Robert Henri, "Isadora Duncan and Walt Whitman," *Dionysion* 1 (1915):n.p.

46   Floyd Dell, "Who Said That Beauty Passes Like a Dream?", reprinted in *Looking at Life* (New York: Alfred A. Knopf, 1924), p. 49.

47   Walt Whitman, *Prose Works* (New York: New York University Press, 1964), II, p. 372. For an extended analysis of the connections Whitman drew between poetic creation and procreation, see M. Jimmie Killingsworth, *Whitman's Poetry of the Body* (Chapel Hill and London: University of North Carolina Press, 1989), pp. 61–72.

48   Walt Whitman, Quoted in Traubel, ed., *With Walt Whitman in Camden* (New York: Appleton, 1908), II, p. 331.

10

ALAN TRACHTENBERG

Walt Whitman: Precipitant of the Modern

"As for Whitman," confessed the young Ezra Pound in England in 1909, "I read him (in many parts) with acute pain, but when I write of certain things I find myself using his rhythms." In the same essay, "What I feel about Walt Whitman," Pound pronounced a judgment already shared by his generation about the redoubtable figure who had died just seventeen years earlier: "He *is* America. His crudity is an exceeding great stench, but it is America. . . . I honour him for he prophesied me while I can only recognize him as a forebear of whom I ought to be proud." And he added, "Mentally I am a Walt Whitman who has learned to wear a collar and a dress shirt (although at times inimical to both)."[1]

Whitman had his own ideas about collars and dress shirts. "Undrape," he cries in "Song of Myself,"

> Undrape! you are not guilty to me, nor stale nor discarded,
> I see through the broadcloth and gingham whether or no,
> And am around, tenacious, aquisitive, tireless, and cannot be shaken away.[2]

As if taunted by the call, Pound called back, naming and renaming Whitman "our American keynote" in 1913 in *Patria Mia* (123), the "pig-headed father" in the poem "A Pact" of 1915 and, in the 1909 essay, the American "genius":

> Entirely free from the renaissance humanist ideal of the complete man or from Greek idealism, he [Whitman] is content to be what he is, and he is his time and his people. He is a genius because he has vision of what he is and of his function. He knows that he is a beginning and not a classically finished work.
>
> (145)

It may still astonish us to learn how much Whitman meant to Pound, how little the young modernist was able to shake off the tenacious Whitman in the early years of the "new poetry." It is as if the young rebel felt obliged, for the sake of proclaiming his own antithetical desire for "a renaissance in America of all the lost or temporarily mislaid beauty, truth, valour, glory of

Greece, Italy, England and all the rest of it" (146), to pin the native genius loci into a manageable hold, to claim for himself, collar, shirt, and inimical refinement, a continuity with something native. "It was you that broke the new wood," he concedes in "A Pact"; "now is a time for carving."[3]

Pound's struggle with Whitman deserves more study in its own right; I evoke it here to introduce the larger matter of Whitman's presence among the American moderns, the young artists who made an aesthetic revolution in the early twentieth century. It should be no surprise to find him there, the author of "Years of the Modern" and similar prophecies, hailed as forerunner, progenitor, mentor by young rebels across the range of the modern arts. A roll call of Whitmanian modernists includes the most prominent names among the innovators who altered the look and sound and expectations in several media: Louis Sullivan and Frank Lloyd Wright in architecture; Robert Henri, Marsden Hartley, John Marin, and Joseph Stella in painting; Isadora Duncan in dance; Pound, William Carlos Williams, Wallace Stevens, and Hart Crane in poetry; and Gertrude Stein, Sherwood Anderson, Jean Toomer, and John Dos Passos in prose fiction – not to mention the provocateurs and agitators who prepared a sympathetic climate for aesthetic change: William James, George Santayana, Horace Traubel, Emma Goldman, Van Wyck Brooks, and Waldo Frank. Source, precursor, native genius, enfranchiser: Whitman looms as the single most revered and honored and idolized figure from the recent past in the minds of artists dedicated to "making it new" from the turn of the century through the 1920s.

Given a story so resonant with implications regarding native aspects of early American modernism, it is striking that Whitman's presence there has not yet been examined in detail. A kind of camouflage may explain the matter. As Pound remarked: "He [Whitman] was so near the national colour that the nation hardly perceived him against that background" (124). Densely saturated in the times, the story still needs trying out, however. We stand to learn from it something about indigenous sources of the modernist impulse, the tendencies toward radical change in the arts. The notion of modernism as a foreign import, an effect of such invasions and interventions as that represented by the Armory Show of 1913, still colors our understanding of the aesthetic movements of the period. The Whitman story not only sheds light on American sources but provides a clue to an American ripeness for change. Tracking his presence and influence can open new routes of investigation into the social history from which artistic modernism sprung, a premodernist genealogy in turn-of-the-century friendships, filiations, and erotic relations among men heartened by what seemed Whitman's example or at least encouragement in the fervid "Calamus" poems.

The Whitman presence helps us identify collectivities of interest, leads us to artists' colonies and little magazines, intersecting networks that trace paths of circulation of ideas and feelings and perceptions forbidden in genteel circles and in a public realm still gripped by puritanical canons. We find Henry James reading and weeping over Whitman with Edith Wharton, among whose papers one finds manuscript notes for an essay on Whitman's language; William James citing Whitman in a place of honor in his revolutionary book *Pragmatism* in 1907, planting the poet-prophet among the foremost examples of the new outlook on experience that would underwrite modernist experiments in America; and others in the Harvard community drawn to Whitman, heartened by his worldly freshness, his tranquil acceptance of emotion, his guiltless eroticism – the philosophers James and Santayana, the poets Edmund Clarence Stedman and William Vaughn Moody, the critic and early biographer of Whitman, Bliss Perry – a community Gertrude Stein passed through on her way toward her own new and "outlaw" method of composition; the Walt Whitman Fellowship, with its dinner meetings presided over by the sweet-spirited socialist Horace Traubel and other "hot little prophets," in Bliss Perry's epithet – Traubel, Whitman's Boswell in the last years in Camden, friend of Marsden Hartley and a familiar among artists like John Sloan and Stieglitz's 291 group; African-American writers like Alain Locke, James Weldon Johnson, and Jean Toomer, finding in Whitman's Dionysian universalism (as they saw it) a ground for the program Locke and others conceived for a New Negro art in the 1920s, a program to transform folk culture into high art.

Indeed, Whitman as influence or forerunner or mentor or any other title signifying historical precedence seems inadequate, too pale to do justice to the enabling power of his image among these and numerous other artists in the generation following his death. He seemed there – in the body of Isadora Duncan dancing, for example: "In seeing Isadora Duncan dance, I am always reminded of the great voice of Walt Whitman," remarked Robert Henri.[4] It was common to hear Whitman hailed, saluted as if in reply to his great voice, as if he himself might yet reply. "The spirit of Walt Whitman stands behind THE SEVEN ARTS," proclaimed the editors of that fervently visionary journal in 1916; "What we are seeking, is what he sought."[5] On the occasion of the exhibition of the Society for Independent Artists in the spring of the same year, where Duchamp made Dada a historic American event by submitting a mass-produced urinal titled "Fountain," his journal *The Blind Man* included this invocation: "May the spirit of Walt Whitman guide the Indeps. Long live his memory, and long live the Indeps."[6] "I don't know why I had that instinctive drive to get in touch with Whitman,"

William Carlos Williams recalled about his youth.[7] And Hart Crane, the poet most fatefully inflamed with the fever of Whitman's presence, in a letter in March 1923, in the exhilarating early stages of his epic of American modernity, *The Bridge,* stated: "I begin to feel myself directly connected with Whitman. I feel myself in currents that are positively awesome in their extent and possibilities."[8]

Modernism emerged in America and shaped itself at least in part as a diverse collective response to Whitman's call, an answer to the Answerer. Why Whitman? What gave rise to this extraordinary sense of presence? The purposes were not simple. Whitman delineates a composite figure: a father fashioned as much to resist as to obey, an older brother sharing secrets, a lover making cryptic signs by which all comrades of manly love might recognize and greet each other, a priestly poet embarked on a sacred mission of redemption and transfiguration for his people. Why did the likes of Williams and Crane and Hartley and Duncan in their several ways fashion such a figure answerable to their needs? How did their invented Whitman define and serve their needs?

William Carlos Williams recalled that when he entered the University of Pennsylvania in 1902 he brought *Leaves of Grass* with him, "absorbed it with enthusiasm," and kept a Whitmanian notebook in which he jotted down "quick spontaneous poems." At the same time he swore by Keats, called him "my God." Curious, he wrote later, "that I was so preoccupied with the studied elegance of Keats on one hand and with the raw vigor of Whitman on the other." In retrospect, he remarked on the aesthetic and emotional schizophrenia this dual love implied. The Whitman notebooks held his "secret life," a "sort of purgation and confessional, to clear my head and my heart from turbid obsessions." Keats represented the conventionally romantic side of that turbidity. What the secret notebooks represented, Williams's desire to write a poetry that was simple, direct, and passional, eventually prevailed and guided Williams to the discovery or invention of his own voice. Whitman helped release the emotional energy Williams required to break with convention. In Whitman, he wrote years later, "we hear the cry of man breaking through the barrier of constraint IN ORDER TO BE ABLE TO SAY *exactly* what was in his mind."[9] Sanctioning desire, rebellion, the urge to be and sing oneself, Whitman's voice spurred Williams to break through the constraints of romantic verse.

Similarly, in an essay in 1909, Robert Henri, painter and teacher and leading figure of the proto-modernist "Ashcan School," wrote: "It seems to me that before a man tries to express anything to the world he must recognize in himself an individual, a new one, distinct from others. Walt Whitman did this, and that is why I think his name so often comes to me."[10] Marsden Hartley, writing of Whitman and Cézanne, said, "they have done more, these modern pioneers, for the liberation of the artist, and for the 'freeing' of painting and poetry than any other men of modern time. Through them, painting and poetry have become literally free, and through them it is that the young painters and poets have sought new fields for self deliverance."[11]

"Liberation of the artist." The phrase needs amendment to read "liberation of the *male* artist" or "liberation of men to *be* artists." And by "artist," what these figures meant, as did Whitman, principally described a passional condition of being, a sense of the oneness of body and mind or spirit. Whitman as male liberator, harbinger of a sensual and sensuous maleness at the core of the modernist rebellion, tells us, symptomatically, of a major current of change in turn-of-the-century America. The figure of the liberator bespeaks a historical rupture, a crisis in the cultural image of manhood. Why such insistence on liberation? Liberation from what? Conventional bourgeois repression of the senses and feelings, a reification of gender roles, goes only partway toward an explanation of the pervasive need for Whitman as a father who, paradoxically, enables rebellion. Needs for change in the understanding and practice of engendered sexual roles have complex sources at this time. They might be linked, for example, to the reconstruction of American business corporations in this era and to the accompanying first wave of mass consumerism in America. Highly stratified, hierarchical forms took over the structure of institutions in which middle-class white males increasingly found their identities within professional vocations. Together with the announced "closing of the frontier" near the time of Whitman's death in 1892, the corporate reorganization of American life drove older models of manhood – the rugged individual, the freebooting entrepreneur, the pioneer – into obsolescence, replaced by the ideal of the complacent, obedient company man. For men of the 1890s troubled by this loss of images of masculine possibility, the picture of Whitman the loafer, the freebooting tramp, provided a beckoning secretive alternative. In 1898 John Jay Chapman imagined just such a Whitman:

> A man who leaves his office and gets into a canoe on a Canadian river, sure of ten days' release from the cares of business and housekeeping, has a thrill of joy such as Walt Whitman has here and there thrown into his poetry. One might say that to have done this is the greatest accomplishment in literature. Walt Whitman, in some of his lines, breaks the frame of poetry and gives us life in the throb.[12]

Life in the throb – on holiday from the office in the remote wilderness: Chapman constructs a Whitman to tease the Walter Mitty fantasies of the corporate drudge. The image brings to mind the secret notebooks of student William Carlos Williams at the University of Pennsylvania.

Another need for Whitman, more elusive, difficult to pin down, is the emergence at the end of the nineteenth century, here and in England especially, of a distinct category of "homosexual," a prohibitive label that outlawed the homoerotic possibility within homosocial relationships, exactly the sort of open, loving relations Whitman celebrated as the defining praxis of democracy. Among the repressive forces at the turn of the century, then, must be counted anxieties produced by thoughts of homosexual possibility, by the public naming of love between men as "queer." Whitman provided an outlet, a sanctioning of male expression of love and desire, whether straight or gay. He seemed a grand model for the alternate possibility of a man's being emotional, expressive, a lover of beautiful bodies (or of all bodies because all are beautiful) – and still a man, still of the masculine gender. And perhaps more important in light of the large number of male artists under his banner who preferred male lovers, he also liberated the closeted male homosexual artist, not to public revelation but at least to self-acceptance as artist and man.[13] Any accounting of the modernist embrace of Whitman in these years must include this dynamic of sexual identity. Of course, the flourishing of bohemian communities such as those formed in Greenwich Village also provided networks of security and encouragement for the artist whose identity as a sexual being threatened risk and danger. But the role of Whitman in providing a model, not simply for gay artists but for men in general who suffered anxiety about the masculine propriety of a career in art, cannot be ignored as a factor in his constructive presence among the moderns. It is likely, especially given the evidence of Isadora Duncan's rapturous remarks about Whitman – she called herself "the spiritual daughter of Walt Whitman"[14] – that the sanctioning effect of his image affected women artists in a similar way.

To be sure, Whitman's presence gave rise to certain questionable effects as well – the bequest, for example, of a style of writing and address we might dub "Whitmanesque." Whitmanesquerie can be recognized by its favoring of a long, engorged, fragmented, and shapeless line of unmetered verse. Many took it as the veritable sign of freedom and authenticity. "Meanwhile the verse of Walt Whitman . . . soaring above as a white aereoplane of Help . . . was leading the sails of my Art through the blue vastity of Phantasy, while the telegraph wires, trembling around, as if expecting to propagate a new musical message, like aerial guides leading to Immensity, were keeping me awake with an insatiable thirst for new adventures."[15] Thus wrote the visionary painter Joseph Stella. Whitmanesquerie – in the declamations of Vachel Lindsay, Stephen Vincent Benet, and Carl Sandburg; in private letters and public essays in the period – is the deceptive guise of a presence that caricatures the serious role of Whitman's afterlife in the generation after his death fired up by new conditions and prospects for change in American life. Whitman's legacy helped them recognize the "modern" in their lives. He was most provocative and nourishing not as a model to mimic but as a force to engage with, as much to resist as to adore. "The only way to be like Whitman is to write *unlike* Whitman,"[16] wrote Williams in 1917.

The perception of modernity Whitman precipitated in his serious readers in the two decades after his death includes a number of key ideas seized and developed by modernists: the idea, known as "organicism," that form follows function; "The cleanest expression is that which finds no sphere worthy of itself and makes one" (717); the identity of body and soul; the notion of the "body electric"; the equality of all persons and things; their eligibility for art and dignity; "All truths wait in all things"; "Every existence has its idiom" (168); the heroism and "divine average" of the common life; "mine a word of the modern, the word En-Masse" (51); the priestly role of the artist; the necessity of art and yet the priority of life over art.

This last phrase assumes the highest priority in Whitman's own theory of modernity, a theory of a poetry that measures its success as its ability to produce discernible effects on readers – literally to produce a future. He writes in one of the original twelve poems of 1855, later titled "Song of the Answerer":

You think it would be good to be the writer of melodious verses;
Well it would be good to be the writer of melodious verses;
But what are verses beyond the flowing character you could have? . . . or beyond
 beautiful manners and behaviour?
Or beyond one manly or affectionate deed of an apprenticeboy? . . . or an old
 woman? . . . or man that has been in prison or likely to be in prison?[17]

"The true question to ask respecting a book," he quotes the librarian of Congress in *Democratic Vistas*, "is, *has it help'd any human soul?*"[18] "Not the book needs so much to be the complete thing, but the reader of the book does."[19] The theory rests on the radical incompleteness of the poem: certainly Whitman's most audacious claim on poetics, that the reader completes the poem as life.

Whitman found such readers among the moderns. "Read some of Whitman's 'Song of Myself.' Then out for a walk in the sunshine," John Sloan noted in his diary in 1909.[20] Not alone among precursors – indeed, his influence was mixed with and mediated by that of Emerson, Nietzsche, and Bergson, among others – but with his own uniquely persuasive voice, Whitman seemed to the early moderns exactly the figure they needed, a figure of possibility who opened doors, indeed removed them altogether: "Unscrew the locks from the doors! / Unscrew the doors themselves from their jambs!" (52). Whitman dilated his readers, led them into the sunshine, staged for them a carnival of release, a free acceptance of the pleasure of things without stint or limit. He taught the sufficiency of the self, the present, the here and now, and provoked dissatisfaction with stasis, with limits: "I open my scuttle at night and see the far-sprinkled systems, / And all I see multiplied as high as I can cipher edge but the rim of the farther systems" (82).

Openness surely lies close to the heart of Whitman's legacy to the early American moderns, openness of form and its corollary, openness of emotion, of being, to the unsung truths and beauties of the modern world, stench and all. But an experimental attitude toward experience and art, the idea of art *as* experience, is not the full message the moderns, or several of them, heard in his call. Openness helped many, Williams high among them, to achieve a voice, to cast off the repression of genteel culture and morality and give sanction to emotional life. Important as this was in the shaping of American modernist art, there was another aspect, more difficult to absorb under the conditions of American modernity, to what Hart Crane called Whitman's as yet unrealized "bequest."

Understandably it was the poets who most rigorously wrestled with their chosen father and in whose works we find the most indelible traces of the Whitman paternity adopted to personal need. "The words of the singers," Whitman wrote in "Song of the Answerer," "are the hours or minutes of the light and dark, but the words of the maker of poems are the general light and dark. . . . The singers do not beget, only the Poet begets" (169). This division between singers (we can understand this to mean the poet as *maker*) and "the Poet" (visionary, prophetic) underlies a division, a slippage of emphasis, within the legacy itself. Not unlike Pound, only without the exile's surly posturing, Williams took Whitman as his genius loci, the breaker of fresh wood, the spirit of the local, the demotic. Doing so, Williams cast in shadow what Hart Crane spent his talent pursuing: the visionary Whitman, the Whitman of the tally, the poet who "places himself where the future becomes the present." For Williams in 1932 Whitman was finally "a magnificent failure. He himself in his later stages showed all the terrifying defects of his own method. Whitman to me is one broom stroke and that is all."[21] For Crane, writing in 1930, Whitman authored "a universal vision which takes on additional significance as time goes on."[22] Between these versions of the precursor the legacy divides: the broom, the breaker of the wood who cleared the field, no more; the visionary, the prophet, the universal brother and lover. Less familiar to us because it has been less palatable to later modernist and academic versions, Crane's prophetic Whitman perhaps requires more attention for the sake of perspective on the story of the modernists' Whitman.

After his remark in 1923 about a direct connection with Whitman, Crane continued: "The modern artist needs gigantic assimilative capacities, emotion, – and the greatest *all – vision*."[23] He has in mind such proleptic passages as this from *Democratic Vistas*:

> America needs, and the world needs, a class of bards who will, now and ever, so link and tally the rational physical being of man, with the ensembles of time and space, and with this vast and multiform show, Nature, surrounding him, ever tantalizing him, equally a part, and yet not a part of him, as to essentially harmonize, satisfy, and put at rest.[24]

In an essay on modern poetry in 1930, after completing his own gigantic enterprise of assimilation, *The Bridge*, Crane appraised more fully, if still cryptically, Whitman's significance for modern poetry and culture:

> The most typical and valid expression of the American psychosis seems to me still to be found in Whitman. His faults as a technician and his clumsy and indiscriminate enthusiasm are somewhat beside the point. He, better than any other, was able to coordinate those forces in America which seem most intractable, fusing them into a universal vision which takes on additional significance as time goes on. He was a revolutionist beyond the strict meaning of Coleridge's definition of genius [that genius creates its own laws], but his bequest is still to be realized in all its implications.[25]

Crane foregrounds two features of the Whitman bequest that by the 1920s had receded from view: one, that the Whitman legacy entails more than a way of writing, a kind of line and poem, but a "universal vision" constructed of "intractable" or contradictory materials; and two, that the bequest remains open-ended, "still to be realized." As Pound had said, Whitman offers a beginning, not "a classically finished work." This lack of finish, the privilege of always seeming to begin anew, is perhaps the American psychosis Crane meant. Whitman bequeathes something not yet coherent, unclear in its details, shaggy at its edges, "unperform'd," as Whitman himself boasted: "Years of the modern! years of the unperform'd!" (489).

In *The Bridge* Crane attempted to realize this heritage of a transfigured modernity. He places the generative poet directly within the text, in the "Cape Hatteras" section, and characterizes him not as the writer of free verse or singer of the body electric or of manly love among comrades, but as a visionary whose future, our present, corrosively mocks the vision. Crane embodies Whitman in order to challenge him with the taunt of failure, of irrelevance.

> "– Recorders ages hence" – ah, syllables of faith!
> Walt, tell me Walt Whitman, if infinity
> Be still the same as when you walked the beach
> Near Paumanok – your lone patrol – and heard the wraith
> Through surf, its bird note there a long time falling . . .
> For you, the panoramas and this breed of towers,
> Of you – the theme that's statured in the cliff.
> O Saunterer on the free ways still ahead!
> Not this our empire yet, but labyrinth
> Wherein your eyes, like the Great Navigator's without ship,
> Gleam from the great stones of each prison crypt
> Of canyoned traffic . . . Confronting the Exchange,
> Surviving in a world of stocks, – they also range
> Across the hills where second timber strays
> Back over Connecticut farms, abandoned pastures, –
> Sea eyes and tidal, undenying, bright with myth![26]

Modernity arrives as a blinding threat to Whitman's myth, and Crane asks for justification, for renewal of the visionary pledge in the face of the world's refusal. He places Whitman at the site of the invention of mechanical flight, an invention not of poets but of engineers, technologists who have preempted and seemingly fulfilled the ancient dream of fusing space and time. "Space, instantaneous, / Flickers a moment, consumes us in its smile" (89), and "Man hears himself an engine in a cloud!" (89). But the modern poet finds himself in a labyrinth, imprisoned in the city's canyons of traffic, a world controlled by the stock exchange; through Whitman's eyes he scans the city's crypt-like buildings and the depleted countryside, two stark denials of what the Saunterer's eyes, "bright with myth," had promised as vision: vibrant city, nourishing country. A scene of fiery disaster embodies the threat, the crash of a flying machine "into mashed and shapeless debris. . . . / By Hatteras bunched the beached heap of high bravery" (93). Can Whitman's myth-laden eyes survive the sight of "the Cape's ghoul-mound" (95), survive the irony of a vision that outstared civil war and assassination – "O, upward from the dead / Thou bringest tally, and a pact, new bound / Of living brotherhood" (93) – now confronted only with evidence of repeated violence, greed, and "fraternal massacre" in place of "living brotherhood"?

In "Years of the Modern" Whitman asks:

What whispers are these O lands, running ahead of you, passing under the seas?
Are all the nations communing? is there going to be but one heart to the globe?
Is humanity forming en-masse? for lo, tyrants tremble, crowns grow dim,

. . .

Years prophetical! the space ahead as I walk, as I vainly try to pierce it,
   is full of phantoms,
Unborn deeds, things soon to be, project their shapes around me,
This incredible rush and heat, this strange ecstatic fever of dreams O years!
Your dreams O years, how they penetrate through me! I know not whether I
   sleep or wake;
The perform'd America and Europe grow dim, retiring in shadow behind me,
The unperform'd, more gigantic than ever, advance, advance upon me.

(490)

Such lines represent the Whitman of Crane's "Cape Hatteras," the figure hailed in the apostrophe: "thou who on boldest heel / Stood up and flung the span on even wing / Of that great Bridge, our Myth, whereof I sing" (94). This is the Whitman of the unperformed, the unrealized bequest, the myth and the prophecy. By its challenge "Cape Hatteras" validates the vision, as by fusing his eyes with Whitman's, the poet comes to see "the rain-bow's arch – how shimmeringly stands / Above the Cape's ghoul-mound, O joyous seer!" (95) – a prefiguration of the Bridge, the route to Cathay, to the promised redemption. Such an imagined Bridge, if the vision will hold, joins East and West, space and time, and reproduces Whitman's "vast Rondure, swimming in space" ("Passage to India," 414), modernity's ghostly vision of a transfigured technological modernity and a new image of the oneness of things and of being.

Crane took Whitman as a type of the modern not only in language, style, and demeanor, but mainly in his perception of a mystical equivalent latent in the instruments of modernity. Crane also acknowledged the homosexual aspects of Whitman's "living brotherhood"; in "Cape Hatteras" the ma-chinery of flight suggests the dangerous pleasures of transgressive passion as the visionary precursor assumes the role of lover: "My hand / in yours, / Walt Whitman – / so –" (95).[27] That wish to transume or tally an unconsciously erotic modernity in the light of Whitman's "unperform'd" recalls another Whitmanian modernist, Frank Lloyd Wright, who in a lecture in 1901 said that "American Society has the essential tool of its own age by the blade, as lacerated hands everywhere testify!"

> But, I say, usurped by greed and deserted by its natural interpreter, the artist, the machine is only the creature, not the creator, of this iniquity! I say the machine has noble possibilities unwillingly forced to this degradation, degraded by the arts themselves. Insofar as the true capacity of the machine is concerned it is itself the crazed victim of artist impotence. Why will the American artist not see that human thought in our age is stripping off its old form and donning another; why is the artist unable to see that this is his glorious opportunity to create and reap anew?[28]

In his work early in the century, Wright submitted the logic of the machine to a logic of the organic, which bears analogies with Crane's "logic of metaphor"; he joined modern materials like steel and concrete and plate glass by means of modern tools and imagined a new form of shelter based on openness: inside open to outside, free flow of space within, rapport with natural site, and the whole contained by a rhythm of repeated decorative forms that impart to his prairie houses the beat of a human heart.

What Wright and Crane share is not a style of machine art but a vision projected by Whitman of a culture founded on an art of transfigured modernity. In his own wish to hold the modern in an "imaged Word," "a visionary company of love" ("The Broken Tower," 193), Crane set himself the task of answering Whitman's call for a poetry whose final measure is whether it helps a human soul, whether it elicits "loving brotherhood," democracy, an ideal America. A monument, along with Wright's Taliesen, his masterpiece in the Wisconsin countryside, of Whitman's propadeutic presence among the moderns, Crane's *Bridge* stands for that visionary modernity that was Whitman's most demanding and troubling bequest – his vision of unqualified oneness, a vision barely traceable in the labyrinth of stocks, tunnels, crypts, and ghoul-mounds in which Crane takes Whitman's hand. Hart Crane imagined a role for Whitman that would answer Whitman's own call in "Poets to Come":

> I myself but write one or two indicative words for the future,
> I but advance a moment only to wheel and hurry back in darkness.

> I am a man who, sauntering along without fully stopping, turns a casual look
>   upon you and then averts his face,

Leaving it to you to prove and define it,
Expecting the main things from you.

(14)

Whitman projects himself ahead and looks back at the reader, as if a memory from the future,[29] awaiting the reader's performance as an unborn deed.
A telling number of young Americans aspiring to a new art and a new
culture took the part of Whitman's "you," shaping an afterlife for the poet's
glance that gave a distinctive note and tone to the initial phase of American
modernism. More than any other, Hart Crane placed himself directly in the
call-and-response circuit with Whitman, dared to take the older poet not
only as breaker of the old wood but visionary of a new life, a Whitman
whose "main thing" is hinted at by the gigantic unperformed, the bequest
whose identifying sign is its inevitable recession into a future already past.

NOTES

1   Ezra Pound, *Selected Prose: 1909–1965* (New York: New Directions, 1973),
    p. 145. Subsequent citations in the text are to this edition.
2   Harold W. Blodgett and Sculley Bradley, eds., Walt Whitman, *Leaves of Grass,
    Comprehensive Reader's Edition* (New York: New York University Press,
    1965), p. 35. Subsequent citations in the text are to this edition.
3   Ezra Pound, *Personae* (New York: New Directions, 1971), p. 89.
4   Robert Henri, *Dionysion* 1, no. 1 (1915):n.p.
5   *The Seven Arts* (November 1916). See James Oppenheim, "The Story of the
    Seven Arts," *American Mercury* 20 (1930):156–64.
6   *The Blind Man* (1917):n.p.
7   Walter Sutton, "A Visit with William Carlos Williams," *The Minnesota Review,*
    1 (April 1961):312.
8   Brom Weber, ed., *The Letters of Hart Crane* (Berkeley: University of California
    Press, 1952), p. 128.
9   Quoted in James E. Breslin, *William Carlos Williams: An American Artist* (New
    York: Oxford University Press, 1970), p. 19. See also Stephen Tapscott, *Ameri-
    can Beauty: William Carlos Williams and the Modernist Whitman* (New York:
    Columbia University Press, 1984).
10 Robert Henri, *The Art Spirit* (Philadelphia: J. B. Lippincott, 1923), p. 135.
11 Marsden Hartley, *Adventures in the Arts* (New York: Boni and Liveright,
    1921), p. 35.
12 Jacques Barzun, ed., *The Selected Writings of John Jay Chapman* (New York:
    Doubleday Anchor Books, 1959), p. 163.
13 In exploring the influence of Whitman on the painter Marsden Hartley, Jon-
    athan Weinberg argues that "the importance of Whitman for Hartley, as well as
    for other homosexuals at the turn of the century, was his poetry's suggestion
    that same-sex love was part of a more universal love of humanity." *Speaking for
    Vice: Homosexuality in the Art of Charles Demuth, Marsden Hartley, and the*

First American Avant-Garde (New Haven, Conn.: Yale University Press, 1993), p. 137. For important recent discussions of homosexuality in Whitman's poetry, see Robert K. Martin, *The Homosexual Tradition in American Poetry* (Austin: University of Texas Press, 1979), and Michael Moon, *Disseminating Whitman* (Cambridge, Mass.: Harvard University Press, 1991).

14 Isadora Duncan, *My Life* (New York: Liveright, 1927), p. 31. In a letter in 1922, Hart Crane describes his "excitement at seeing Isadora Duncan dance" in Cleveland and recounts her comments to the audience after the performance: "[she] told the people to go home and take from the bookshelf the works of Walt Whitman, and turn to the section called 'Calamus'." Weber, *The Letters of Hart Crane,* p. 109.

15 Quoted in Alan Trachtenberg, *Brooklyn Bridge: Fact and Symbol* (Chicago: University of Chicago Press, 1979), p. 190.

16 "America, Whitman, and the Art of Poetry," *The Poetry Journal* 8 (November 1917):31.

17 Walt Whitman, *Complete Poetry and Collected Prose* (New York: Library of America, 1982), pp. 131–2.

18 Ibid., p. 987.

19 Ibid., p. 993.

20 Bruce St. John, ed., *John Sloan's New York Scene* (New York: Harper & Row, 1965), p. 314.

21 John C. Thirlwall, ed., *The Selected Letters of William Carlos Williams* (New York: McDowell, Obolensky, 1957), p. 135.

22 Hart Crane, "Modern Poetry," in Brom Weber, ed., *The Complete Poems and Selected Letters and Prose of Hart Crane* (New York: Doubleday Anchor Books, 1966), p. 263.

23 Weber, *The Letters of Hart Crane,* p. 129.

24 Whitman, ibid., p. 988.

25 "Modern Poetry," p. 263.

26 Weber, ed., *Complete Poems and Selected Letters,* p. 89. Subsequent citations in text are to this edition.

27 See Thomas E. Yingling, *Hart Crane and the Homosexual Text* (Chicago: University of Chicago Press, 1990), pp. 209–15, for a perceptive and subtle reading of homosexual allusion in "Cape Hatteras," and pp. 186–226 of *The Bridge* as a whole.

28 Frank Lloyd Wright, "The Art and Craft of the Machine," reprinted in Lewis Mumford, ed., *Roots of Contemporary American Architecture* (New York: Grove Press, 1952), pp. 177–8.

29 I borrow this happy phrase from an unpublished paper by Donald Pease.

II

FERNANDO ALEGRÍA

Borges's "Song of Myself"

Years ago, in a first attempt to describe Whitman's presence in Latin America, I said: "Studying Whitman in the poetry of Hispanic America is like searching for the footprints of a ghost that can be felt everywhere but is nowhere to be seen."[1]

At the University of Iowa's international meeting in homage to Whitman in 1992, once again I felt the presence of this familiar ghost. It was springtime. Observing known and unknown faces, listening to foreign accents, and deciphering allusions made with fascinating ambiguity created a certain magic among us. We were participants in a chorus that, in strange harmony, expressed the frustration of not being able to communicate all that we were saying to each other.

Then I thought that just as every generation of Whitmanists conceives a Whitman model that is characteristically related to its concept of poetic art, each culture also finds a way of translating Whitman in order to integrate him into its own conception of life.

Our Chinese colleagues explained why Whitman cannot be translated into their language in the way Westerners translate him. They gave the name of the insurmountable barrier: sex. Then I understood their long metaphorical tangents, their omissions, and their strange rhetoric. Indirectly, they were telling us that each people makes of Whitman's art an overwhelming metaphor and of his person an imposing, intricate symbol. Whitman's followers accommodate him to the size of the dream that is, in truth, his peculiar poetic art.

Whitman, then, survives *nationalized* in the language of his admirers, translated into different realities.

"As time passes," said Gay Wilson Allen, "I am more convinced that Whitman is a symbol."

A symbol? Not a myth? Not the prophetic poet who creates a character, becomes the incarnation of that character, and, with the creature on his back, becomes the hero of a legendary text?

The face of Jorge Luis Borges appeared to me at that moment, with all its shades of light and shadow. I had the sensation that he was both with us and not with us. He should have been because, of all the Whitman followers in Latin America, I think Borges was the one who understood him the best.

Let me explain.

Borges had no illusions about heroes. He saw the common man behind every monument. He understood the virtues and the dangers facing an artist who adopts a historical pose. Borges respected the courage of a poet who assumes a pose and dedicates the rest of his life to making sure that he deserves it, without arrogance, naturally, like the blind man that he was, for whom the abyss of darkness that surrounded him was never emptiness, but a mold in which to fit his solitude.

Face to face with Whitman's poetry, Borges seems to prefer a literal translation:

> I bequeath myself to the dirt to grow from the grass I love,
> If you want me again look for me under your boot-soles.

Says Whitman, and Borges translates:

> Si quieres encontrarte conmigo, búscame bajo la suela de tus zapatos.[2]
> (If you want to meet me, look for me under your boot-soles.)

Then Borges looks up at the empty sky, smiling, as sure of the ghost who speaks as he is of the cane that he holds in his hands.[3]

Borges's literalness results in accurate translations of Whitman's symbolism: He gives us the only possible reading of a text that is, from beginning to end, a deliberate and powerful metaphor.

However, if we are going to consider Borges's translation of "Song of Myself" from a critical point of view, it might be helpful to establish some premises:

1. In the brief preface to his translation, Borges refers only to two Hispanic versions of "Leaves of Grass": Armando Vasseur's and Francisco Alexander's.[4] With respect to Vasseur, he makes no judgment whatsoever; with regard to Alexander, he expresses limited reservations, warning that he is "too literal."

2. Borges was thoroughly familiar with the English language, although his familiarity was more with the British form than with the North American.

3. Borges does take liberties as he translates, but always making an effort to stay close to Whitman's directness and bluntness. He is protected by his sense of rhythm and his understanding of lyrical nuances. We know that Borges *knows,* and that though he may replace some words, he does it in

order to remain faithful to Whitman's *sense*, not only to *form*. He eliminates or adds words if it seems to him that by simplifying he will strengthen the text. Here are some examples:

Whitman says:

> The atmosphere is not a perfume, it has no taste of the distillation,
> it is odorless.

(29)

Borges abbreviates:

> El aire no es un aroma, no huele a nada.
> (The air is not a perfume, it is odorless.)

(40)

Whitman synthesizes:

> A few light kisses, a few embraces, a reaching around of arms.

(30)

Borges expands:

> Un beso fugaz, un abrazo, los pechos se buscan . . .
> (A light kiss, an embrace, breasts seeking each other . . .)

(30)

Whitman describes in detail:

I am satisfied – I see, dance, laugh, sing;
As the hugging and loving bed-fellow sleeps at my side through the night, and
  withdraws at the peep of the day with stealthy tread,
Leaving me baskets cover'd with white towels . . .

(31)

Borges – modest and proper – makes the "bedfellow" feminine, and the towels "linen":

> Estoy satisfecho, veo, bailo, me río y canto:
> Cuando la compañera amorosa que comparte mi lecho duerme a mi lado
>   y se retira al amanecer con pasos furtivos,
> Dejándome canastas cubiertas con lienzos blancos . . .
> (I am satisfied, I see, dance, laugh and sing:
> As the loving woman-partner who shares my bed sleeps by my side
>   and withdraws at dawn with stealthy tread,
> Leaving me baskets covered with white linen . . .)

(42)

4. Borges makes no attempt to beautify Whitman's language, a temptation that has seduced numerous translators. I am convinced, however, that some of Borges's own images surpass Whitman's lyric discourse. The best example of this is Borges's translation of Section 5, a translation that is full of frank and direct sensuality:

Creo en ti, mi alma, el otro que soy no se rebajará ante ti,
Y tú no te rebajarás ante él.
Tiéndete en el pasto conmigo, desembaraza tu garganta,
No son palabras ni música, ni versos los que preciso, ni hábitos,
   ni discursos ni aún los mejores,
Sólo quiero el arrullo, el susurro de tu voz suave.
Recuerdo cómo nos acostamos una mañana transparente de estío,
Cómo apoyaste la cabeza sobre mis caderas y la volviste a mí dulcemente,
Y abriste mi camisa sobre el pecho y hundiste tu lengua hasta tocar
   mi corazón desnudo,
Y te estiraste hasta tocarme la barba, y luego hasta tocarme los pies . . .
Velozmente se irguieron y me rodearon el conocimiento y la paz que trascienden
   todas las discusiones de la tierra,
Y desde entonces sé que la mano de Dios ha sido prometida a la mía,
Y sé que el espíritu de Dios es hermano del mío,
Y que todos los hombres que han nacido son mis hermanos,
Y las mujeres mis hermanas y mis amantes,
Y que el sostén de la creación es el amor,
Y que son innumerables las hojas rígidas o que se curvan en los campos,
Y las negras hormigas en las grietas bajo las hojas,
Y las mohosas costras del seto, las piedras hacinadas, el saúco, la candelaria
   y la cizaña.

(I believe in you, my soul, the other I am will not abase to you,
And you will not abase to the other.
Lie down on the grass with me, clear your throat,
Not words, not music, or verses I want, not habits or lectures not even the best,
Only the lull, the whisper of your soft voice.
I remember how once we lay in a transparent summer morning,
How you put your head upon my hips and sweetly turned it over upon me,
And opened my shirt over my chest, and plunged your tongue until you touched
   my bare heart
And you stretched until you touched my beard, and then until you touched
   my feet.
Swiftly arose and surrounded me the knowledge and the peace that transcend all
   the arguments of the earth,
And ever since I know that the hand of God has been promised to mine,
And I know that the spirit of God is the brother of my own,

And that all the men ever born are my brothers,
And the women my sisters and my lovers,
And that the support of creation is love,
And limitless are leaves stiff or drooping in the fields,
And the black ants in the cracks under the leaves,
And the rusty cracks in the hedge, the piled up rocks, the elder, mullein
and poke-weed.)

(43–4)

The dubious translations don't matter: *mohosas* for *mossy*, *seto* for *wormfence*. These are details. The tone, the rhythm, and the modulation of Borges's text, the alliterations – *el arrullo, el susurro* – and the smooth sliding toward a mystical transcendence are the elements of an exemplary translation.

5. The reader must not forget that Borges's translation is fragmentary. It includes the fifty-two sections of "Song of Myself," but some are considerably shortened. In others, some lines have been moved from their original place; for example, twenty-three lines belonging in Section 24 end up in Borges, page 67 (Blodgett and Bradley, 54). The ten lines that Borges (or a playful typesetter) moved begin "Contemplar el amanecer!" ("To behold the day-break!"; Blodgett and Bradley, 54).

All of this, of course, concerns the formal aspect of the work. It has no relation to the essential problem I would like to discuss here, which can be summarized in a few questions:

Can we say that through his translation Borges makes an attempt to identify himself with Whitman? If so, does he identify with Whitman's ideology? With his social behavior? With the symbolic content of his poetry? What elements essential to Whitman does he reject? His sexual attitude? His political ideology? What does Borges see in Whitman that Whitman never considered to be fundamental aspects of his poetics?

In his famous "Note on Whitman,"[5] Borges proposes a surprising incongruity:

> Let us imagine that a biography of Ulysses (based on the testimonies of Agamemnon, Laertes, Poliphemus, Calypso, Penelope, Telemachus, the swineherd, Scylla and Carybdis) suggests that he never left Ithaca. The deception such a book would produce in us – happily, a hypothetical one – is the deception that all the biographies of Whitman produce. To pass from the heavenly orbit of his verses to the insipid chronicle of his life is a melancholy transition. Paradoxically, that inevitable melancholy is aggravated when the biographer tries to conceal the fact that there are two Whitmans: the "friendly and eloquent savage" of *Leaves of Grass* and the poor man of letters that

invented him. This one was chaste, reserved and rather taciturn; but the other, effusive and orgiastic. It is easy to find other discrepancies, but it is more important to understand that the happy vagabond described in the poems of *Leaves of Grass* would not have been capable himself of writing them.   (99).

In defining Whitman as a double, Borges failed to point out a surprising detail: The person who wrote the poems, a "chaste, reserved, and rather taciturn" man, is very much like Borges himself. The fact of the matter is that Borges left a testimony of his own conception as a double in a little masterpiece called "Borges y yo":[6]

> It's Borges, the other, to whom things happen. I walk around Buenos Aires and pause, perhaps mechanically, to contemplate an old entrance hall and its heavy wood-framed door. I get news about Borges in the mail, I see his name listed with two other professors being considered for a position, or in a biographical dictionary. I like sand-clocks, maps, 18th century typography, etymologies, the taste of coffee and Stevenson's prose; the other Borges shares these preferences, but with vanity, so they become an actor's attributes. It would be an exaggeration to say that our relationship is a hostile one; I live, I allow myself to live, so that Borges can work out his literature and this literature justifies me. I can easily grant that he has succeeded in writing some worthy pages, but these pages cannot save me, perhaps because what is good doesn't belong anymore to anyone in particular, not even to the other Borges, but to language or tradition. Besides, I'm destined to be lost, definitely, and only an instant of myself will be able to survive in the other. Little by little, I give to him everything, although I'm aware of his malignant habit of falsifying and magnifying all. Spinoza understood that all things want to persevere in their own being: the stone wants to be eternally a stone, and the tiger a tiger. I must remain in Borges, not in me (if I'm somebody), but I recognize myself less in his books than in many other things, as in the complicated playing of a guitar. Years ago I tried to liberate myself of him, and went from the barrios' mythologies to games of time and infinitude; but those games now belong to Borges, so I'll have to think of other things. Thus, my life is a continuous escape, and I lose everything, and all belongs to forgetfulness or to the other.
>
> I don't know who is writing this page.   (164)[7]

So I believe that Borges, the imaginative, playful, and ironic writer, has truly identified himself with the "rather taciturn" man who wrote "Song of Myself" – not exactly with the boisterous, cosmic, powerful bard, but with the secluded, bearded man of the soft, melancholy and dubious, amorous voice. Regardless of whether Whitman can be judged as a many-sided symbol or not, Borges seems convinced at least that he had a double, and it's with this double that he sympathizes and sings along.

It is quite possible that no Hispanic translator has ever equaled Borges in
his masterful versions of Whitman's ambiguous sex poems. Let's consider
Section 11 as an example:

Veintiocho muchachos bañándose en la orilla,
Veintiocho muchachos tan llenos de vida,
Veintiocho años de vida de mujer y tan solitarios.

Es dueña de la linda casa de la barranca
Se oculta hermosa y bien vestida tras el postigo de la ventana.

Cuál de los muchachos le gusta más?
El menos agraciado es para ella hermoso!

Adónde va usted señora? Porque la he visto,
Juega usted en el agua y, sin embargo, permanece en la casa.

Bailando y riendo viene una mujer por la orilla,
Los hombres no la ven, pero ella los ve y los ama.

El agua brilla en la barba de los muchachos,
Se escurre por sus largos cabellos,
Leves arroyos corren por sus cuerpos.

Una invisible mano también acaricia sus carnes,
Desciende trémula por las sienes y por los pechos.

Los muchachos nadan de espaldas, sus blancos vientres se curvan al sol, no se
    preguntan quién se une a ellos,
No saben quién jadea y se hunde con la espalda curvada,
No saben a quién están salpicando con la espuma del agua.

(Twenty-eight young men bathing at the edge,
Twenty-eight young men so full of life
Twenty-eight years of womanly life and so lonely.

She owns the pretty house on the cliff,
She hides beautiful and well dressed behind the shutters of the window.
Which of the young men does she like the best?
The homeliest of them is beautiful to her!

Where are you going, lady? For I have seen you,
You play in the water and yet you stay in the house.

Dancing and laughing comes a woman along the beach,
The men do not see her, but she sees them and loves them.

The water shines in the young men's beards,
It runs down their long hair,
Little streams run down their bodies.

An unseen hand also caresses their bodies,
It descends trembling over their temples and their breasts.

The young men swim on their backs, their white bellies curve
under the sun, they do not ask themselves who joins them,
They don't know who puffs and submerges with a curved back,
They don't know whom they souse with the spray.)

(51)

The two sections that follow this one express similar examples of lyrical voyeurism and deep attraction for nude male bodies. In Sections 12 and 13 the voyeur observes first a young butcher and then a black coachman:

The butcher-boy puts off his killing-clothes, or sharpens his knife at the stall
   in the market,
I loiter enjoying his repartee and his shuffle and breakdown . . .

From the cinder-strew'd threshold I follow their movements,
The lithe sheer of their waists plays even with their massive arms . . .

(39)

Borges translates with sensuous enjoyment, creating a dancing movement of his own:

El muchacho del carnicero se quita los avíos de matar, o afila el cuchillo
   en la tabla del mercado,
Me distraen sus zafadurías y sus pasos de baile.

Herreros de tiznados y velludos pechos rodean el yunque,
Cada uno tiene su martillo, todos trabajan, hace mucho calor en la fragua.

Desde el ceniciento umbral sigo sus movimientos,
El vaivén de sus talles armoniza con el de sus fornidos brazos . . .

(The butcher-boy takes off his killing-clothes, or sharpens his knife at the stall
   in the market,
I enjoy his impudence and his dancing-steps.
Blacksmiths with grimed and hairy chests surround the anvil,
Each one has his main-sledge, they are all working, it's very hot in the forge.)

(51)

Describing the coachman, Borges emphasizes love and desire over mere description:

El negro sujeta con firmeza las riendas de sus cuatro caballos . . .
Firme y alto guía el carro de la cantera y se sostiene con un pie en el estribo,
Su camisa azul descubre el amplio cuello y el pecho, y cae sobre el cinturón,
Su mirada es tranquila e imperiosa, se echa para atrás el chambergo y descubre
   la frente,

El sol da en su bigote y en su pelo ensortijado, y en la negrura de sus miembros
pulidos y perfectos.
Miro a este gigante pintoresco y lo quiero, y no me detengo ahí,
Voy con los caballos también.

(The negro holds firmly the reins of his four horses . . .
Firm and tall drives the dray of the stone-yard he holds on with a foot
    on the board,
His blue shirt exposes his ample neck and breast and loosens over his belt,
His glance is calm and commanding, he tosses back his hat and displays
his forehead,
The sun falls on his mustache and on his crispy hair, on the black of his polished
and perfect limbs.
I look at this colorful giant and I love him, and I don't stop there,
I'm going with the horses as well.

(51–2)

This is the language that Borges never used as an expression of sensuality
in his own poetry. He has availed himself of Whitman's feelings and symbols
in order to make a metaphor of his own chastity and daring.

Speaking of chastity and bravery, I would like to refer here to a couple of
anecdotes, without the slightest intention of attributing unwarranted importance to them.

One has to do with an incident, witnessed by me, in which Borges was
verbally attacked in a public event held in New York during the Vietnam
War. The attacker threw every conceivable insult at Borges, while Borges –
blind and decrepit – limited himself to repeat, as an echo, every word
thrown at him, so that if one had only recorded his words, and not those of
his assailant, Borges would have entered history as the master of the foulest
form of diatribe. A supreme act of irony?

My observations: Borges's courage had no limits; he was ready to be
killed but not to remain silent. His courage was an act of total lunacy,
defying the fury of a senseless attacker.

After the incident, I told Borges to remember the legend of the *Popol Vuh,*
which concerns the revolt of things and objects against man.

The second anecdote: An American professor, a devoted student of Borges's works and life, told me that among old papers given to him by the
master himself, he found a note in which Borges tells about his old habit of
turning all the lights off before undressing and going to bed. Borges, the
admirer of manliness and courage, the glorifier of folk toughness in his
bloody descriptions of knife fights, appears to have been as shy and reticent
as a young girl in his private life.

It may come as a surprise to know that a German admirer of Borges, Ernst Jünger, the philosopher of Nazi inclinations, identified him as the champion of an aesthetic of aggression. The evidence? His gaucho poems!

Whitman's metaphysical nuances became games of mystery and fatality in Borges's own poems. Borges admired men in the midst of heroic violence, patriotism, and decorum. Whitman responded to a type of manhood that could be described as domineering and sensually passionate, direct in its sexual tenderness.

Professor Víctor Farías, an expert on both Bürger's essays and Borges's stories and poems – has written the following:

> The question I would like to deal with is the relation between Borges's works and an Aesthetic of Aggression, the poetization of active and free violence of man against man and its magnification. It is a legitimate question not only because Borges has publicly saluted well known and irreducible military dictatorships in Latin America, but also because reflection, affirmation, and magnification of aggressive violence truly constitute one of the leading currents of his literature.[8]

Professor Farías makes special reference to Borges's last visit to Germany in 1982 and to his statement, published in the *Frankfurter Allgemeine Zeitung* (October 28), to the effect that of all the German writers he knew, he was interested in talking only to Bürger.

"Borges," commented Bürger, "has been following my development for the last seventy years. The first book of mine that he read was *In Stahlgewitter,* translated and published under the Spanish title *Bajo la tormenta de acero* in 1922 by the initiative of the Argentine army."[9]

Literarily speaking, Borges's chauvinism is harmlessly romantic. It never achieved the stentorian echoes of Lugones or José Santos Chocano. Moreover, there is always a trace of irony in Borges's exaltation of old generals and popular outcasts. This is a typical comment of his: "Perhaps this is the tango's mission: to give Argentines the assurance of having been brave men, of having already fulfilled the demands of honor and valor."[10]

Few, if any, Hispanic commentators of Whitman have ever referred to him as an exponent of an aesthetic of aggression or as a speaker for the Manifest Destiny of the United States. As a matter of fact, at a writers' gathering in a Latin American country, I heard someone attack Whitman in this respect. Lo and behold, it was no less than the Cuban poet Roberto Fernández Retamar who rose to his defense. Male worshipper, maybe. Chauvinistic bully, never.

Borges's translation of "Song of Myself" faithfully expresses Whitman's passionate admiration for youthful, virile beauty.

If throughout his translations Borges approached Whitman as a mystical companion who thoroughly understands love calls and occasional erotic encounters in which one lover covers another while lying in the grass, opening his shirt with his tongue in order to reach his heart, filling him with his breath, so that both become flames of a single body and a single soul, shouldn't we conclude that their union was nothing more than love and fulfillment in communion with God?

What other reason could there have been for Borges's devotion to Whitman? We can agree, as we have said, that Borges admired Whitman's cult of manly strength, of the spirit of a visionary conquerer, discoverer, and creator of new worlds. Would this mean that Whitman and Borges were both exponents of an "aesthetic of aggression"? I think not.

In "Canto a mí mismo" and "Song of Myself" Borges and Whitman are, truly, as much symbols as paradigms. They represent and they preach, creating, as they speak, different echoes. Whitman is historical, biblical, sensuous, and transcendent. Borges is anti-epic, intimate, and modest, suggesting symbols that immediately call up doubts.

Since Borges has chosen to explain himself within his own mystery using the most eloquent, resonant, and programmatic words of Whitman's, together they have produced a text – "Canto a mí mismo" – that, in affirming itself, also casts doubts on itself. They have given birth to a mystery about what, in fact, they really are: one might say, the mystery of that which in living negates itself: the metaphoric power of impotence.

NOTES

1 See F. Alegría: *Walt Whitman en Hispanoamérica* (México City: Ediciones Studium, 1954), p. 9.

2 *Leaves of Grass: Comprehensive Reader's Edition,* ed. Harold W. Blodgett and Sculley Bradley (New York: New York University Press, 1965), p. 89. Quotations from Whitman's poetry are taken from this edition and noted parenthetically by page in the text.

   Jorge Luis Borges, *Hojas de hierba* (Buenos Aires: Juárez Editor. Selección, traducción y prólogo de J. L. Borges; estudio crítico de Guillermo Nolasco Juárez; grabados de Antonio Berni, 1969), p. 108.

3 We musn't forget that Gabriela Mistral paraphrased Whitman's words in one of her "Motivos del barro" (*Desolación,* 1922).

4 Armando Vasseur, *Walt Whitman. Poemas* (Montevideo: Claudio García Cía, 1939). Francisco Alexander, *Hojas de hierba* (Quito, Ecuador: Casa de la Cultura, 1953).

5 *Otras Inquisiciones* (Buenos Aires: Emecé, 1960), pp. 97–104.

6 See "Borges y yo" in *Genio y figura de Jorge Luis Borges* (Buenos Aires: Editorial Universitaria, 1964), p. 164.

7   My translation.
8   See Víctor Farías, "La estética de la agresión. Reflexiones en torno a un diálogo de Jorge Luis Borges con Ernst Jünger," *Araucaria de Chile*, no. 28 (1984):83–98.
9   Ibid.
10 Ibid., p. 92.

EZRA GREENSPAN

Suggestions for further reading

"I am big – I contain multitudes" boasts the speaker in "Song of Myself." The same thing can be said of Whitman commentary, which grows so rapidly that readers may be left feeling that they need a "guide to the perplexed." The following list of works is designed to orient them to the body of commentary on Whitman and to help them to improve their knowledge and appreciation of Whitman and his writing.

Readers coming to Whitman should be aware that they do so with the advantage of two superb bibliographical tools: for primary bibliography, Joel Myerson's *Walt Whitman: A Descriptive Bibliography* (Pittsburgh: University of Pittsburgh Press, 1993), which sets a new standard for Whitman bibliography and provides an encyclopedia of factual information regarding the textual and material history of *Leaves of Grass* and other Whitman works; and, for secondary bibliography, the lists regularly compiled in the *Walt Whitman Quarterly Review* by its editor, Ed Folsom. The *WWQR* also publishes a variety of articles, notes, and book reviews on Whitman well worth the attention of students.

PRIMARY BIBLIOGRAPHY

Original Editions of Leaves of Grass

The publishing history of *Leaves of Grass* is so unusual and interesting; the individual editions so strikingly variant from each other (both inside and out); and the distance between original editions individually, and between them and modern editions collectively, so considerable that students may wish to see Whitman's volume in the original (or in the various facsimile editions issued over the course of the twentieth century). Alternatively, readers may simply wish to have a convenient record of the first editions of *Leaves of Grass*.

First edition – *Leaves of Grass* (Brooklyn, 1855)
Second edition – *Leaves of Grass* (Brooklyn, 1856)
Third edition – *Leaves of Grass* (Boston, 1860)
Fourth edition – *Leaves of Grass* (New York, 1867)
Fifth edition – *Leaves of Grass* (Washington, D.C., 1871)
Sixth edition – *Leaves of Grass* (London, 1872 – actually, an unauthorized type facsimile issued in 1873)
Seventh edition – *Leaves of Grass* (Boston, 1881–2; Philadelphia, 1882)

Complex though this publishing history may seem for a single title, readers should understand that it is actually a simplification of a much more tangled printing history. Works such as *Drum-Taps* (1865) and *After All, Not to Create Only* (1871) were subsequently incorporated into late editions of *Leaves of Grass;* and other works, such as *Democratic Vistas* (1871) and *Passage to India* (1871), as well as various prefaces to editions of *Leaves of Grass,* were worked into and out of the late editions or incorporated only in part.

Various of these editions have been issued in modern facsimiles or in look-alike reprints. Although fancy facsimile editions, especially of the 1855 *Leaves,* have been issued periodically throughout the years, particularly popular with recent readers have been the inexpensive reprints of the first edition, edited by Malcolm Cowley (New York: Viking, 1959); the second edition, edited by Gay Wilson Allen (Norwood, Pa.: Norwood Editions, 1976); and the third edition, edited by Roy Harvey Pearce (Ithaca, N.Y.: Cornell University Press, 1961).

Two other modern scholarly works deserve mention here for making available proof texts that allow readers a vantage point from which to view the way Whitman proceeded from text to text and from edition to edition: Fredson Bowers, ed., *Whitman's Manuscripts: Leaves of Grass (1860)* (Chicago: University of Chicago Press, 1955); and Arthur Golden, ed., *Walt Whitman's Blue Book: The 1860–61* Leaves of Grass *Containing His Manuscript Additions and Revisions,* 2 vols. (New York: New York Public Library, 1968).

Modern Edition of Whitman's Writings

The standard modern edition of *Leaves of Grass* and of Whitman's other writings is the one that has been issuing, in fits and starts, from New York University Press since 1961. It includes the following titles:

The Correspondence, ed. Edwin Haviland Miller, 6 vols. (New York: New York University Press, 1961–1977).

The Early Poems and the Fiction, ed. Thomas L. Brasher (New York: New York University Press, 1963).

Prose Works 1892, ed. Floyd Stovall, 2 vols. (New York: New York University Press, 1963–1964).

Leaves of Grass, Comprehensive Reader's Edition, eds. Sculley Bradley and Harold W. Blodgett (New York: New York University Press, 1965).

Daybooks and Notebooks, ed. William White, 3 vols. (New York: New York University Press, 1978).

Leaves of Grass: A Textual Variorum of the Printed Poems, eds. Sculley Bradley et al., 3 vols. (New York: New York University Press, 1980).

Notebooks and Unpublished Prose Manuscripts, ed. Edward F. Grier, 6 vols. (New York: New York University Press, 1984).

SECONDARY BIBLIOGRAPHY

The following list includes many of the most important scholarly studies of Whitman, weighted somewhat toward recent criticism. For evaluations of the contents of these works, readers are advised to consult the *Walt Whitman Quarterly Review, American Literary Scholarship,* and *American Literature,* all of which issue reviews of the latest Whitman scholarship.

Allen, Gay Wilson. *The Solitary Singer: A Critical Biography of Walt Whitman.* 1955; rev. ed. Chicago: University of Chicago Press, 1985.

The New Walt Whitman Handbook. New York: New York University Press, 1975.

Arvin, Newton. *Whitman.* New York: Macmillan, 1938.

Aspiz, Harold. *Walt Whitman and the Body Beautiful.* Urbana: University of Illinois Press, 1980.

Asselineau, Roger. *The Evolution of Walt Whitman: The Creation of a Poet.* Cambridge, Mass.: Harvard University Press, 1960.

The Evolution of Walt Whitman: The Creation of a Book. Cambridge, Mass.: Harvard University Press, 1962.

Bauerlein, Mark. *Whitman and the American Idiom.* Baton Rouge: Louisiana State University Press, 1991.

Black, Stephen A. *Walt Whitman's Journey into Chaos.* New Brunswick, N.J.: Rutgers University Press, 1975.

Blodgett, Harold. *Walt Whitman in England.* Ithaca, N.Y.: Cornell University Press, 1934.

Brasher, Thomas L. *Whitman as Editor of the* Brooklyn Daily Eagle. Detroit: Wayne State University Press, 1970.

Burroughs, John. *Notes on Walt Whitman as Poet and Person.* New York: American News Company, 1867.

Carlisle, E. Fred. *The Uncertain Self: Whitman's Drama of Identity.* East Lansing: Michigan State University Press, 1973.

Cavitch, David. *My Soul and I: The Inner Life of Walt Whitman.* Boston: Beacon Press, 1985.

Chari, V. K. *Walt Whitman in the Light of Vedantic Mysticism: An Interpretation.* Lincoln: University of Nebraska Press, 1965.

Chase, Richard. *Walt Whitman Reconsidered.* New York: William Sloane, 1955.

Dougherty, James. *Walt Whitman and the Citizen's Eye.* Baton Rouge: Louisiana State University Press, 1993.

Eby, Edwin Harold. *A Concordance to Walt Whitman's "Leaves of Grass" and Selected Prose Writings,* 5 parts. Seattle: University of Washington Press, 1949–55.

Eitner, Walter H. *Walt Whitman's Western Jaunt.* Lawrence: Regents Press of Kansas, 1981.

Erkkila, Betsy. *Walt Whitman Among the French.* Princeton, N.J.: Princeton University Press, 1980.

Whitman: The Political Poet. New York: Oxford University Press, 1989.

Fishkin, Shelley Fisher. *From Fact to Fiction: Journalism and Imaginative Writing in America.* Baltimore: Johns Hopkins University Press, 1985.

Folsom, Ed. *Walt Whitman's Native Representations.* New York: Cambridge University Press, 1994.

ed. *Walt Whitman: The Centennial Essays.* Iowa City: University of Iowa Press, 1994.

Fone, Byrne R. S. *Masculine Landscapes: Walt Whitman and the Homoerotic Text.* Carbondale: Southern Illinois University Press, 1992.

Giantvalley, Scott. *Walt Whitman, 1838–1939: A Reference Guide.* Boston: G. K. Hall, 1981.

Greenspan, Ezra. *Walt Whitman and the American Reader.* New York: Cambridge University Press, 1990.

Hayman, Ronald. *Arguing with Walt Whitman.* London: Covent Garden Press, 1971.

Hindus, Milton, ed. Leaves of Grass: *One Hundred Years After.* Stanford, Calif.: Stanford University Press, 1955.

Walt Whitman: The Critical Heritage. London: Routledge and Kegan Paul, 1971.

Hollis, C. Carroll. *Language and Style in* Leaves of Grass. Baton Rouge: Louisiana State University Press, 1983.

Hutchinson, George B. *The Ecstatic Whitman: Literary Shamanism and the Crisis of the Union.* Columbus: Ohio State University Press, 1986.

Kaplan, Justin. *Walt Whitman: A Life.* New York: Simon and Schuster, 1980.

Killingsworth, M. Jimmie. *Whitman's Poetry of the Body: Sexuality, Politics, and the Text.* Chapel Hill: University of North Carolina Press, 1989.

The Growth of Leaves of Grass: *The Organic Tradition in Whitman Studies.* Columbia, S.C.: Camden House, 1993.

Krieg, Joann P., ed. *Walt Whitman: Here and Now.* Westport, Conn.: Greenwood Press, 1985.

Kuebrich, David. *Minor Prophecy: Walt Whitman's New American Religion.* Bloomington: Indiana University Press, 1990.

Kummings, Donald D. *Walt Whitman, 1940–1975: A Reference Guide.* Boston: G. K. Hall, 1982.

Larson, Kerry C. *Whitman's Drama of Consensus*. Chicago: University of Chicago Press, 1988.

Lawrence, D. H. *Studies in Classic American Literature*. New York: Thomas Seltzer, 1923.

Lewis, R. W. B., ed. *The Presence of Walt Whitman*. New York: Columbia University Press, 1962.

Loving, Jerome M. *Emerson, Whitman, and the American Muse*. Chapel Hill: University of North Carolina Press, 1982.

Marki, Ivan. *The Trial of the Word: An Interpretation of the First Edition of Leaves of Grass*. New York: Columbia University Press, 1976.

Martin, Robert K. *The Homosexual Tradition in American Poetry*. Austin: University of Texas Press, 1979.

   ed. *The Continuing Presence of Walt Whitman: The Life After the Life*. Iowa City: University of Iowa Press, 1992.

Matthiessen, F. O. *American Renaissance: Art and Expression in the Age of Emerson and Whitman*. New York: Oxford University Press, 1941.

Middlebrook, Diane Wood. *Walt Whitman and Wallace Stevens*. Ithaca, N.Y.: Cornell University Press, 1974.

Miller, Edwin Haviland. *Walt Whitman's Poetry: A Psychological Journey*. Boston: Houghton Mifflin, 1968.

   Walt Whitman's "Song of Myself": A Mosaic of Interpretations. Iowa City: University of Iowa Press, 1989.

Miller, Edwin Haviland, ed. *A Century of Whitman Criticism*. Bloomington: Indiana University Press, 1969.

   ed. *The Artistic Legacy of Walt Whitman: A Tribute to Gay Wilson Allen*. New York: New York University Press, 1970.

Miller, James E., Jr. *A Critical Guide to* Leaves of Grass. Chicago: University of Chicago Press, 1955.

   The American Quest for a Supreme Fiction: Whitman's Legacy in the Personal Epic. Chicago: University of Chicago Press, 1979.

Moon, Michael. *Disseminating Whitman: Revision and Corporeality in* Leaves of Grass. Cambridge, Mass.: Harvard University Press, 1991.

Myerson, Joel, ed. *Whitman in His Own Time: A Biographical Chronicle of His Life, Drawn from Recollections, Memoirs, and Interviews by Friends and Associates*. Detroit: Omnigraphics, 1991.

Nathanson, Tenney. *Whitman's Presence: Body, Voice, and Writing in* Leaves of Grass. New York: New York University Press, 1992.

Nolan, James. *Poet-Chief: The Native American Poetics of Walt Whitman and Pablo Neruda*. Albuquerque: University of New Mexico Press, 1994.

Pearce, Roy Harvey, ed. *Whitman: A Collection of Critical Essays*. Englewood Cliffs, N.J.: Prentice-Hall, 1962.

Pease, Donald. *Visionary Compacts: American Renaissance Writings in Cultural Context*. Madison: University of Wisconsin Press, 1987.

Perlman, Jim, Ed Folsom, and Dan Campion, eds. *Walt Whitman: The Measure of His Song*. Minneapolis: Holy Cow! Press, 1981.

Price, Kenneth M. *Whitman and Tradition: The Poet in His Century*. New Haven, Conn.: Yale University Press, 1990.

Reynolds, David S. *Beneath the American Renaissance: The Subversive Imagination in the Age of Emerson and Melville*. New York: Knopf, 1988.

Rubin, Joseph Jay. *The Historic Whitman*. University Park: Pennsylvania State University Press, 1973.

Shively, Charley, ed. *Calamus Lovers: Walt Whitman's Working-Class Camerados*. San Francisco: Gay Sunshine Press, 1987.

  Drum Beats: Walt Whitman's Civil War Boy Lovers. San Francisco: Gay Sunshine Press, 1989.

Sill, Geoffrey M., and Roberta K. Tarbell, eds. *Walt Whitman and the Visual Arts*. New Brunswick, N.J.: Rutgers University Press, 1992.

Stovall, Floyd. *The Foreground of Leaves of Grass*. Charlottesville: University Press of Virginia, 1974.

Sweet, Timothy. *Traces of War: Poetry, Photography, and the Crisis of the Union*. Baltimore: Johns Hopkins University Press, 1990.

Thomas, M. Wynn. *The Lunar Light of Whitman's Poetry*. Cambridge, Mass.: Harvard University Press, 1987.

Warren, James Perrin. *Walt Whitman's Language Experiment*. University Park: Pennsylvania State University Press, 1990.

Waskow, Howard. *Whitman: Explorations in Form*. Chicago: University of Chicago Press, 1966.

Woodress, James, ed. *Critical Essays on Walt Whitman*. Boston: G. K. Hall, 1983.

Zweig, Paul. *Walt Whitman: The Making of the Poet*. New York: Basic Books, 1984.

Cambridge Companions to Literature